Beyond the Light

Beyond the Light

What Isn't Being Said About Near-Death Experience

P. M. H. Atwater, Lh.D.

A BIRCH LANE PRESS BOOK
Published by Carol Publishing Group

A Birch Lane Press Book
Published by Carol Publishing Group
Birch Lane Press is a registered trademark of Carol Communications, Inc.
Editorial Offices: 600 Madison Avenue, New York, N.Y. 10022
Sales and Distribution Offices: 120 Enterprise Avenue, Secaucus,
N.J. 07094

In Canada: Canadian Manda Group, P.O. Box 920, Station U, Toronto, Ontario M8Z 5P9
Queries regarding rights and permissions should be addressed to Carol Publishing
Group, 600 Madison Avenue, New York, N.Y. 10022

Carol Publishing Group books are available at special discounts for bulk purchases, for
sales promotion, fund-raising, or educational purposes. Special editions can be created to
specifications. For details, contact: Special Sales Department, Carol Publishing Group, 120
Enterprise Avenue, Secaucus, N.J. 07094

Manufactured in the United States of America
10 9 8 7 6 5 4 3 2 1

Library of Congress Cataloging-in-Publication Data

Atwater, P. M. H.
    Beyond the light : what isn't being said about near-death
experience / P. M.H. Atwater.
       p.   cm.
    ISBN 1–55972–229–0
    1. Near-death experience.   2. Near-death exerience —Case
studies. I. Title.
BF1045.N4A86 1994
133.9'01'3—dc20   93–42169
                                                CIP

To my husband, Terry Young Atwater. He sacrificed his own career advancement so I could continue my research, thus sharing in what came next—derision, heartbreak, joy, wonder. He has ever been my best soundingboard, my severest critic, confidant, and friend extraordinaire. And he is love incarnate, proof to me that humans really can be angels in disguise. *Thank You!* is hardly enough to say, but I will say it anyway.

Contents

Foreword

I am an experiencer. I have lived my research, it has been my life.

This fact—that I have experienced near-death—has created a quandary for me right from the beginning. How do you maintain distance, objectivity, detachment, if you are both a researcher and an experiencer of the very phenomenon you seek to study?

To do this, I have been demanding of myself, exceedingly so. I have not allowed my multiple experiences with death, what I learned while on The Other Side, my personal bias, or anyone else's research findings to interfere with my work. To ensure clarity, I have double-checked and triple-checked everything—conducting rounds of interviews, taking time out for analysis and contemplation; more interviews, walks in the woods to rethink; more travel and more interviews; phone calls to groups of people to see what input they could offer; meditation and prayer; more analysis. My interviews and dialogues have not only been with near-death survivors but, whenever possible, with their spouses, children, relatives, friends, neighbors, co-workers, and health-care providers. And this activity has been ongoing.

My work schedule, since deciding to research the near-death phenomenon the week before Thanksgiving in November 1978, has been intense. This schedule intensified further in November 1983, after Kenneth Ring, an internationally known near-death researcher, convinced me to write a book about my observations. I then switched to day and night, seven-days-a-week, nonstop labor. Very seldom have I taken any breaks, except when sidelined by a rib injury and surgery. My husband, Terry, nicknamed me "the monk in the monastery."

My dedication has been so focused that one night, while we were living in Harrisonburg, Virginia, I did not recognize Terry when he walked in the door. That embarrassing incident occurred when he was working two full-time jobs so I could quit my outside employment and concentrate on research. He had an hour between jobs to rush home for dinner, which I always had prepared and waiting for him. On this particular night, however, not only had I forgotten to cook, but I had no idea who the "stranger" was who stood staring at my blank face with such utter puzzlement. Needless to say, I have kept several photographs of my husband next to my typewriter and computer ever since to ensure that this never happens again.

This determination of mine to "step apart" and be absolutely objective and detached in my work, is the reason behind my choice of words when I described the seven major aftereffects as "the inability to personalize"..."the inability to recognize."...and so forth. When my book *Coming Back to Life: The After-Effects of the Near-Death Experience* first came out, reviewers reacted sharply, claiming I made near-death survivors sound like "a bunch of sickies" (my mother agreed, by the way). Never was it my intention to be "negative," and I apologize to anyone who might have been offended by the words I used. However, since clarity has always been my goal, viewing the phenomenon of near-death from as many *different* angles as possible. I'll stick with my original assessments. I'll save romanticism for fiction, if I ever get around to writing any.

Where did this obsessive behavior, this driving need of mine to explore and probe, question and challenge, come from? To answer that, you need to know three things about me.

First, at the age of five I began "tearing up" my environment; dissecting, separating, studying, watching, observing, and challenging everything I saw, heard, touched, or felt. I became distrustful of authority, including parental figures, at this tender age and insisted on finding my own truth my own way. To say I was a difficult child to raise would be an understatement.

My adoptive father, Kenneth L. Johnston, entered my life when I was a third-grader. I was frightened of him at first and refused to cooperate. Perhaps in retaliation for my behavior, or simply because he, a newly hired police officer, sincerely wanted to sharpen his interviewing skills, I unwittingly became the subject of an experiment of his.

We'd be shopping in the dime store (usually Woolworth's), me agog at the kind of glitter that attracts children, when Dad would suddenly grab me by the shoulders, jerk me around, glare at me, and command, "All right, describe that woman who just walked by. What color and length was her hair? Was there a part? Any eyeglasses? What was she wearing? Describe her clothing in detail. Any handbag or watch? What shoes and stockings was she wearing? Did you notice any scars or distinguishing features?" Or we'd cross the intersection of Main and Shoshone Streets in Twin Falls, Idaho, our hometown, and Dad would grab me by the shoulders again and away he'd go: "Describe that man. . . . " This checklist routine continued off and on for three years. I swear the man was trying to create the world's most perfect witness. Today, I lavish my dad with praise and love and thanksgiving. That early training he foisted upon me has made a significant and important difference throughout my entire life.

Second, when I recovered from my three near-death experiences, everything I had previously known had lost its value and meaning. I needed to reidentify my place in the scheme of things, to understand what had occurred and what was still happening to me. My desire to research the near-death phenomenon was plainly not research to begin with; it was survival! Never was there any question in my mind of how I could conduct this research or finance it, how long it might take, or even if I was qualified to do it. I began, and "the way" revealed itself as I went along.

Third, while on The Other Side I had been told, "One book for each death." Instructions had been given, but were forgotten. It wasn't until three days after Ken Ring suggested that I write a book about my research when I was standing atop the massive granite boulders that define the coastline of Maine, that those original instructions given in death returned to my awareness. Books two and three were given their names while I was on The Other Side, *Future Memory* and *A Manual for Developing Humans*. The first, *Coming Back to Life*, although nameless for a time, eventually took its title from a column I had been writing for the International Association for Near-Death Studies (IANDS) in their magazine at the time, *Vital Signs.* I had been shown what each book was to contain, but not how to write them. Because of publishing considerations, *Coming Back to Life* will continue in print as long as it will; *Beyond The Light,* however, will take its rightful place as book one of the trilogy. This threesome should be completed by the close of 1995.

As of this writing, I have spent a total of fifteen years fulfilling the task I agreed to do in death and chose to do in life. This dedication has been both a burden and a joy. Disappointments and delays have been many. In order to help my husband keep the bills paid, I have worked as a psychic counselor on the nation's largest 900 line [1]. I am uncomfortable admitting this, for I find the term *psychic counselor* laden with more nonsense than I care to be associated with. Yet there are wonderful, gifted sensitives working the line as I do, and I am proud to be in their number. Continued research without this additional income source would have been impossible.

When I am finished with the trilogy, yours truly is taking up painting. Obsessions, no matter how magnificent, are too much work.

Acknowledgments

I extend my deepest gratitude to the following:

The near-death survivors I have spoken to or interviewed during the course of my research. Thousands in number, they are scattered throughout the United States, Canada, Russia, Egypt, Haiti, and several other countries. All had the courage to speak openly about their joy and their pain, revealing intimate facts about their personal lives—sometimes at risk to their reputations and personal relationships.

David McKnight, who, without my knowledge, arranged for the first talk I ever gave on near-death. Several other experiencers attended, and I interviewed them, thus beginning the research that would span fifteen years. He continued as my mentor afterward, quietly ensuring that I stayed "on course" so I would meet more people and ask more questions.

Wabun Wind and Sun Bear, who were the first to publish articles about my near-death experiences. There were so many requests for reprints that I compiled those articles into a small, self-published book called *I Died Three Times in 1977*. It was Wabun who insisted that I meet David McKnight. "You need to know him," she said.

Arthur E. Yensen, who introduced me to what heaven might be and became a treasured friend and a beloved member of our family. Without his financial assistance, *I Died Three Times in 1977* would never have been printed. It was this book that Kenneth Ring found in a Connecticut bookstore. He traced me by phone because of it.

Kenneth Ring, who asked that I write a column for near-death survivors in *Vital Signs* magazine, and then urged me to do a book based on my research of the phenomenon. His guidance through the scientific labyrinth of statistical facts was invaluable, as was his advice to trust my own insights and observations.

Merelyn McKnight and Charles C. Wise, Jr., who were editors during different stages of production for the books I have written, and Liz St. Clair, who rescued me from "mountains" of typing and last-minute corrections during the course of my work.

Tam Mossman, who located the publisher for *Coming Back to Life*, and Sallie Gouverneur, whose foresight in tossing my first attempts at writing in the wastebasket prompted me to do better.

Stephany Evans, who located the publisher for this book, and my new editor, Kevin McDonough, who is like "a breath of fresh air."

Machaelle Small Wright and Clarence Wright, who decided it was time that I modernized. When they updated their equipment at the Perelandra Gardens, they gave me their original computer. "Pere" has since become my technological angel.

Nancy Evans Bush, a gracious and endearing saint, who shared with me the pain of undeserved criticism and personal attacks. Her courage brought light to the dark side of near-death research.

Marianne Paulus and OSO (formerly Diane K. Pike and Arleen Lorrance), who introduced me to The Love Project Principles many years ago, principles that have become more valuable with the passing of time as I have confronted both the darkness and the light within myself.

M. Elizabeth Macinata, Terry Macinata, and Thomas More Huber (now Thomas Shawnodese Wind), three strangers who came to my aid after my near-death experiences, and nourished and guided the babe I was while I struggled to relearn and redefine my life.

William G. Reimer, who taught me the real meaning of health and, in so doing, proved to me that alternative sources of medicine and natural therapies are credible aids in the healing process.

My three children, Kelly John Huffman, Natalie Gae Huffman Rowell, and Pauline Ann Huffman Coiner, who put up with me and loved me in spite of all, at a time when I was barely functional and had nothing left to give.

And my adoptive father, Kenneth L. Johnston, who, when I was but a third-grader, taught me the fine art of observation, insisting that I learn how to see what most people don't. I never realized how invaluable his teaching was until I returned from death, opened my eyes, and breathed in the newness of air.

Introduction

With her 1988 book *Coming Back To Life: The Aftereffects of the Near-Death Experience*, P. M. H. Atwater staked her claim as one of the pioneers of near-death research. In that book she describes her own spiritual awakening after having a near-death experience. She is at her most eloquent when describing the psychological changes that lead to awakening. For her this awakening has meant: to live with small means, to seek elegance rather than luxury, to study hard, to think quietly, to talk gently, to act frankly, to listen to the stars and birds and to babes and sages with an open heart, and to let the spiritual unconscious grow through the common.

The theme of spiritual awakening has been at the core of her work, both as researcher and author. For her there is nothing "freakish" or "abnormal" about the near-death experience. It is a normal event that gives meaning and understanding to our lives.

Atwater's insights and predictions about the nature of the near-death experience came years before the hard medical research that backed them up. For instance, she was one of the first to say that the near-death experience changes the brain's physiology, actually altering its structure. She was also among the first to say that near-death experiences significantly change the electromagnetic fields that surround the average person. This particular claim was looked upon with great skepticism at first, but subsequent research on the nature of these electromagnetic fields has shown her to be right again. Now when people who have had near-death experiences say that their watches stop running with great frequency, we can tell them why it happens.

Atwater is among this field's best researchers. Her new book reflects her honesty and devotion to science. It provides a comprehensive overview of near-death research, skillfully combining science, religion, metaphysics, and her own research; synthesizing the entire field. She discusses the practical aspects of having a near-death experience and makes the point that it can involve a state of spiritual emergency and crisis. She gives suggestions on how to help survivors, speaking as one who has had the experience. She also discusses the negative near-death experience, a fascinating and little-known area of the near-death phenomenon that will provoke intense debate and controversy.

I am deeply flattered to write the introduction to this book. P. M. H. Atwater's books have profoundly influenced my own work and inspired many of my thoughts. Her book is must reading for those who want to learn more about themselves and what will happen when we die. The knowledge in this book can be used to learn more about the nature of reality and the meaning of life itself.

Melvin Morse, M.D.
Author of *Closer to the Light*
and *Transformed by the Light*

ANOTHER DEFINITION OF DEATH

The Aramaic word for death translates:
not here
present elsewhere.

This ancient concept of death best
describes the near-death experience and
what happens to those who go through it.

These people were present—elsewhere!

Although my near-death experience was nearly thirty-four years ago, there is virtually not a day that goes by that I am not aware of making decisions based on that experience.
—Geraldine F. Berkheimer

I

Aspects
of
Near-Death

ONE

The Near-Death Phenomenon

Death is our eternal companion. It has always been watching you. It will until the day it taps you.

—Carlos Castaneda

Death surprised me when it came to call.

Twice in January of 1977 and once two months later I passed *through* death to The Other Side and returned to speak of it. I've never been the same since. How could I? When you know what death is, when you have glimpsed its secrets, your concept of life alters radically.

My first death was caused by a miscarriage and severe hemorrhaging; the second, two days later, by a major thrombosis in the vein in my right thigh. The clot dislodged and was followed by the worst case of phlebitis the specialist had ever heard of, let alone seen. Then, on March 29, I suffered a complete physical, mental, and emotional collapse. Each time death came to call I had a near-death experience, and each was different, yet each one seemed somehow to lead into the next, as if the experience were progressive. I was not seen by doctors until after the fact—our family doctor first, later a specialist who was able to diagnose what happened to me by the condition I was in. The specialist felt the worst was over, so I was allowed to convalesce at home. Hindsight reveals the folly of that judgment, for, that fall, I had three major relapses, one of which was adrenal failure. My blood pressure registered sixty over sixty when I was examined by William G. Reimer, the Naturopathic physician who literally saved my life. When symptoms could finally be controlled, I was challenged to relearn how to crawl, stand, walk, climb stairs, run, tell the difference between left and right, rebuild my belief systems, as well as train myself to see and hear without distortion. This means I wound up remodeling an old house—my body and me with it.

Since I was never hospitalized, I lack clinical proof that I actually died. It was the specialist's opinion that I did die, however, and that is my opinion as well.

The following year, I encountered Elisabeth Kübler-Ross, and she described the near-death phenomenon to me and identified me as a near-death survivor. Our talk at Chicago's O'Hare Airport was my turning point. I had never heard of Raymond Moody, Jr., M.D., who had originated the term *near-death* and popularized the phenomenon in his bestseller *Life After Life*. All I knew was that I was a medical miracle, a woman three times dead who was now alive.

Elisabeth's description helped, but it was not enough. I wanted to know more. I had to. My response to this inner need was characteristic of the way I had lived my entire life: Go out and do your own research, deal direct, go to the source. I did, sometimes even door-to-door. I usually found other near-death survivors in the audience whenever I gave a talk about what I had gone through. Yet just as often I simply "bumped" into people like me during the routines of daily living and, later on, because of the employment I had accepted, which required constant travel. Thus I met near-death survivors in every possible locale—a truck-stop near Macon, Georgia; the streets of Minneapolis; an intersection in Washington, D.C.; the lobby of a hotel in Miami, Florida. These survivors must have "smelled" me coming, for no sooner did I meet someone than we would be deep in conversation about that person's near-death scenario. Me, popping questions as fast as I could; them, reveling in the attention they almost never received. It was uncanny how this happened.

And so it went. I asked more questions than I had ever thought I could. Not only did I learn a lot from doing this, I was also able to view my own experiences reflected back to me in the eyes of over three thousand near-death survivors—spread out across most of the states and including experiencers from Canada, England, France, Belgium, Mexico, Egypt, Saudi Arabia, Russia, Ukraine, Georgia, Haiti, and Kenya.

Let's make no mistake here. I had no idea my quest to understand what had happened to me would develop into a fifteen-year-long, nonstop, day and night, all-consuming research project. Initially, I was just trying to save my sanity. That first time, a deliriously happy encounter with two other near-death survivors who gathered after a talk I had given the week before Thanksgiving, 1978, in Middletown, Virginia, set the pace for how I would conduct myself as a researcher: Invite the individual to share his or her experience while listening intently; probe further with lots of "ands" and "oh, reallys" and "tell me mores"; carefully note the individual's body and eye movements; observe how interested others respond to the individual, and note their body language as well as their words; whenever possible visit in the person's home so family members can be interviewed, maybe friends, co-workers, and health-care providers, as well. Instinct drove me to examine the phenomenon from many diverse points of view.

Kenneth L. Johnston, my police-officer father (now retired), trained me in the fine art of observation from the time I was a third-grader. I still tend to function like a "cop on the beat" when I'm investigating anything, a skill honed by years of analytical employment and as a professional writer/reporter.

"Don't take anyone's word at face value," Dad would often say to me. "Double check, cross-examine, seek out witnesses, double-check again, cover every lead—and be alert. Then balance your observations with what your gut tells you. Intuition is a tool— use it." I learned a lot from my father. Frankly, he gave me no other choice.

I tell you this because many people have questioned how I do my research. The Resource Methodology section at the back of this book provides more detail, but I wanted to at least give you an idea of what I do and why. Listening to people's stories has never been enough for me, nor have I been satisfied with what I learned from my own. The near-death phenomenon is a complex dynamic, much richer in what it can tell us about ourselves, our lives, and our deaths, than has been previously told. You'll get a sense of what I mean as you read through these pages. Since my past observations have proved accurate and have been verified by the likes of more scientific researchers such as Melvin Morse, M.D., I feel at liberty to reveal the rest of my findings. Far from reaching a saturation point, the field of near-death study has only just begun to address the incredible scope and breadth of the subject. An international measurement study is now a must, and I make an appeal for that, to establish funding and direction, at the close of this book.

The initial observations I made about near-death are contained in *Coming Back to Life: The Aftereffects of the Near-Death Experience* [2]. That book resulted from a column I wrote for *Vital Signs* magazine (a publication of the International Association for Near-Death Studies [IANDS]), starting in 1981, and at the urging of Kenneth Ring, a well-known researcher of near-death states who found my discoveries about the aftereffects intriguing [3].

I wrapped the book around two hundred indepth interviews of near-death survivors plus a questionnaire I sent out in two separate mailings: one to people whose names and addresses I had obtained from the archives of IANDS, and the other to survivors I had already interviewed and/or whose homes I had visited. This double mailing enabled me to compare what was going on with people I knew versus those I had never met. A pattern of aftereffects emerged that has since become universally recognized. (A brief summary of the seven major elements of this pattern is presented in Chapter Eight under the heading "Psychological Aftereffects.")

This current rendering advances what I have observed and cross-checked to the next level of discovery. To accomplish this feat, I have prepared a veritable compendium of material on the near-death phenomenon, its aftereffects and implications, and I have pursued positives and negatives with equal vigor. My findings are based on original fieldwork (i.e., interviews, observations, analysis), plus a mailed questionnaire that explored the range of electrical sensitivity experiencers claim to exhibit. The case studies that appear throughout the book are representative of what I have found to be typical during the course of my research. Any percentages used come from my own analysis of the observations I have made, unless otherwise stated.

Of the three thousand plus sessions I have had with near-death survivors during the course of these last fifteen years, I claim a conservative figure of seven hundred interviews (which includes my first two hundred) as the basis of the findings I now offer, since the smaller figure more closely addresses those I have interviewed in greatest depth. One hundred and five of these seven hundred people reported having had a hell-like or unpleasant near-death experience. Hence, one out of seven of those I interviewed spoke of hell rather than heaven. And this isn't the only area where what I have observed in fieldwork tends to deviate from precedent.

Too often what has been revealed about the near-death phenomenon, either by professionals or through the media, has been geared more to what the public might want to hear rather than to what could be said. This has created a myth, and the myth goes like this: As a compensatory gift, near-death experiencers are privileged to survive the immediacy of death and witness, in so doing, the realms of heaven. They return utterly transformed, eschewing greed and materialism for selfless service and love for all humankind.

Not so!

Certainly the myth can apply, and you do encounter that sort of thing when researching, in fact, frequently. But the actual phenomenon, as well as its aftereffects and implications, are not so easily categorized. Along with the brilliant light you hear so much about these days, there is every imaginable shade of darkness and confusion. In near-death research, there has been, and still is, a tendency, even a preference, to mistake the greater story for its "trappings," to focus on the "light show" instead of the fuller drama.

Myths stem from truth. They interweave fact and fantasy into a fabric of symbolic metaphor so codes of conduct, individual and collective growth and transformation, can be recognized and taught. This universal pattern of myth-making applies to near-death mythology as well. Thus, my goal in writing this book is to place "The Myth of Amazing Grace" in context with the reality it sprang from.

As you turn these pages, I think you will come to realize as I have that each near-death episode, no matter how poignant or unique (including my own), is but one piece of a bigger picture—partial, at best.

No single experiencer is a "superstar," since the power of the near-death phenomenon lies not in its storyline but in what occurs *because* the story ever happened. The consequences, what comes afterward, are where you find real value and meaning. As persuasive as near-death reports are about life beyond death, in truth these reports reveal much more about the amazing, absolutely awesome *aliveness* life has. This revelation challenges societies across the globe to reassess and redefine what is presently known about human faculties, the broad sweep of mind, and the presence of soul.

Hardly the medical anomaly first thought, the near-death experience has earned the distinction of being a factual, documentable occurrence that can happen to anyone at any age, anywhere, anytime. A Gallup poll survey conducted in 1992 sets the figure at around thirteen million experiencers in the United States, up from eight million ten years earlier. This statistic does *not* factor in infants or children, though, nor is it indicative of the kind of numbers being submitted today from a multitude of professional researchers in other countries who interview cases within their own population groups. Thanks to this new wealth of data, we now know that experiencers in China, for instance, although coloring their episode with cultural nuances, will undergo the same basic episode as experiencers in Norway, Israel, Brazil, or Zaire. Regardless of descriptive variants, the overall pattern remains the same for what happens to someone who dies or nearly dies, and then revives, describing life on the other side of death.

Here is the overall pattern:

1. **A sensation of floating out of one's body,** often followed by an out-of-body experience where all that goes on around the "vacated" body is both seen and heard accurately and in detail.
2. **Passing through a dark tunnel** or black hole or encountering some kind of darkness. This is usually accompanied by a feeling or sensation of movement or acceleration. "Wind" may be heard or felt, or a swooshing sound may predominate.
3. **Headed toward and entering into a light at the end of the darkness,** a loving light of warmth and brilliance, with the possibility of seeing people, animals, plants, lush outdoors, and even cities within that light.
4. **Greeted by friendly voices, people, or beings,** who may be strangers, loved ones, or perhaps religious figures. Con-

versation can ensue, information or a message may be given, as part of the "scenario."

5. **Seeing a panoramic review of the life just lived,** from birth to death or in reverse order, sometimes becoming a "reliving" rather than a dispassionate viewing. The person's life can be reviewed in its entirety or in segments. This is often accompanied by a feeling or need to assess gains or losses made during the life, so the individual can be aware of what was learned or not learned. Other beings can participate in this assessment or offer advice. It is possible for such "memories" to be open ended and to include all existent knowledge, not just personal revelations.

6. **A different sense of time and space,** discovering that time and space do not exist, along with losing the need to recognize such measurements as either valid or necessary.

7. **A reluctance to return to the earthplane,** but invariably coming to realize that either one's job on earth is not finished or a mission is yet to be performed before one can return to stay.

8. **Disappointment at being revived,** feeling a need to shrink or somehow squeeze to fit back into the physical body. There can be unpleasantness, even anger or tears, at the realization that one is now back in his or her body and no longer on The Other Side. Fear of death either subsides or disappears altogether.

Although it is rare for any single case to include all the components just given, most report experiencing at least half of them. And all manner of variations can occur. There are even reports of experiencers who, in their out-of-body state, floated outdoors or traveled to see friends and relatives who lived far away. A few of these "travelers" were *physically seen and recognized* when they arrived at their destinations—appearing as perfectly normal, totally alive, even audibly speaking—while their "corpses" remained unmoved and unmoving on-site at the death event. Some "were home" when the call came through from the hospital announcing their deaths. These "invisible" experiencers, once they returned to their bodies and revived, were able to describe what transpired at home at the moment of the phone call—who was there, what each person was wearing, and what was said—and to do so without flaws in the narrative.

As an example of what an out-of-body state can entail, here is what happened to Jazmyne Cidavia-DeRepentigny of Hull, Georgia, when she died on the operating table during surgery in late 1979:

> I must say that this experience was quite unsettling to say the least. I was floating over my body. I could see and hear everything that was being said and done. I left the room for a short while and then returned to where my body lay. I knew why I died. It was because I couldn't breathe. There was a tube down my throat and the medical staff did not have an oxygen mask on my nose. I had also been given too much anesthetic.
>
> In my out-of-body state, I'm using my mind to try and make my right arm and hand move—my arms are extended parallel to my physical body. I want my right hand to move, anything to move. I was trying to pull the tube out of my mouth. I looked down at my face and tears were streaming. One of the nurses blotted the tears from my face but she didn't notice my breathing had stopped, nor did she see me next to her. At this point, I'm trying really hard to make my physical arm move, but it's like my whole body is made of lead.

Cidavia-DeRepentigny's determination in her out-of-body state to make an arm move finally paid off; and, with great clamor and commotion, the tube was pulled out, an oxygen mask attached, and her breathing restored. She had a similar near-death episode when she was hospitalized at thirteen, and again in 1991 when she faced death a third time. The more recent occurrence resulted from a nearly fatal bout with pneumonia, only this time she witnessed her own soul as a spirit residing outside of her body:

> I could see my spirit standing before me. My spirit was so beautifully perfect, dressed in a white gown that was loose, free-flowing, and below the knee. From my spirit there emanated a bright, soft-white halo. My spirit was standing six to eight feet from my body. It was so strange, for I could see my spirit and my spirit could see my pathetic body. I had not an ounce of color and I looked all withered and cold and lifeless. My spirit felt warm and so, so celestial. As my spirit slowly moved away, my spirit told my body goodbye, for my spirit saw the light and wanted to go into it. The light was like a circular opening that was warm and bright.

Cidavia-DeRepentigny spoke of feeling torn between two worlds—wanting to remain on earth while at the same time feeling a strong pull to unite with her spirit self and pass into the light. After another round of hospitalization, she was left confused and disoriented, ready to change her life yet hesitant to begin. She lamented about the lack of people she could discuss her situation with, although her church bishop did express some degree of understanding. Her lament is commonly shared by most experiencers.

Fewer than half of the people I interviewed encountered a tunnel, yet the majority described a life review that was facilitated either by a tribunal of some sort or self-judgment. This life review, by the way, was in some cases so profound that it included the consequences of the individual's actions on others. One woman described in anguish how, during her scenario, she experienced the pain felt by each bug she had ever killed. Today she refuses to harm even a fly.

Of the phenomenon's many components, the most frequently reported was the overwhelming sense of love experiencers encountered in the light. To them, this love incorporated perfect peace, total acceptance, and the presence of God.

The case of Robin Michelle Halberdier of Texas City, Texas, illustrates this. Her near-death episode took place in a hospital when she was between one and two months of age. Born prematurely, and with Hyaline Membrane disease, she was not expected to live:

> My first visual memory was looking forward and seeing a brilliant bright light, almost like looking directly at the sun. The strange thing was that I could see my feet in front of me, as if I were floating upward in a vertical position. I do not remember passing through a tunnel or anything like that, just floating in that beautiful light. A tremendous amount of warmth and love came from the light.
>
> There was a standing figure in the light, shaped like a normal human being, but with no distinct facial features. It had a masculine presence. The light I have described seemed like it emanated from that figure. Light rays shone all around him. I felt very protected and safe and loved.
>
> The figure in the light told me through what I now know to be mental telepathy that I must go back, that it was not time for me to come here. I wanted to stay because I felt so full of

joy and so peaceful. The voice repeated that it wasn't my
time; I had a purpose to fulfill and I could come back after I
completed it.

The first time I told my parents about my experience was
right after I began to talk. At the time, I believed that what
happened to me was something everyone experienced. I told
my mom and dad about the big glass case I was in after I was
born, and the figure in the light and what he said to me.
They took my reference to the glass case to mean the
incubator. My father was a medical student at the time, and
he had read a book about near-death experiences. From
comparing the information in the book with what I told
them, they decided that's what I was describing. My mom
told me all of this years later when I brought the subject up
again.

I began attending church at the age of five, and I would
look at the picture of Jesus in the Bible and tell my mom that's
who it was in the light. I still have many physical difficulties
with my health because of being premature. But there is a
strong need inside me that I should help others with what
death is, and talk to terminally ill patients. I was in the other
world and I know there is nothing to be afraid of after death.

I found that both adults and children occasionally report being
greeted on The Other Side by animals, especially if favored pets
have previously died. But it is the children who describe an
animal heaven, some even insisting that they must go through it
before they can reach the heaven where people are. Adult cases
can be equally compelling.

Several years before his death, Bryce Bond, a famous New York
City media personality turned parapsychologist, shared with me
the story of what happened to him when he once collapsed after a
violent allergic reaction to pine nuts and was rushed to a
hospital. He remembered suddenly passing through a long
tunnel toward a brilliant light, and then:

I hear a bark, and racing toward me is a dog I once had, a
black poodle named Pepe. When I see him, I feel an emotional floodgate open. Tears fill my eyes. He jumps into my
arms, licking my face. As I hold him, he is real, more real
than I had ever experienced him. I can smell him, feel him,
hear his breathing, and sense his great joy at being with me
again.

I put my dog on the ground, and step forward to embrace my stepfather, when a very strong voice is heard in my consciousness. Not yet, it says. I scream out, Why? Then this inner voice says, What have you learned, and whom have you helped? I am dumbfounded. The voice seems to be from without as well as within. Everything stops for a moment. I have to think of what was asked of me. I cannot answer what I have learned, but I can answer whom I have helped.

I feel the presence of my dog around me as I ponder those two questions. Then I hear barking, and other dogs appear, dogs I once had. As I stand there for what seems to be an eternity, I want to embrace and be absorbed and merge. I want to stay. The sensation of not wanting to come back is overwhelming.

Bryce was also greeted by all of his relatives who had passed on before him. He experienced these loved ones as somewhat younger in form and face than when he had last seen them, healthier and happier. He remembered racing backward through the same tunnel he had entered when it was time to leave and reviving in time to witness a hypodermic needle being plunged into his arm. "I heard a voice say, 'Welcome back.' I never asked who said that nor did I care. I was told by the doctor that I had been dead for over ten minutes."

Another feature I noticed was that adult experiencers will occasionally be met in death by the children they will eventually father or mother. Women reported this more than men. Children, however, even infants, were invariably greeted during their death episode by any siblings who died before they did. These siblings told them how they passed over, whether from stillbirth, death shortly after birth, miscarriage, or because of an abortion when they were but a fetus. Future siblings sometimes appeared as well, introducing themselves and giving the names they would someday have. I have yet to come across an incident where the child experiencer was incorrect about any of these past or future siblings, even when it was *absolutely impossible* for the child to possess such knowledge.

What I've mentioned thus far is but a sampling of the phenomenon's pattern. Now, let's get more specific.

About one-third of the adults who face death or who clinically die have a near-death experience. With children, the figure is over 75 percent, as established by the research of Melvin Morse, M.D., and Kimberly Clark Sharp, M.S.W., in Seattle, Washington. The closer one is to actual death the more apt one is to undergo such an incident. Modern technology and advanced resuscitation measures seem to account for this. Drugs don't.

Take note: Most reports come from individuals who were not given drugs until after their experiences were over, if at all. Research has consistently shown that drugs actually impede the phenomenon, especially drugs like Valium, chemicals used in most types of anesthesia, and alcohol.

Sue Schoenbeck, RN, MSN, director of nursing at Oakwood Health Care and Retirement Community in Madison, Wisconsin, and a researcher of near-death for many years, is quoted in the *Wisconsin State Journal* as saying that lack of oxygen does not explain near-death episodes either. And she is one of many confirming this fact. Hallucinations that occur when oxygen levels change produce confusion in patients, yet a striking aspect of near-death is the similarity in people's descriptions and the clarity of what they remember, even in minute detail, and often for years afterward.

I've heard it stated that since no one who was a real corpse ever revived to report a near-death experience, the phenomenon must obviously be a ploy the brain uses for reassurance when death seems near. If that is true, how do you explain the case of Ricky Bradshaw, currently of Staunton, Virginia?

In 1975, the torso of Bradshaw's body was literally ground in half when he became trapped between two automobiles backing into each other at a grocery store parking lot. Only his spine and a few cords around it were left intact before the panic-stricken drivers let up on the gas. He was rushed to a hospital and pronounced dead, his body heaped in a corner. A group of medical students noticed the cadaver and requested that they be allowed to experiment with it (the hospital was a teaching facility). With their new acquisition laid out like "a real patient," the would-be doctors began to stretch this and attach that. After an hour of such "high jinks," one of the students noticed that the heart monitor they had attached to the body "for fun" was starting to register bleeps. A superior was summoned out of concern for the equipment, not because they thought the corpse was coming back to life. The experienced physician recognized the by-then frequent bleeps and took over. Two years and twenty-four surgeries later, Ricky Bradshaw's survival made medical history nationally. And, you guessed it, the man had a near-death experience, a long one. In it he not only saw what the students were doing to his body, but also visited other realms of existence and was shown all of history from beginning to end as a "reward" for agreeing to return to earthlife. Surely this man was stone-cold dead, or was he?

And how do you explain the case of George Rodonaia?

A vocal communist dissident in Tbilisi, Georgia, in 1976 Rodonaia was twice run over by a car driven by a member of the KGB (the second time was to make certain there was no slipup in the assassination attempt). He was rushed to the hospital, pronounced dead, and his body was taken to the morgue. Morgues in Tbilisi are not like those in the United States. There, bodies are quick-frozen immediately and kept in that state a full three days before any autopsy is performed or the body is dispensed with. After the three days, Rodonaia's body was removed from the freezer vault and wheeled to the autopsy room. A team of doctors then commenced splitting apart his lower torso. As the blade cut through flesh, he managed to force open his eyes. One doctor, thinking this a mere reflex, promptly closed them. He opened his eyes again. Again the doctor closed them. Once more his eyes popped open, only this time the doctor jumped backward—and screamed. Believe it or not, Rodonaia's own uncle was one of the attending physicians! I will discuss the case of George Rodonaia in more detail in the chapter on transcendent cases, for his is the most unusual near-death experience in modern history; plus his death and the frozen state of his body have been verified. Doubt is not a factor here. This man really was stone-cold dead.

The case of George Rodonaia challenges the entire field of near-death studies and the very definition of the term *near-death*. So does the story of Julian A. Milkes.

I met Milkes on a bumpy train ride to Long Island Sound, where I was slated to speak at a near-death study group meeting in Syosset, New York. He is a retired teacher, and was returning that day from buying concert tickets in Times Square. Here is what he told me:

> My mother and I were driving out to the lake one afternoon. My dad was to follow later when he finished work. We were having company for dinner, and, as we rode along, my

mother spotted some wild flowers at the side of the road. She asked if I wouldn't stop the car and pick them as they would look nice on the dinner table. I pulled over to the right side of the road (it was not a major highway), parked the car, and went down a small incline to get off the road to pick the flowers. While I was picking the flowers, a car came whizzing by and suddenly headed straight for me.

As I looked up and saw what I presumed would be an inevitable death, I separated from my body and viewed what was happening from another perspective. My whole life flashed in front of me, from that moment backwards to segments of my life. The review was not like a judgment. It was passive, more like an interesting novelty.

I can't tell you how many times I think of that near-death experience. Even as I sit here and write my story for you, it seems as though it happened only yesterday.

Milkes suffered no injury. The speeding car veered off just as suddenly as it had appeared, and sped away. I have observed that the terror of an ultimate end, the kind of terror that sees no hope, no other alternative except death itself, is sometimes enough to shift people into a near-death mode. Illness, injury, or body trauma is not necessary.

Cases like the ones offered here demand that we reconsider what is presently known about the near-death phenomenon. And to do this we must broaden the scope of our inquiry. Obviously, the experience far exceeds the sweetly simple wonderment depicted on television talk shows or in the popular press. There is more to the story—surprisingly more.

To begin reconsidering the phenomenon, let's start with suicides. Seldom are they hell-like. Contrary to popular notions, most suicide near-death scenarios are positive, or at least illustrative of the importance of life and its living. Although I have yet to find a suicide experience that was in any way transcendent or in-depth, just to have something happen, anything that affirms that he or she is loved and special, seems miracle enough for the one involved. Near-death survivors from suicide attempts can and often do return with the same sense of mission that any other experiencer of the phenomenon reports. And that mission is usually to tell other potential victims that suicide is not the answer. For example, this young man (he asked not to be identified):

Since then, suicide has never crossed my mind as a way out. It's a copout to me and not the way to heaven. I wish you luck in your research and hope my experience will help stop someone from taking his own life. It is a terrible waste.

Suicide near-death episodes can lay to rest problems and conflicts, explain away confusions, and emphasize the need to remain embodied. Experiencers usually return with a feeling that suicide solves nothing, and they are notably renewed and refreshed by that feeling, using their near-death event as a source of courage, strength, and inspiration.

But not all suicide scenarios are positive.

Some are negative, and these can be so negative that they upset the individual more than the original problem that precipitated the suicide. This kind of devastation *can* be transforming if used as a catalyst to help the person make the kind of changes that comprise constructive, long-term solutions. Such changes can come from an inner awakening, or from the fear that what was experienced may indeed herald the individual's final fate if something is not done to turn things around.

Yet, there is another aspect to the suicide issue. Just because an individual has had a near-death experience *does not* prevent him or her from considering and perhaps attempting suicide at a later date. I am aware that most researchers in the field claim the opposite, but that is not what I have observed. The near-death experience, especially if heaven-like, *can* be a suicide deterrent, but not always. We are not "saved" by having a near-death experience, not even from ourselves.

One woman who contacted me spoke of having been hospitalized twice for attempting suicide many years after her near-death event. She had experienced a scenario that was both soul stirring and uplifting; but, with the passing of years and a life filled with tragedy and pain, the positive upliftment she had previously received seemed to fade. Memories of how wonderful it was on The Other Side prompted her to try killing herself so she could return. She failed at each attempt and caused herself unbelievable grief. When I last heard from her, she seemed reasonably back on her feet and more practical, stating that she now realized there was no escape and she had better get busy and solve her problems herself.

Another woman, who repeatedly brushed death and had a

heavenly near-death episode each time, seriously considered suicide so she could be free from the horrors of her life and return to the wonders she knew existed beyond death. Although this woman never followed through on her threats, neither did she follow through on advice to seek help. What has become of her I do not know.

Regardless of how meaningful the near-death phenomenon is, it will not necessarily protect or shield anyone from the realities of life. The experience is not magic, even though it may seem so. Being a near-death survivor does not automatically make one enlightened or superhuman or holy. Aftereffects from the event can be just as negative as positive.

Yet miracles are numerous. For example, spontaneous healings can occur after the individual revives. People have suddenly become cancer free; brain tumors have vanished; one man with AIDS emerged without a trace of the disease left in his body. The medical community is at a complete loss to explain any of this. It is a fact that near-death survivors can become so transfigured and transformed, they are as if strangers to those who once knew them; even before and after photographs can differ.

Equally true are the periods of confusion, disorientation, and depression that often follow. Brain structure seems to shift around, while personal skills alter. The family unit can become "foreign territory": Its members changing along with the experiencer if they are open-minded, separating or divorcing from the individual if they are more fixed in their beliefs. Readjusting to "life as always" takes time and effort—years of it!

Not all survivors are survivors.

While we are reconsidering what is known about the near-death phenomenon, I want to point out that one of the reasons I used observation/analysis as my primary mode of research rather than control-group testing, was because I felt that racking up numbers on lists of statistics from questionnaire studies might leave me with too many blind spots. As a former professional analyst, I knew all too well how easy it was to manipulate numbers or fool myself by the very bias I sought to avoid. I also knew that studies based solely on control groups often overlook the very details that can later turn out to be crucial. I'm not saying this to be critical of other researchers, for more empirical study methods are absolutely necessary. But observational work is important, too. Actually, we need both types—for one will tend to highlight what the other often downplays.

My decision was initially influenced by a discovery I made: The vast majority of experiencers claimed that what had happened to them was *needed*, that it was somehow *ordered*.

The idea that the experience could be "needed" prompted me, at least as much as possible, to keep the individual's near-death scenario in context with the life he or she had previously lived and was living presently. Doing this enabled me to find multiple connections, correlations, and parallels between the two. Not that these connections invalidated the "unexpectedness" of the phenomenon, but they somehow seemed to influence how the phenomenon tended to arrange itself—the imagery and dialogue present in the scenario. It's almost as if the near-death experience can be, and quite probably is, one of nature's more accelerated growth events, a powerful and complex dynamic that not only can foster psychological changes in both adults and children, but can cause physiological mutations the equal of species evolution.

Viewing the near-death phenomenon in this manner, I was able to identify four distinctive types of experiences plus a general psychological profile that seemed predominant within each category.

The Four Types of Near-Death Experiences

Initial Experience (sometimes referred to as the "non-experience")
  Involves elements such as a loving nothingness or the living dark or a friendly voice. Usually experienced by those who seem to need the least amount of evidence for proof of survival, or who need the least amount of shakeup in their lives at that point in time. Often, this becomes a "seed" experience or an introduction to other ways of perceiving and recognizing reality.

Unpleasant and/or Hell-like Experience (inner cleansing and self-confrontation)
  Encounter with a threatening void or stark limbo or hellish purgatory, or scenes of a startling and unexpected indifference, even "hauntings" from one's own past. Usually experienced by those who seem to have deeply suppressed or repressed guilts,

fears, and angers and/or those who expect some kind of punishment or discomfort after death.

Pleasant and/or Heaven-like Experience (reassurance and self-validation)

Heaven-like scenarios of loving family reunions with those who have died previously, reassuring religious figures or light beings, validation that life counts, affirmative and inspiring dialogue. Usually experienced by those who most need to know how loved they are and how important life is and how every effort has a purpose in the overall scheme of things.

Transcendent Experience (expansive revelations, alternate realities)

Exposure to otherworldy dimensions and scenes beyond the individual's frame of reference; sometimes includes revelations of greater truths. Seldom personal in content. Usually experienced by those who are ready for a "mind stretching" challenge and/or individuals who are more apt to utilize (to whatever degree) the truths that are revealed to them.

I have noticed that all four types can occur during the same experience for the same person at the same time, can exist in varying combinations, or can spread out across a series of episodes for a particular individual. Generally speaking, however, each represents a distinctive type of experience occurring but once to a given person.

What may seem as negative or positive concerning any of these four types is strictly misleading. *Value and meaning depend on each individual involved and his or her response to what happened* (including the aftereffects).

A chapter on each of these four experience types follows, as well as a separate chapter for near-death-like experiences, anomalies, and psychological and physiological aftereffects. Topics such as spiritual implications, Kundalini, brain shift, and the revelatory aspects of the episodes themselves are all covered in a way that I hope provokes questions and elicits further examination.

To reconsider the field of near-death, we must shine the light of inquiry on *all* of it . . . including what we don't want to see or can't prove. To do any less, now, at this juncture in the history of the phenomenon's research, would be a copout.

TWO

Initial Experience

The modern tradition of equating death with an
ensuing nothingness can be abandoned. For
there is no reason to believe that human death
severs the quality of oneness in the universe.
—Larry Dossey, M.D.

Initial Experience (sometimes referred to as the "non-experience")
*Involves elements such as a loving nothingness or the living dark or a
friendly voice. Usually experienced by those who seem to need the least
amount of evidence for proof of survival, or who need the least amount of
shakeup in their lives at that point in time. Often, this becomes as if a
"seed" experience or an introduction to other ways of perceiving and
recognizing reality.*

There is a whole segment of people who have very brief
experiences or ones that consist of but one or two elements.
Hardly more than "snatches" of anything otherworldly, these
seemingly inconsequential events can have an impact on an
individual every bit as powerful as a full-blown near-death
scenario. Uncomplicated or simple out-of-body episodes account
for about half of these.

What happened to the famous novelist Ernest Hemingway is an
example of the typical initial experience. During World War I,
Hemingway was wounded by shrapnel while fighting on the

21

banks of the river Piave, near Fossalta, Italy. He convalesced in
Milan. In a letter from there to his family, he made this cryptic
statement: "Dying is a very simple thing. I've looked at death and
really I know." Years later, Hemingway explained to a friend what
had occurred on that fateful night in 1918 [4]:

> A big Austrian trench mortar bomb, of the type that used
> to be called ash cans, exploded in the darkness. I died then. I
> felt my soul or something coming right out of my body, like
> you'd pull a silk handkerchief out of a pocket by one corner.
> It flew around and then came back and went in again and I
> wasn't dead anymore.

Hemingway remained deeply affected by this out-of-body/
initial near-death experience throughout his life, and was never
again as "hard-boiled" as he once had been. *A Farewell to Arms*
contains a passage where the character Frederic Henry undergoes
the same confrontation with death that Hemingway did:

> I ate the end of my piece of cheese and took a swallow of
> wine. Through the other noise I heard a cough, then came
> the chuh-chuh-chuh-chuh—then there was a flash, as when
> a blast-furnace door is swung open, and a roar that started
> white and went red and on and on in a rushing wind. I tried
> to breathe but my breath would not come and I felt myself
> rush bodily out of myself and out and out and out and all the
> time bodily in the wind. I went out swiftly, all of myself, and
> I knew I was dead and that it had all been a mistake to think
> you just died. Then I floated, and instead of going on I felt
> myself slide back. I breathed and I was back.

What happened to John R. Liona of Brooklyn, New York, is also
typical of the initial experience:

> Mine was a difficult birth, according to my mother. She
> said she didn't hear me cry after I was born because I was a
> "blue baby." They did not bring me to her for two days. My
> face was black and blue, and she said the skin was all cut up
> on the right side of my face. That's where the forceps slipped.
> I was given a tracheotomy to help me breathe. I am totally
> deaf in my right ear. Also, the right side of my face and head
> is less sensitive than the left. When I get tired, the right side
> of my face droops a little, like Bell's palsy.

I am forty years old now. All my life going back to my childhood I can remember having this same recurring dream. It is more vivid than any other dream. It starts and ends the same—I am kneeling down and bent over, frantically trying to untie some kind of knots. They almost seem alive. I am pulling on them and they are thick and slippery. I am very upset. Pulling and snapping. I can't see what they're made of. I remember getting hit in the face while trying to untie or break free of the knots, and waking up crying. Then I would go back to sleep thinking it was only a dream or a nightmare. When the dream would happen again on another night, I would sleep through it longer, as I began to get used to it.

After I am able to sleep through the knotty part, suddenly my struggling stops. I feel like a puppet with all the strings cut. My body goes limp. All the stress and struggle is drained right out of me. I feel very calm and peaceful, but wonder what caused me to lose interest in the knots. They were important one minute; the next minute I am floating in this big bright light. I know I can't touch the ground because there is light there, too. I look at the light and try to move toward it. I can't, and this upsets me. There is a woman in a long, flowing gown floating away to my left. I call and call to her but the light is so bright sound does not travel through it. I want to talk to the woman. My dream ends there.

About a year ago, I walk out of my house to go to work. The ground is wet from rain, yet I find this book lying there—*dry*. No one is around, so I pick it up. The book is called *Closer to the Light*, by Melvin Morse, M.D., and Paul Perry. It is on the near-death experiences of children. That night I start reading it and cannot put it down. For the first time in my life, I now understand my dream. Those knots were when I struggled in the womb with the umbilical cord; getting hit in the face is when the doctor grabbed me with the forceps, then I died. After that, I went into the light.

But, wait a second. You're not supposed to remember being born. We don't just sit around at parties and talk about what we remember of our birth. We only talk about what our parents tell us. I look forward to having my dream again. I'm ready now to experience more of it than before, and without being upset.

It can be argued that since Liona's birth was so intensely traumatic, his repetitive dream may be more of the trauma's replay than any memory of a near-death experience. And that argument carries considerable weight, as prebirth awareness is commonly reported and often verified. For instance, David Cheek, past president of the American Society for Clinical Hypnosis and a retired obstetrician, believes that humans are remarkably capable while still in the womb. He is quoted as saying: "Babies are at least somewhat aware from the moment their mothers become aware of their pregnancy."

Yet this supposition does not take into account the woman in the long flowing gown who is also part of Liona's dream sequence. The antiseptic uniforms of attending physicians and medical personnel do not explain away this "gossamer" figure, nor does the idea of a mental replay account for how these images have haunted him. Neither does it explain why, since earliest childhood, he has displayed the typical aftereffects of a near-death survivor. The aftereffects of near-death are discussed in more depth in Chapters Eight and Nine.

What we are seeing here, and why I have used Liona's case as an example of the initial experience, is that current near-death research has shown that more and more children are being discovered who remember having had a near-death experience, either before, during, or after the moment of birth. This memory usually remains vivid in children's minds either from repeated storytelling after they learn how to talk, or because of repetitious imagery that intrudes upon their dreamlife, as in the case of John R. Liona. By the way, I have found that interviewing children can be as surprising as it is revelatory, for children seem able to hear parental conversations while still in the womb, and can repeat what was heard once they are old enough to talk—with embarrassing exactness.

The first of my three near-death experiences I would classify as "initial" in the sense that it was relatively brief (it probably lasted about five minutes) and consisted of few elements. Primarily an out-of-body episode, it was precipitated by a miscarriage and extreme hemorrhaging. It occurred on January 2, 1977, in Boise, Idaho.

What impressed me most about my first experience was the difference in spatial relationships; one minute I was standing at the toilet horrified to recognize a small fetus bobbing around in the blood I had just expelled, the next minute I was little more than a fetus myself, bobbing along the ceiling and bumping into the bathroom light bulb. Every time I formed a question in my mind about this state of affairs, strange blobs would form in the air around me. So many appeared that they nearly crowded me out of airspace. A loud "snap" ricocheted around my small bathroom, as I felt myself suddenly jerked back into my body like an overstretched rubber band (entering through the top of my head where I had once had a soft spot as a baby) and somehow "shrinking" so I could once again fit into my body's lesser size. The whole episode was unforgettably puzzling. It challenged me to rethink "the self" I thought I was.

A college professor I interviewed told of dying on the operating table and then instantaneously finding himself walking down the gentle slope of a bright greensward. No one else was there. Nothing else happened. Yet to hear him speak of it, it was as if the greatest of miracles had happened to him and he now knew, absolutely knew, that there was life after death. This brief incident completely transformed his life. Even today he lights up when describing the incredible aliveness of the green grass he once walked upon on The Other Side of death.

I have spoken with many people who have described "the living dark" that greeted them after dying with words like "soft velvety blackness" and "warm inviting blanket." Being engulfed by this type of darkness seldom impressed anyone as something negative or somber, or anything dreadful. Contrary to how such an experience might seem to affect one, most of these people felt awed by the wonderment of a black aliveness that appeared intelligent, emoted feelings, and instilled in the experiencer a sense of peace and acceptance.

Those who reported "a loving nothingness" told similar stories. Even though both light and darkness were absent in their brief near-death scenarios—only utter blankness existed—each reported great surges of overwhelming warmth and compassion, and they felt loved.

The ones who encountered light and light alone are no different in their praise. They claim that the radiant brilliance of this special light does not blind or burn; it simply accepts, embraces, and loves. A sense of worthiness can remain afterward, changing forever how the experiencer regards him or herself.

Often I've heard experiencers recount hearing a friendly voice during their short "time out," a voice they cannot place as belonging to anyone they know—yet the voice unmistakably knows them. A mind-to-mind or telepathic dialogue invariably ensues. No other senses or sensations are activated, only the faculty of hearing. Men usually hear a woman's voice when this happens and women, a man's (although not always). I can offer no reason for this.

Yes, some individuals can be apprehensive or anxious when faced with an "otherness" devoid of recognizable form or content. Seldom does this reaction last, though, since feelings of blissful ease quickly replace anything negative. Once revived, people who have initial experiences express true amazement. Then they start asking questions. Did they imagine it all? Did this really happen to them? Was their mind playing tricks? Can they believe their own perceptions? Can an explanation be found for a nothingness that is lively and intelligent?

I find it fascinating that those who have this type of near-death episode respond as if they had been suddenly "stimulated" afterward. They appear to be more alert, curious, and open than they were before. Their sensory faculties sometimes heighten. It's almost as if what they went through functions like yeast does when you bake bread, a little bit raises the whole loaf. Another comparison I could make would be that of a "seed" event, an experience that grows like a seed does over time, inspiring the individual to think more creatively and abstractly. This can lead to some lifestyle or personality changes. Lengthy or complicated near-death scenarios seem somehow unnecessary for these individuals. It's almost as if a little bit of exposure to otherworldly realities is quite enough for this stage of their development.

It seems to me that brain chemistry must be affected or altered to some extent during an initial near-death experience, perhaps there is a rush of endorphins that leads to permanent or lasting mood adjustments. The way people emphasize feelings over interpretation suggests this. Yet there is more involved here. People who undergo such an event are far more than just "stimulated." They seem to "wake up," sometimes in substantial ways that can affect them for a lifetime.

It takes more than chemicals to accomplish something like that.

THREE

Unpleasant and/or Hell-like Experience

The process of learning anew is more the process of unlearning that which is not true.
                                    —Paul V. Johnson

**Unpleasant and/or Hell-like Experience (inner cleansing and
self-confrontation)** *Encounter with a threatening void or stark limbo or
hellish purgatory, or scenes of a startling and unexpected indifference,
even "hauntings" from one's own past. Usually experienced by those
who seem to have deeply suppressed or repressed guilts, fears, and
angers, and/or those who expect some kind of punishment or discomfort
after death.*

The following story from Jeanne L. Eppley of Columbus, Ohio,
may seem like another rendering of an initial near-death experience to you. Elements are few, and it is brief, as are the others I
wrote about in Chapter Two. But it is different...unpleasant.

My experience happened during the birth of my first
child. For many years I blamed it on the anesthetic. I had
three more children without pain because I believed that if
there wasn't any pain, I wouldn't have to have anesthetics
that caused experiences like this. Living proof of mind over
matter, right?

What happened was this: Everything was bright yellow. There was a tiny black dot in the center of all the yellow. Somehow I knew that the dot was me. The dot began to divide. First there was two, then four, then eight. After there had been enough division, the dots formed into a pinwheel and began to spin. As the pinwheel spun, the dots began to rejoin in the same manner as they had divided. I knew that when they were all one again, I would be dead, so I began to fight. The next thing I remember is the doctor trying to awaken me and keep me on the delivery table, because I was getting up.

When my daughter was born, her head was flattened from her forehead to a point in back. They told me that she had lodged against my pelvic bone. But the doctor had already delivered two others that night and was in a hurry to get home. He took her with forceps. I've often wondered if my experience was actually hers, instead.

Although distressing to her, Eppley had this to say about her experience:

I survived and became very strong. Before it happened I was a very weak person who had depended on others all my life. It constantly amazes me that people talk about how much they admire my strength. I developed a lot of character having lived this life and raising four children alone. I can honestly say that I like and respect myself now. I did not when the near-death experience happened. I believe maybe it was sent to show me that I could be strong. I certainly needed that strength in the years that came after.

She expressed disappointment that her case did not match all the wonderful stories other near-death survivors tell. A fellow experiencer suggested that maybe the reason for this was her refusal to "let go" and surrender to the experience, that the battle she had waged so fiercely may have blocked any further development of an uplifting scenario. This idea is not so far-fetched, since recent research suggests that "surrender" may indeed be the factor that determines not only depth of experience but who might possibly have one to begin with, i.e., people who refuse to relinquish the power of their will seldom report the phenomenon.

Yet, if you explore Eppley's life before and after her experience, a startling pattern emerges: This disappointing experience presaged two disappointing marriages, the birth of three more children, verbal and physical abuse, an attempt on her life, plus the ordeal of raising her family without support. The battle fear generated in her near-death episode was *the first time* she had ever stood up for herself. By her admission, the strength she gained from that fight enabled her to call upon deep reservoirs of power she never knew she had. Thus, winning one battle gave her the courage to win many. She has since remarried, and is now a radiantly happy woman. What was originally fearsome turned out to be a godsend.

Eppley's case is an example of why I challenge the surrender theory. Yes, research is persuasive on this issue: It does appear that people who fight the experience seldom have much of an experience, if any. Still, there is a question worthy of asking here, and that question is: Would Eppley have benefited as much as she did had her scenario been sweetly angelic? No one can say, of course, but the question is a valid one, for in asking it we broaden the base of our inquiry from concentrating on the event alone to an equal consideration of the one who experienced the event.

Whether you consider Eppley's case drug induced, undeveloped, or happenstance, the fact remains it did occur during a time in her life when developing psychological "muscle" was more advantageous than becoming spiritually "pious." She needed to get tougher and the experience helped her do it. I have continually observed that all near-death experiences tend to provide the experiencer with an opportunity to rectify a major character flaw or fulfill an emptiness or in some way challenge him or her to loosen up, open up, and grow.

Gloria Hipple of Blakeslee, Pennsylvania, was brought to my attention by Gracia Fay Ellwood (an individual who is investigating hell-like near-death scenarios):

My incident took place in August of 1955. I had been taken to Middlesex Hospital in New Brunswick, New Jersey, due to a miscarriage. Placed in a ward because I was a military dependent, the doctor who was to care for me never came. I was placed at a forty-five-degree angle due to bleeding and was left that way for almost eight days. No one heard my pleas. By the eighth day, I could not hear anyone, my eyes could not see, and I was later told that my body temperature registered 87.6 degrees. I should have been dead.

I recall being pulled down into a spinning vortex. At first, I did not know what was happening. Then I realized my body was being drawn downward, head first. I panicked and fought, trying to grab at the sides of the vortex. All I could think of was my two children. No one would care for them. I pleaded, Please, not now, but I kept moving downward.

I tried to see something, but all there was to see was this cyclonic void that tapered into a funnel. I kept grabbing at the sides but my fingers had nothing to grasp. Terror set in, true terror. I saw a black spot, darker than the funnel and like a black curtain, falling in front of me. Then there was a white dot, like a bright light at the end of the funnel. But as I grew closer, it was a small white skull. It became larger, grinning at me with bare sockets and gaping mouth, and traveling straight toward me like a baseball. Not only was I terrified, I was really livid, too. I struggled to grab hold of anything to keep me from falling, but the skull loomed larger. "My kids, my baby is so little. My little boy, he's only two years old. No!" My words rang in my head and ears. With a bellowing yell, I screamed: "No! damn it, no! Let me go. My babies need me! No! No! No! No!"

The skull shattered into fragments and I slowed in movement. A white light, the brightest light I have ever known or will ever see again was in place of the skull. It was so bright yet it did not blind me. It was a welcome, calming light. The black spot or curtain was gone. I felt absolute peace of mind and sensed myself floating upward, and I was back. I heard my husband calling me, off in the distance. I opened my eyes but could not see him. Two doctors were at the foot of my bed—both were angry and compassionate at the same time. I was taken to the operating room, given several pints of blood and was released one week later.

No one would believe my handshake with the grim reaper. Scoffers almost put me in tears. Everyone laughed at me, including my husband, so I never told my story again—until I wrote to you. It was the most horrendous, yet the most gratifying experience I've ever had in my life.

A flood of memories poured forth once Hipple started talking about her experience, including a nearly forgotten incident that had occurred in 1943 when she had a tonsilectomy:

Ether was the sedation used to put me to sleep. I recall being terrified by the mask and the awful smell. I can still taste it as I think about it. As the sedation took hold, there was the vortex, the dizzy spinning sensation, as I was dragged downward into sleep. I screamed, not knowing what was happening to me.

As she compared the two episodes, she recognized that the vortex experienced during surgical anesthesia in childhood was the same as the one she had encountered as an adult—minus the smell and taste. This association underscores what you find in medical literature. It is well known and documented that certain chemicals, especially ether, can cause vortex or spinning hallucinations. Missing from medical literature, however, is mention of anything more significant than this imagery. No attention is given to possible *after*effects (above and beyond chemical *side* effects). Hipple suffered no side effects from the sedation she was given in 1943, nor any aftereffects from being pulled into the vortex, except for a dislike of ether. But her adult confrontation with the same type of vortex *did* have aftereffects, the kind associated with the near-death phenomenon.

Unlike Eppley, Hipple's hellish near-death scenario was lengthy, intense, fully involved, and resolved in "heavenly" light. A dream? "Absolutely not!" She continues:

My near-death experience has made me quite sensitive to many more things than my mind understands. It also helped me to be less serious about myself. I'm dispensable. I have discovered I do not value "things" as I once did. I befriend people in a different way. I respect their choices to be the people they want to be. The same for my own family. I will guide, but not demand. As for the "Light"—it was then and remains so, my encounter with the most powerful of all entities. The giver of life on both sides of the curtain. After all, I was given a second chance. I am blessed and cannot ask for more.

A closer examination of Hipple's life reveals the sudden development of unique sensitivities afterward. The pending death of an unborn daughter was revealed to her in an unusually detailed vision. When her husband died in a trucking accident at

4:15 A.M., she was up and prepared for it, and even heard a thump against her trailer home at the exact moment he was killed some distance away. Strange sensations about her sister awakened her from a deep sleep at the exact moment her sister died. "I am more sensitive to people's thoughts and actions than before. I follow hunches that are sometimes quite accurate."

Like Eppley, Gloria Hipple now glows with a special confidence, charm, and wisdom. She speaks effusively of God and angels. "The curtain, the darkness, the skull, the void, the terror, the anger, the fight, the light. There was nothing more than that, but it changed my life." Her hellish experience transformed her from being dependent on outer circumstances and material possessions to the realization of greater truths and the power of inner peace. No drug-induced hallucination ever recorded fostered the kind of life-shift that happened to this woman, and she is one of millions.

(Hipple drew the four-part picture on the next page to illustrate the four major segments of her trip into the depths of death.)

Next is a case of a haunting, and of an experiencer assaulted by entities awaiting her arrival in the tunnel. But there is more to the story of Sandra H. Brock of Staunton, Virginia, than first glance reveals—proof that one cannot judge a near-death scenario solely by its description. You must investigate before and after conditions in the person's life to reach any kind of meaningful context within which to consider the experience:

> I had a stomach stapling in 1980 and, in the process, had to have a deformed spleen removed. I hemorrhaged on the operating table, and the doctor said that at three times he thought he was going to lose me. The first day after surgery I had to have transfusions. During one of the transfusions I started feeling really weird. I felt like if I shut my eyes I would never open them again. I called a nurse. Of course, she said it was all in my head, and left the room. I remember she just walked out the door and I started being pulled through a tunnel. It was a terrible experience because all I could see were people from my past, people who were already dead, who had done or said something to me that had hurt me in one way or another. They were laughing and screaming, until I thought I could not stand it. I begged and begged that I be allowed to go back. I could see a light at the

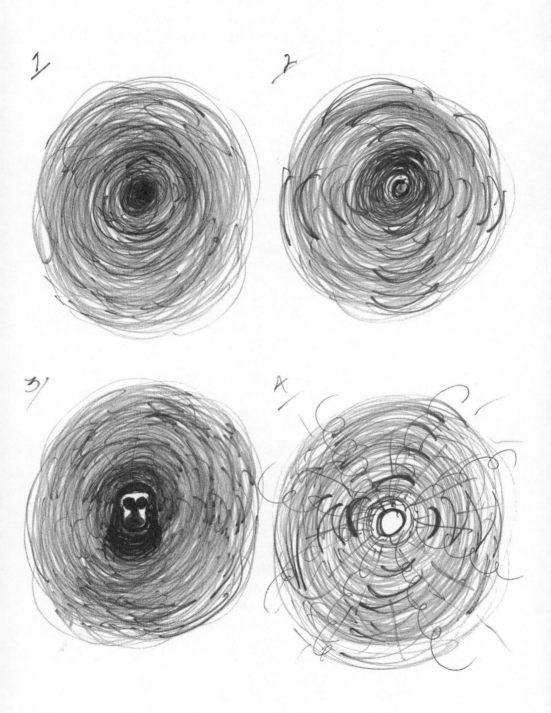

end of the tunnel, but I never really got close to it. All of a sudden I was back in my bed, just thankful I had not died.

Brock, as it turns out, has had several near-death-type experiences, scattered over a long life.

My mother told me that when she found she was pregnant with me, she prayed that I would die. They were just coming out of the depression and they already had a baby and could not afford another. When I was born, I was born with a harelip. Mother thought that was her punishment for wanting me dead. Within several days, and without any surgery, my harelip healed itself, and to this day I do not carry a scar. She also told me that when I was only a few weeks old, she came to my bassinet and found me not breathing. I had already turned purple. She grabbed me, shook me, and blew in my face until I started breathing again. I don't remember this experience, but I do remember being in a bassinet that had no liner. I remember studying my hands and what my hands looked like as an infant. My mother said I couldn't possibly remember this, but I did, and I was right.

Until the age of four, Brock survived numerous nearly fatal accidents that caused cessation of breath. Her memory of each is detailed and verified by relatives, even though several occurred when she was only a toddler. Right from her earliest years (I suspect from when she was but a few weeks old), she displayed the typical aftereffects of the near-death phenomenon, including stunningly accurate psychic abilities, extended perceptual range, and heightened faculties. Like Hipple, she has been visited by the dead, "advised" of pending deaths, and has known the exact moment individuals died.

Yet Brock has been haunted throughout her life, and not just by the deceased who grabbed at her in death's tunnel. An overshadowing theme of "Why would anyone want to harm me?" seems to have permeated every aspect of her life's experiences, from her memory of frightening creatures crawling into her bed when she was young and making her scream and cry, to adult misunderstandings and distressing dreams. It's almost as if her mother's prayer that she die imprinted her brain in some manner. I say that because Brock's many brushes with death, even as an infant, were precipitated by acts of self-destructive behavior. That single overshadowing theme continued to undermine the satisfaction that her many accomplishments in life should have given her. This did not change until after her husband's suicide in 1983. At that time, according to Brock, her father and son, long since dead, and her recently deceased husband, physically and in broad daylight, drove up to her front door in an old Cadillac, honked the horn, and called out, "We're together now and we're okay. We just wanted you to know." With that said, the group, car and all, disappeared. This ghostly spectacle gave Brock the reassurance she needed to finally free herself from the "ghost" of her own past. Her mother's death decree, which she had subconsciously been trying to both justify and nullify throughout her life, was finally put to rest when her husband's suicide forced her to confront her own life's issues as she came to terms with his.

In Brock's case, her near-death episode was but one in a long series of similar events that finally brought her to that point of peace within herself where true forgiveness and understanding reside.

Some researchers think unpleasant or hell-like near-death episodes are partial, incomplete experiences, perhaps aberrations of some kind, or a confrontation with the issue of mortality. I've even heard it said that you can recognize a hellish one by the direction an individual travels in the tunnel—down for hell, up for heaven. Since the ones discussed so far in this chapter have involved several directions of tunnel traveling, obviously, this assumption isn't true. Nor is it true that only Bible Belters and fundamentalists (people who profess belief in devils and damnation), will necessarily experience a hell.

Back in the sixties, my very first encounter with the near-death phenomenon involved people who had experienced the hellish version. What I discovered back then about the reality and the power of these episodes made a significant difference in the way I would interview experiencers many years later.

My encounter took place at St. Alphonsus Hospital in Boise, Idaho, when I was visiting a woman who had suffered a heart attack. She had just moved to town from southern California and, because I had previously befriended her, she requested that I come. She was chalk white with fear when I arrived. While clinically dead, she had experienced an incident that went like this: She floated out of her body and into a dark tunnel, then headed through the tunnel toward a bright light ahead. Once the light was reached, she came to view a landscape of barren, rolling hills filled to overflowing with nude, zombie-like people standing elbow to elbow doing nothing but staring straight at her. She was so horrified at what she saw that she started screaming. This snapped her back into her body, where she continued screaming until sedated. As she relayed her story, she went on to declare death a nightmare, then cursed every church throughout all history for misleading people with rubbish about any kind of heaven. She was inconsolable.

As I patiently listened, two other people entered the room, an elderly man and woman, both walking with canes. Each of them had suffered heart failure, too, and had later revived after being declared dead. Both relayed substantially the same story as the woman I knew. And they were equally frightened. The three had found out about each other from nurses who had been comparing notes on patients they felt were having strange hallucinations.

This was such a coincidence that I instinctively began asking confrontational questions. This is what my questions revealed: None of these three people had the same religion, background, or lifestyle. None had mutual friends or common interests, nor did they have the same doctor in attendance. They had never seen each other before. All had lived long lives of various degrees of hardship and success; two were still married to their original spouses and had several grown children apiece; the woman from California had been divorced several times and had no children. The only link I could find, besides their heart ailments and the fact that their rooms were on the same hospital floor, was this: *All three confessed to having hidden within their deepest selves varying types of guilt.* This guilt seemed quite painful to them and the strange "vision" they experienced while "dead" only served to deepen that pain. They admitted to me that they met what they most feared in dying, which confirmed and strengthened their already strong belief that their "sins" would be punished.

Before I left, a nurse took me aside and said there was one more experiencer, a man recovering from surgery who was so shaken he refused to speak with anyone, but kept muttering words like "hills and hills of nude people, all staring." I was not allowed to see him.

Why four people within a span of two days at the same hospital had the same basic experience brought on by the same type of ailment is a mystery to me. I could offer no consolation to any of them. I could only listen and ask questions. The whole thing was so unnerving I was shaking when I left the hospital. What became of these four people, I do not know. The woman from California became so irrational and rude afterward that I stopped visiting her. Had I known then what I know now, I would have handled the situation differently. These people were absolutely convinced there is a hell.

Since 1978, when I began to do serious research on near-death, I have at times been almost engulfed with reports of hellish cases...like the man in his middle thirties who stopped at my table during a book signing in a large mall, and yelled: "You've got to tell people about hell. There is one. I know. I've been there. All them experiencers on television telling their pretty stories about heaven, that's not the way it is. There's a hell, and people go there."

Initially, I asked such people, Why are you telling me this and not other researchers? Their answers: "You're a fellow experiencer and you know I'm not lying" or "I don't trust the others" or "You understand."

Other researchers claim that hell-like cases account for less than 1 percent of the total, a mere anomaly. I have always claimed the opposite is true—one out of seven in my present study. Why the disparity?

Consider this: At the 1990 Washington, D.C., conference of the International Association for Near-Death Studies (IANDS), Bruce Greyson, a psychiatrist noted for his long-term commitment to near-death research, admitted that people like him had not been asking the right questions to identify those who might have undergone "dark" or distressing episodes. He confessed: "We didn't try to find them because we didn't want to know." His comment underscored the fact that, for the most part, published reports of near-death studies have sidestepped negative accounts.

Since his admission, Greyson and Nancy Evans Bush, president of IANDS, have completed a descriptive study of fifty terrifying near-death cases they have collected over the past nine years. It was published in *Psychiatry*, in February 1992. British researcher Margot Grey [5] and sociologist Charles Flynn [6] have also acknowledged the existence of such experiences in their work. Yet only cardiologist Maurice Rawlings and I have actively pursued near-death reports of a hellish nature since the beginning of our involvement in the field, and we have found many.

Beyond Death's Door, Rawlings's first book [7], focused on his observations of people in the process of being resuscitated after clinical death. In it, he recounts story after story of near-death survivors describing unpleasant or threatening scenarios: being surrounded by grotesque human and animal forms, hearing other people moaning and in pain, violence and demonic types of torture. Rawlings believed that since he was present when the phenomenon actually occurred, he was able to obtain pure and unrepressed reports. This led him to formulate his theory that at least half of near-death experiences begin as hell-like, then become heaven-like as the episode progresses, with the average individual able to remember only the heavenly segment once revived.

Rawlings's second book, *Before Death Comes*, and his latest, *To Hell and Back* [8], add to his original claims that in order for people to die a good death and avoid the horrors of what must assuredly be hell, they should commit themselves to the doctrines of Christianity. Needless to say, Rawlings created quite a stir in the research community. So far, no other physician has been able to substantiate either the extent of his anecdotal findings or his theory, even when present during ongoing resuscitation procedures conducted in clinical settings.

Rawlings's observations have been confined to experiencers either in a particular locale, or to those who have been heavily influenced by fundamentalist religious teachings. He does not have a diverse or cross-cultural research base. Neither do several other researchers in the field, for that matter. And I can appreciate this to a point, given the time and money constraints we all work under. But a narrow research base can bias your findings no matter how careful you are, and sometimes in unexpected ways. Thus, numbers are not always as valuable as broadness of scope. I have noticed that: *Deeply rooted belief systems and regionalisms can color an individual's description and interpretation of his or her experience.* Although the pattern of the near-death phenomenon remains the same for all, imagery can and does vary across population groups and continents.

For this reason, I'd like to put a few things in perspective about hell. Historically, hell is not a biblical concept, although many people like to think it is. What came to be translated as hell was a peculiar idiom in the Aramaic language that used the name of a city dump where trash was burned to signify "mental torment" and "regret." Centuries later, and after numerous translations of the Bible, what was originally expressed as *Gehenna of Fire* was changed to *hell*.

The word *hell* is actually Scandinavian and refers to Hel, the Teutonic queen of the dead and ruler of "the other world." According to Norse myth, "to Hel" is where people went who were good, but not quite good enough to transcend to Valhalla, that heavenly hall reserved for heroes killed in battle and other special folk. Unlike more modern symbols depicting satanic figures and being burned for one's sins, there was nothing evil or scary about Hell (or Hel herself, except her looks). She was said to be deformed, with half of her face human and the other half featureless. Over time allusions to Hel connoted "an abode of the dead," not some place of everlasting punishment.

Today, the type of hell most people visualize when they say the word is a European conceptualization used during the early days of Christianity to scare converts into obedience. Depictions in such classics as Dante's *The Divine Comedy* [9] and Dickens's *A Christmas Carol* [10] further popularized this concept. Thornton Wilder's clever play *Our Town* [11] used comedy to explore how the deceased could linger in cemeteries before making their final "crossover." Many modern Christians, especially fundamentalists, continue to foster notions such as these—which are more political than biblical.

A reference to the hell an individual might encounter during the death process and after passing through death's "door" is found in *The Tibetan Book of the Dead* [12]. This ancient text describes three stages, or *bardos*, said to follow death, and explains how each stage represents an opportunity for the departed to inhabit a different level of existence beyond that of embodiment. According to this book, heavenly visions resembling what are now referred to as states of consciousness occur during the first week after death, hellish ones during the second week, and various opportunities for judging one's life in the third. Unlike Dante's *Divine Comedy*, this traditional Tibetan view chronicles the various gateways it is possible for one to enter after death, and between incarnations. Specifically detailed is a period of twenty-eight to forty-nine days after a person has died.

Heaven-like scenarios outlined in *The Tibetan of the Dead* book are strikingly similar to current near-death reports: visions of pure light, vibrant landscapes as if in springtide, blindingly open clear skies, dazzlement. Equally similar are the hell-like versions: terrifying deities, gruesome apparitions, racking and painful torture. Also described are the life-review process, judgment, and a disembodied state; then rebirth into this or other worlds for further growth and learning.

In 1980, Kenneth Ring reported the finding that those with prior knowledge of the near-death phenomenon were less likely to experience it, while those with no prior knowledge were more likely to do so. A clue as to why this could be true is mentioned in the Tibetan book as well. There the claim is made that all postmortem visions, regardless of type, are actually projections from the mind of the participant. This implies that the next world may be structured by the subconscious mind, that mental imagery somehow determines what is met after death. Also implied is that both heavenly and hellish scenarios might well represent part of the natural course of consciousness as it shifts from one state of awareness to another, and through numerous levels of existence.

Oddly, the realness of near-death experiences is not diminished by this claim, or others like it. The phenomenon instead becomes subjected to psychic rather than physical laws, which I believe accounts for the variation of details and descriptions from culture to culture, group to group.

During my own interviews of experiencers, for instance, I discovered little difference between heavenly and hellish near-death episodes in consideration of how elements unfolded in sequence. By that I mean the universal elements now identified as central to the phenomenon can and often do appear in both types and in the same basic sequence pattern: an out-of-body experience, passing through a dark tunnel or some kind of darkness, seeing a light ahead, entering into that light, and suddenly finding one's self in another realm of existence usually replete with people, landscapes, and, occasionally, animals. Hellish episodes can also include dialogue with beings on the other side of death along with glimpses of the life just lived—

features once thought to occur only in heaven-like cases. Both types are, in fact, a lot alike. Yet they do differ in the specifics of detail, interpretation, and emotional response.

To illustrate these differences, here is a comparison chart from my original study that focuses on the language experiencers used to describe what they encountered. Notice consistent settings yet obvious contrasts with interpretation of detail:

Heaven-like Cases	Hell-like Cases
Friendly beings	Lifeless or threatening apparitions
Beautiful, lovely environments	Barren or ugly expanses
Conversations and dialogue	Threats, screams, silence
Total acceptance and an overwhelming sensation of love	Danger and the possibility of violence and/or torture
A feeling of warmth and a sense of heaven	A feeling of cold (or of temperature extremes), and a sense of hell

In the hell-like cases I've dealt with, seldom does anyone mention fiery hot or burning sensations; rather, most comment on how cold it was, or clammy or shivery or somehow "hard" or empty. Also mentioned is the dullness of the light, sometimes gray or "heavy" as if overcast, foggy. Many experienced a bright light beckoning to them initially, but when they entered the light it promptly dimmed or darkened. Invariably, an attack of some kind or a shunning would take place, and pain would be felt or surges of anxiety. Any indifference would be severe, as would the necessity of the experiencer to defend him or herself and/or fight for the right to continued existence. I found themes of good and evil, beings like devils and angels, to be commonplace.

Also common are reports of hauntings after the individual revives and resumes the routines of daily living. These are perceived as physical, very solid and real. The numerous claims that a "devil" can suddenly appear and disappear, as he chases the experiencer in broad daylight to try and capture his or her soul or do battle, are an example. Manifestations such as this are depicted in the 1990 movie *Flatliners* (directed by Schumacher,

1990). Sometimes fearful scenes and sensations can manifest themselves later on, as when an experiencer is unexpectedly faced with an onslaught of the storm, whirlpool, or tidal wave faced in death, or finds him or herself suddenly falling unchecked into what seems to be a bottomless void.

My third near-death experience was like this. Precipitated by a complete physical, emotional, and mental collapse (that I believe was triggered by the emotional despair I felt at the time), my body fell away as I, the soul I perceived myself to be, took leave and soared high through the night sky, drawn to a "lip of light." Once absorbed into that light, I was surprised at what I saw. There before me was a gigantic form, like two cyclones one above the other in an hourglass shape, spinning at tremendous speeds—the one on top was moving clockwise and the bottom one, counterclockwise. Where the two cyclones should have touched but didn't, there burst forth rays of the strangest light I have ever seen—piercing in its intensity. After I revived and was given the medical care I needed, a peculiar thing happened: The cyclones began to physically manifest themselves. I'd be speaking with my oldest daughter, Natalie, when she'd disappear and in her place would be the cyclones. I'd be at the kitchen sink doing dishes, look up, and be taken aback by the sudden emergence of these massive shapes. It made no difference what I was doing, where I was, or the time of day, as to when they'd appear. Their intrusion was always totally and completely real. This was not as frightening to me as it was unnerving.

The cyclone affair haunted me in varying degrees of frequency and intensity for more than a decade. I was deep into writing the book that will follow this one when, as part of the project, I needed to recreate my third near-death experience from memory and confront the cyclones. As I relaxed in front of my computer, more details revealed themselves until the image on the screen took on their shape—literally! The middle, where the spouts should have touched but didn't, rapidly expanded to be larger and larger until it physically exploded right through the monitor screen, flinging sparkly particles of a radiation-type substance all over me, my office, and the nearby hallway. The smell was awful—a kind of flat, acrid ozone odor. I was shaken, but unhurt. When I took the monitor in for a replacement, the computer technician shook his head and said it was impossible for a monitor to blow up like that—yet in his hands was proof positive. This peculiar event laid to rest thirteen years of avoidance, during which I had steadfastly refused to confront what the image of those cyclones might mean. The cause of my haunting was not the cyclones, it was unexpressed fear.

And fear, I discovered, is the causal factor in *every single case of hauntings* claimed by near-death survivors.

Three puzzles emerged from my research on unpleasant and/or hell-like experiences:

Elements—The same thing that one person would describe as "horrendous," another would term "wondrous."

Scenarios—Whether or not an individual could handle the experience, cope with it, had more to do with the labeling of "heavenly" or "hellish" than the actual content.

Experiencers—Only adults reported unpleasant and/or hell-like episodes; children didn't.

Hellish near-death scenarios are easy to generalize about, or toss off as mental projections from "sinners" or religious zealots, or brand as so rare they are hardly worth the effort to investigate. Yet to do this is a mistake. These cases are worth serious study.

The common denominator I found in unpleasant and/or hell-like experiences is a process of inner purification, a fantastic "house cleaning" of sorts, which seems to operate on levels more powerful than personal or religious belief.

What happened to a Connecticut woman addresses this. The daughter of Unitarian ministers, she was married and worked as an academic administrator when, during the premature delivery of her second child, things went awry.

I knew the hospital and the world were receding below me, very fast; to this day my mind holds a sharp picture of them down there, though I don't know how I could so clearly have seen something I didn't look at. I was rocketing through space like an astronaut without a capsule, with immense speed and great distance. A small group of circles appeared ahead of me, some tending toward the left. To the right was just a dark space. The circles were black and white, and made a clicking sound as they snapped black to white, white to black. They were jeering and tormenting, not evil, exactly, but more mocking and mechanistic. The message in their clicking was: Your life never existed. The world never existed. Your family never existed. You were allowed to imagine it. You were allowed to make it up. It was never there. There is nothing here. There was never anything there. That's the joke—it was all a joke.

She commented on the malicious laughter the circles made and on the lengthy argument she gave to prove life did indeed exist. Then the darkness thinned into a never-ending void that went on and on.

The grief was just wrenching; this world gone, and grass, and my first baby and all the other babies, and hills. I knew no one could bear that much grief, but there didn't seem to be any end of it, and no way out. Everyone I loved was gone. It was more than real: absolute reality. There's a cosmic terror we have never addressed. The despair was because of the absolute conviction that I had seen what the other side was— I never thought of it as hell—and there was no way to tell anyone. It wouldn't matter how I died or when, damnation was out there, just waiting.

She was leafing through a book six years later and happened upon a page picturing the circles from her near-death experience. She threw the book across the room in one shudder. That was a moment of both terror and corroboration for her—as the circles turned out to be the yin/yang symbols of polarity from traditional Eastern teachings.

Years later, she answered a newspaper ad for the position of office manager with a nonprofit organization operating out of a small office at the University of Connecticut in Storrs. Kenneth Ring hired her. Thus, Nancy Evans Bush became the first and only executive director IANDS ever had.

Evans Bush was frustrated during her early days on the job, and more than just a little confused, when she came to realize that she, too, was an experiencer—but of the "dark" kind rarely mentioned. Her administrative position came and went as the organization restructured, but her growing awareness of what she had once gone through during childbirth, and what it might mean, became the impetus she used to finally accept her own goodness and her own worth. She is now a pastoral counselor and poet with an exceptional understanding of people and their problems. She was elected president of IANDS's board of directors and has become a researcher of "distressing" near-death cases. What she learned from coming to terms with her own experience she is now using to help thousands of others come to terms with theirs.

Stigmatizing the unpleasant and/or hell-like scenario is wrong.

What I have observed in every case I have investigated is that the hellish version of near-death is a confrontation with one's shadow (that aspect of self either repressed or denied). It is a mechanism the psyche uses...for healing and for growth.

FOUR

Pleasant and/or Heaven-like Experience

A billion stars go spinning through the night,
blazing high above your head. But in you is the
presence that will be, when all the stars are
dead.
                                    —Rainer Maria Rilke

Pleasant and/or Heaven-like Experience (reassurance and self-validation) *Heaven-like scenarios of loving family reunions with those who have died previously, reassuring religious figures or light beings, validation that life counts, affirmative and inspiring dialogue. Usually experienced by those who most need to know how loved they are and how important life is and how every effort has a purpose in the overall scheme of things.*

More men than women spoke to me of encountering a hellish environment during their near-death experiences, yet when I asked for material I could quote, not a single man cooperated. Hence, only the cases of women were offered in the last chapter. For the heavenly version, gender made no difference. Both sexes were equally open verbally, and, when I asked them to draw what they had seen in dying, equally hesitant. What few pictures I was able to obtain are scattered throughout this book.

Since pleasant and/or heaven-like scenarios constitute the vast bulk of reported cases, it is no wonder that the basic storyline has become virtually mythologized in the last two decades. Just as there is more to the hellish version than meets the eye, so, too, is there more to the tales of heaven than is generally acknowledged.

Our investigation begins with what happened in the spring of 1987 to Jennine Wolff of Troy, New York. She was thirty years old at the time. Due to complications from endometriosis, she suffered numerous bouts of hemorrhaging, several surgeries (including a hysterectomy), an additional hemorrhage of massive proportions, and, finally, emergency surgery. During the final operation, she floated out of her body and entered another realm of existence:

> Suddenly I was aware of being in the most beautiful garden I've ever seen. I felt whole and loved. My sense of well-being was complete. I heard celestial music clearly and saw vivid colored flowers, like nothing seen on earth, gorgeous greenery and trees.
>
> As I looked around, I saw at a distance, on a hill, Jesus Christ. All he said to me was that it was up to me whether to come back to earth or not. I chose to come back to finish my work. That is when I was born again.
>
> The changes in my life? I am now more aware of people's feelings, beliefs, and needs. I am more compassionate and considerate of others. Also more confident in God's love.

When you delve into Wolff's history, a fascinating pattern emerges—one of disciplined devotion to the spiritual path. Raised in a strict but loving Presbyterian home, she suddenly developed the ability to have visions when but a teenager. Her concerned parents took her for evaluation to the spiritualist camp of Lily Dale, located in New York State [13]. These experienced psychics advised them that their daughter had a special gift, and that she must decide whether to go on with a normal teenage life or commit herself to spiritual training. She chose to develop her gift. At the age of twenty-one and after seven years of instruction, Wolff met Sam Lentine, a blind biophysicist. He had the scientific background; she had the spiritual. Together they formed a professional partnership dedicated to the restoration of true health and wholeness throughout humankind. Fourteen years later, after the partners had tremendous strides in the health field and were becoming internationally known for their ability to facilitate the healing process, Lentine died. Today, Wolff is a waitress at a senior citizens' facility.

Reflecting on her own death experience, as well as her present situation, she had this to say:

It was my mother who came into my hospital room and said, "You have died and come back." I knew I had died, but she confirmed it. I felt like a baby afterward, and, at the age of thirty, was faced with learning about life all over again. I couldn't stand light at first. When I could, everything became brighter and better than before. My whole perspective drastically improved; I felt more grounded, solid, okay. My psychic gifts skyrocketed. But it still took me a long time to readjust. The doctors said, Oh, it's just the stress of what you've been through. I disagreed. What I was going through was unrelated to the surgery. My mother and father understood, and, especially, my mother's constant love and support made it possible for me to grasp hold of my new life and deal with it. My death stepped up my original commitment to serve as a healer.

Afterward, my abilities sharpened, were better and more attuned. I was much more understanding of others. When I went back to work, Sam and I peaked in our performance—we did our best work. Five years later Sam died. You have to understand how close we were, how bonded our families. Even though I knew death didn't end anything, Sam's transition threw me. I had to readjust all over again. I work with older people now, giving them my love with each touch. I don't know what's ahead for me or where I'll go, but I am taking massage classes—learning to heal in a different way. My life is now in God's hands. New opportunities for me to serve are opening up.

Back in 1932, Arthur E. Yensen, a university graduate and staunch-materialist-turned-syndicated-cartoonist, decided to take some time off to research his weekly cartoon strip, *Adventurous Willie Wispo*. Since his main character was a hobo, Yensen became one for a while, blending in with the over sixteen million unemployed at that time in our nation's history. He bummed rides from Chicago through Minnesota, until a young man in a convertible coupe picked him up on the way to Winnipeg. Going too fast for the road conditions, the car hit a three-foot-high ridge of oiled gravel and flipped into a series of violent somersaults. Both men were catapulted through the cloth top before the car smashed into a ditch. The driver escaped unharmed, but Yensen was injured, losing consciousness just as two female spectators rushed to his aid:

Gradually the earth scene faded away, and through it loomed a bright, new, beautiful world—beautiful beyond imagination! For half a minute I could see both worlds at once. Finally, when the earth was all gone, I stood in a glory that could only be heaven.

In the background were two beautiful, round-topped mountains, similar to Fujiyama in Japan. The tops were snowcapped, and the slopes were adorned with foliage of indescribable beauty. The mountains appeared to be about fifteen miles away, yet I could see individual flowers growing on their slopes. I estimated my vision to be about one hundred times better than on earth.

To the left was a shimmering lake containing a different kind of water—clear, golden, radiant, and alluring. It seemed to be alive. The whole landscape was carpeted with grass so vivid, clear, and green, that it defies description. To the right was a grove of large, luxuriant trees, composed of the same clear material that seemed to make up everything.

I saw twenty people beyond the first trees, playing a singing-dancing game something like Skip-to-My-Lou. they were having a hilarious time holding hands and dancing in a circle—fast and lively. As soon as they saw me, four of the players left the game and joyfully skipped over to greet me. As they approached, I estimated their ages to be: one, thirty; two, twenty; and one, twelve. Their bodies seemed almost weightless, and the grace and beauty of their easy movements was fascinating to watch. Both sexes had long, luxuriant hair entwined with flowers, which hung down in glossy masses to their waists. Their only clothing was a gossamer loin cloth with a loop over one shoulder and a broad ribbon streaming out behind in graceful curves and curlicues. Their magnificence not only thrilled me, but filled me with awe.

The oldest, largest, and strongest-looking man announced pleasantly, "You are in the land of the dead. We lived on earth, just like you, 'til we came here." He invited me to look at my arm. I looked, and it was translucent; that is, I could dimly see through it. Next they had me look at the grass and trees. They were also translucent. It was exactly the way the Bible had described heaven.

Then I noticed that the landscape was gradually becoming familiar. It seemed as if I had been here before. I remembered what was on the other side of the mountains. Then with a sudden burst of joy, I realized that *this was my real home!* Back on earth I had been a visitor, a misfit, and a homesick stranger. With a sigh of relief, I said to myself, Thank God I'm back again. This time I'll stay!

The oldest man, who looked like a Greek god, continued to explain. "Everything over here is pure. The elements don't mix or break down as they do on earth. Everything is kept in place by an all-prevading Master-Vibration, which prevents aging. That's why things don't get dirty, or wear out, and why everything looks so bright and new." Then I understood how heaven could be eternal.

Yensen's rapturous visit was lengthy; more details are contained in his self-published book, *I Saw Heaven* [14]. He did not want to leave, but was told:

You have more important work to do on earth, and you must go back and do it! There will come a time of great confusion and the people will need your stabilizing influence. When your work on earth is done, then you can come back here and stay.

Born on a Nebraska sandhill during the blizzard of 1898, Yensen recalled being force-fed religion as a youngster. Not only did he turn against it, but he started challenging his parents at every turn—including questioning the way they ate. He observed that their farm animals did just fine on a diet of fresh greens and whole grains, yet family members were always suffering indigestion and constipation from the white flour, sugar, and grease they consumed. Behind his parents' back, he cured himself by eating bran flakes. He continued to defy the conventions of his day, switching from atheism to mysticism after his near-death experience at the age of thirty-four. Yensen went on to serve as a muleskinner during World War I, married when the war was over, and built his own home in Parma, Idaho, from pumice blocks he and his sons quarried. He later became an educator, public speaker, was active in politics, specialized in historical sculpture (his work adorns Parma's city park), was a movie extra in several Hollywood films, an authority on organic gardening and nutrition, and was singled out as one of Idaho's "Most Distinguished Citizens."

Although a public figure, Yensen was frequently at odds with the school boards where he taught: opposing any procedure that capped a child's creative drive; speaking out against the incarceration of American citizens of Japanese ancestry during World War II; and ignoring school rules by sharing his near-death experience in class as proof to his students that morality matters and life really has a purpose. Ironically, Yensen was still questioning whether or not he had fulfilled his life's work when he returned "home" in 1992, the quiet benefactor of thousands.

On the next page is his depiction of what it was like to see both worlds at the same time, as he passed into the realms of radiance after being "killed" in a car accident.

Alice Morrison-Mays nearly died at the Marine Hospital in New Orleans, Louisiana, after being rushed there in a coma. She had given birth to her third son two weeks before. It was in May 1952.

From my position near the ceiling, I watched as they began to wrap both my legs from tips of the toes up to my hips, then my arms and hands up to the shoulders. This was to keep what blood remained for my heart and lungs. Then they tilted my body so my legs were up in the air and I was standing on my head!

I was furious about the way they had handled Jeff's birth and now they were running around like chickens with their heads cut off squawking loudly; and here I was looking at that silent, bandaged body lying on a tilt table, head to the floor, legs and feet in the air. I was venting my anger and frustration from the corner of the ceiling on the right side of my body. I can remember the anger vividly, fury at the powerless position this whole event put me in, and I was very "verbal" about it—silently—up there, as my mind raced

Used with permission from *I Saw Heaven* by Arthur E. Yensen.

to express its reaction, worry, and concern. Their statements "We're losing her! We're losing her!" frightened me and I'd get pissed all over again.

The scene changed and I was no longer in that room. I found myself in a place of such beauty and peace. It was timeless and spaceless. I was aware of delicate and shifting hues of colors with their accompanying rainbows of "sound," though there was no noise in this sound. It might have felt like wind and bells, were it earthly. I "hung" there— floating. Then I became aware of other loving, caring beings hovering near me. Their presence was so welcoming and nurturing. They appeared "formless" in the way I was accustomed by now to seeing things. I don't know how to describe them. I was aware of some bearded male figures in white robes in a semicircle around me. The atmosphere became blended as though made of translucent clouds. I watched as these clouds and their delicate shifting colors moved through and around us.

A dialogue softly started with answers to my unfinished questions almost before I could form them. They said they were my guides and helpers as well as being God's messengers. Even though they were assigned to me as a human—and always available to me—they had other purposes, too. They were in charge of other realms in creation and had the capacity of being in several places simultaneously. They were also "in charge" of several different levels of knowledge. I became aware of an ecstasy and a joy that permeated the whole, unfolding beyond anything that I had experienced in my living twenty-five years, up to that point. Even having my two previous children, whom I wanted very much, couldn't touch the "glow" of this special experience.

Then I was aware of an Immense Presence coming toward me, bathed in white, shimmering light that glowed and at times sparkled like diamonds. Everything else seen, the colors, beings, faded into the distance as the Light Being permeated everything. I was being addressed by an overwhelming presence. Even though I felt unworthy, I was being lifted into that which I could embrace. The Joy and Ecstasy were intoxicating. It was "explained" that I could remain there if I wanted; it was a choice I could make.

There was much teaching going on, and I was just "there" silently, quietly. I felt myself expanding and becoming part of All That Was in Total Freedom Unconditionally. I became aware again that I needed to make a choice. Part of me wanted to remain forever, but I finally realized I didn't want to leave a new baby motherless. I left with sadness and reluctance.

Almost instantly I felt reentry into my body through the silver cord at the top of my head. There was something akin to a physical bump. As soon as I entered, I heard someone near me say, "Oh, we've got her back." I was told I had had two pieces of placenta as large as grapefruits removed.

Morrison-Mays told no one except her husband about the monumental experience she had just had. She managed to squelch any noticeable aftereffects until 1967, when developing psychic sensitivities warned her of a need to make a major change in her life or die.

My inner voice burst into activity, somehow picking up the loose threads of my near-death experience. The growth effect was propelling me to move on and develop my own responsibility and talents. I finally listened. My spiritual life was beginning. I divorced and started a career as a musician (cellist) in a major symphony orchestra.

Twelve years later, because of serious difficulty walking and severe hip pain, she had a right hip osteotomy to reduce arthritic damage (the joint in her hip was placed in a different weight-bearing position). The operation went well, but upon reviving, Morrison-Mays entered an altered state of consciousness similar to a near-death episode that she continued to slip in and out of for six months. Throughout this lengthy visionary experience, she received lessons from The Other Side. These "etheric" teachings covered such topics as the geography of the soul, karma, advanced physics, and the cosmology of the Human Experiment. Again her life was profoundly affected. She began volunteering in a hospice afterward and enrolled in a three-year spiritual psychology course.

A second near-death event seven years later plunked her right back in that same etheric classroom she had "attended" after hip surgery. This occasion was precipitated by the sudden onslaught of a severe type of emphysema and the collapse of her adrenal system (Addison's disease). Severe shakes from what she feels was a Kundalini episode complicated the situation. (Traditionally, Kundalini is said to be a powerful energy that lies dormant in a person's sacrum until he or she begins to develop spiritually. Then it supposedly rises up the spine, stimulating the glandular centers until it bursts out a person's head.) Morrison-Mays turned to a chiropractic physician when medical treatment failed her and, once more, completely changed her life. She left the world she had created for herself after her divorce and moved bag and baggage to Quincy, Illinois, the city of her birth.

Virtually wheelchair bound, and robbed by illness of much of her energy, Morrison-Mays has instituted a series of classical music concerts for the public that are staged in her own living room. Newspaper headlines label her concerts "Healing Music." You would never know by the glow on her face and her ever-present smile that she lives in almost constant pain.

> I chose a "big one" this lifetime. The spiritual guidance I receive makes living this life possible. I have walked through the Dark Side and have no fear of my Shadow anymore. I am here to heal my life and do serious writing, though I'm not certain if I am ready to write about the teachings I have been given. What I want is to do a book about the memories I have of choosing my parents before I was born, my experience in the womb, and my rebirthing through the near-death phenomenon.

A role model for the handicapped, Morrison-Mays has become a living legend. She offered this about the severity of her situation: "There's still a quality of life available. You just have to be open enough to explore it. You can empower yourself."

"It happened one bright sunshiny day in the summer of 1973," explained Steven B. Ridenhour of Charlottesville, Virginia. He and his friend Debbie had decided to run the rapids at the bullhole, part of the river that runs behind an old cotton mill in Cooleemee, North Carolina. Both had been smoking pot and were easily bored. There decision to run the knee-high rapids meant that they had to start at the beginning of the rock incline, run down about twenty feet, and start skiing barefooted until they reached the moss beds. The sport could have been great fun, but not on this trip:

We smoked another joint and then headed toward the rapids. Debbie begins laughing, and the next thing I know we're overtaken by laughter. The giggling stops as we're swept off our feet and dragged downriver. Debbie cries out, "Steven I can't swim, I'm drowning." I feel powerless because I can't get to her and I'm yelling, "Hang on, don't panic," when I take in a tremendous mouthful of water. Without any warning, time, as I know it, stops.

The water has a golden glow and I find myself just floating as without gravity, feeling very warm and comfortable. I'm floating in a vertical position with my arms outstretched and my head laying on my left shoulder. I feel totally at peace and full of serenity in this timeless space. Next I go through a past-life review. It was like looking at a very fast slide show of my past life, and I do mean fast, like seconds. I don't quite understand the significance of all the events that were shown to me, but I'm sure there is some importance. When this ended, it was as if I was floating very high up and looking down at a funeral. Suddenly I realized that I was looking at myself in a casket. I saw myself dressed in a black tux with a white shirt and a red rose on my left lapel. Standing around me were my immediate family and significant friends.

Then, as if some powerful force wrapped around me, I was thrust out of the water, gasping for air. There was Debbie within arm's reach. I grabbed her by the back of her hair and I was able to get us both over to the rocks and out of the water. After lying on the rocks for a while, I glance over at Debbie and it's like looking at a ghost. As she describes what she went through, it became apparent that we both had the same experience underwater—the golden glow, the serenity, seeing our lives flash before us, floating over a funeral, and seeing ourselves in a casket. That's the only time we ever talked about it. I haven't seen or talked with Debbie since.

For the next eleven years, Ridenhour tried practically every drug in the universe in an attempt to recapture the euphoria of his near-death experience, but to no avail. All he found was loneliness, prisons, and a failed marriage. He entered a treatment center for drug and alcohol abuse in December 1984, and has been in various stages of recovery ever since. Finally, he was able to find a counselor who knew something about the phenomenon he had experienced and she put him in touch with a near-death researcher. He told his story, then quickly disappeared—unable to face the truth of what he had been through. It wasn't until 1993, after suppressing the aftereffects of his experience for a total of twenty years, that Ridenhour found himself flat on his back because of a work-related injury and with no choice but to surrender. "My life started changing right then and I can't stop it, so I'm opening up my heart and my soul to see where this takes me."

Ridenhour is now in nurse's training, determined to repay society for his previous mistakes and to help heal people. His youth was wrapped around horrific incidents of child abuse and abandonment. He grew up thinking he was unlovable and bad. His near-death experience so challenged this distorted self-image that, although he wanted the euphoria back, he could not accept the rest of it. Confused and frightened by the incident, he flung himself into a seemingly endless nightmare of self-destruction.

"None of the drugs worked," he confessed. "They couldn't even come close to matching my near-death experience." Later he was stunned to learn that many of the problems he had afterward are in fact typical aftereffects of the phenomenon.

> I thought it was all me. I never made the connection between my experience and why I felt so lost. It took getting injured at work before I stopped trying to run away and just relaxed and let all that love and joy back, and the golden glow. I had no choice, really. I had to accept the truth that there is a power in me, and I can use it to help others.

Drug and alcohol free, Ridenhour has helped to organize an IANDS chapter in the Washington, D.C., area, one of many dedicated to providing informational meetings for near-death survivors and the interested public.

One evening in January of 1974, Jeanie Dicus of Sterling, Virginia, was lying on the sofa watching television. She remembers feeling strange, then waking up in an ambulance and being told she had had a seizure. Nothing like that had happened to her before, nor was there any family history of such a condition. This event was followed by a migraine headache and more seizures. Later, she, her husband, and her daughter drove to Baltimore where her father was a psychiatric consultant at Johns Hopkins

Hospital and where they were assured she would receive the finest care. Her case was given to the head of neurology and she was put on Dilantin and phenobarbital, normal medications for what appeared to be epilepsy. However, Dicus got much worse and was given yet another drug in addition to the two she was taking. Within three months she had become schizophrenic and was given Valium, as well. She steadily advanced into insanity, was straitjacketed, and confined to isolation in a mental ward. Her medication was increased and Thorazine was added to the concoction she was forced to take. She became suicidal and lapsed into one seizure after another. More drugs. More compounding effects, until, by summer, she was engulfed in a catatonic coma that lasted two months. A ward doctor finally noticed what was going on, went to Dicus's father and said, "All her symptoms are the result of the medications, not from mental illness. Stop the drugs." The physician in charge was immediately pulled off the case and shock treatments were applied in an attempt to free Dicus from the coma. By the time this decision was reached, her hands and feet had atrophied and were twisted and paralyzed, her skin was covered with pimples. Electric shocks did make a difference, but during the tenth treatment her heart went into fibrillation—a nurse had forgotten to give her a necessary shot of potassium—and she died:

> I was floating above my body. I saw green shower caps. The people in the room all wore those stupid caps. There were five or six caps and they were panicky. Their fear was so thick I could feel it. I kept thinking, Hey, I'm okay, don't worry, but they didn't get my message. This was a little frustrating.
>
> I found myself in the right-hand corner of the room. I lifted my arm and stretched. I had been immobile for so long. It felt like I had taken off a body girdle, and it was so delicious to get out of that cramped body. I felt a wonderful feeling wash over me—a sense of peace and power. I felt love and a sense of wonder as I realized that any question I could come up with would be answered.
>
> There was Jesus. I was stunned and said, "I don't believe in you." He smiled and said the etheric equivalent of tough shit, here I am. Looking at his eyes, I asked, "You mean, you've been with me the whole time and I didn't know?" And his reply was: "Lo, I am with thee, always, even beyond

the end of the world." Now, I wasn't into *lo* so I said, "Hey, man, this is the seventies and we don't say *lo*. Come on." He kind of grinned, I guess I was amusing him, and answered, "you want to be reincarnated?" "Hey, give me a break," I yelled (only I made no sound). "I just died. Don't I get a chance to rest?" "Take it easy, hold on, it's alright. You can change your mind at any time." I gasped, "I don't even believe in you and now you want me to reincarnate. Help!"

Our conversation continued. He even asked me to kiss his feet. No way. I gave him a bear hug and kissed his cheek. I got the equivalent of a belly laugh. I was so happy with him that words were no longer necessary. We then communicated mind-to-mind. Suddenly I was aware God was coming. I came to know that I had needed a human-looking Christ to relate to so I wouldn't be scared. The Light came and I was given a choice—I could remain trapped in earth, seeing and hearing everything, but unable to help anyone, not even my daughter (I was told this was limbo), or I could stay with God. I chose God.

The White Light in front of me was sorta like a white light bulb only it was so strong. I remember thinking my eyes should be burning, but then I remembered that I didn't have any eyes to burn. God was love and love was light, and it was warm and it permeated every molecule of me. This was so delicious, I was crying with torrents of tears that didn't exist. It was so enormous. I was loved. I didn't feel irrelevant. I felt humble, awed, and amazed. For a long time after my near-death experience, I ended my prayers with, "You are soooooo big!" It was my way of expressing appreciation.

Then I was instantly zapped to a domed room with square screens up and down the walls, on the ceiling—hundreds of television screens. On each screen was a home movie of one event in my life. The good, the bad, the secret, the ugly, the special. Everything was going on at once; nothing was chronological. All was silent. When you looked at one screen, you focused in, and you could hear what was there. Not only words, but your thoughts, your feelings, everything; and when you looked at the other people or animals, you could hear their thoughts, their feelings, too. And you made the connection between these and the events which ensued. You were filled with, not guilt, but a strong sense of responsibility.

God said to me: "I gave you the precious gift of life. What did you do with this gift?" I answered in a puny, wimpish voice, "I'm only twenty-three. I didn't know I was supposed to do anything. I have a two-year-old daughter. I spend my time and energy on her." It wasn't a good answer, but it was the truth. I was the judge and I was satisfied. I guess that was what God wanted. But the next time this happens, I'm having a list ready. I now have a card on my fridge door that says, "Practice random kindness and senseless acts of beauty." I asked a lot of questions, about sin, murder, and such, and I got a lot of answers. I was told that before we're born, we have to take an oath that we will pretend time and space are real so we can come here and advance our spirit. If you don't promise, you can't be born.

I truly wish I had enough space in this book to carry all of Jeanie Dicus's story. Certainly, it is filled with mind-numbing tragedies. But to hear her describe what happened, especially when she was talking to Jesus, well, it's the funniest thing I have ever come across. Amazingly, she was able to hear what the medical personnel said when near her body during the time she was in the coma.

I understand that the reason I was ripped away from paradise was for my father. He could not have taken my death. He had a Jewish surname and a Jewish nose, lived in France, and was a doctor and captain in the French army during World War II. At that time, the French believed the Nazis were their allies. He was on a hill when he looked down and saw the German army invading France. He fled and just barely made it out alive. He wound up in New York, turned against any form of God or religion, and became a staunch Freudian psychoanalyst. He married a psychiatric nurse and had three daughters, of which I am the oldest. As I grew, I became an atheist just like my father and married another one, a freshman at Princeton who did not believe in God or anything—yet he earned his Ph.D. in philosophy so as a professor he could get paid for arguing about religion and still get six months' paid vacation each year. When I revived, I had tubes all over me. Dad was sitting next to my bed humming French songs, and had been for weeks, which is a monumental feat considering that he is almost tone deaf. I hummed back. He shot up about three feet in the air, landed flat on top of me, gave a war whoop, and hugged me and cried. You have to remember he is a dignified psychoanalyst going on sixty, trained never to blink an eye—so much for promising him I wouldn't tell.

No one would accept Dicus's near-death experience afterward, especially not her father or husband. Wheelchair bound, she was put on Haldol, a chemical lobotomy, and given a bleak prognosis. Over time she was able to eat again and was allowed to go home. What she went through in the hospital and afterward is frightful. After several surgeries to repair some of the damage to her hands and feet, she decided on her own to decrease and finally stop all dosages of Haldol, and did so without its deadly side effects. Although she had two more children, life with her husband became impossible. He couldn't handle her "newness" or her claim that the Light she had come to love so dearly had guided her to take up palm reading. He left. She later remarried, this time to a gentle man who supports her "strange" ideas even though he doesn't understand them. They have a child, her fourth. A self-taught palmist, she continues to amaze people with her ability and the power of her love.

I am psychic, whether I believe it or not. I'm a stay-at-home mother. I don't have dynamic thoughts about the world of business or politics. Yet I feel an internal pressure, *a need to move,* to find a direction to be of more service. I'm still adjusting to the earthplane. It's been twenty years and my experience is clearer to me than yesterday.

The five cases we have just discussed are each a little different than the other.

Jennine Wolff's near-death experience intensified her original commitment to heal, made when a teenager. Even though her associate's death challenged her in unexpected ways, she has opened up to the true power of healing—faith and love. Arthur E. Yensen's introduced him to a whole new way of living, convincing him of his connectedness to all things and the importance of helping others, a conviction that dominated his daily activities until his death in 1992. Alice Morrison-Mays was shown that she had the ability to access multiple dimensions of knowledge in her episode, so she could empower herself and accomplish the impossible. She has continued her "classroom attendance" in those etheric levels ever since. Steven B.

Ridenhour discovered the love of his soul, faced his past and a possible future, only to flee, turning what could have been heaven into hell until an injury forced him to surrender—to the love he had previously rejected. Jeanie Dicus lived out her father's worst-case scenario after a life filled with the loneliness of never quite fitting in, and discovered in the process the wonderment of her own unique abilities—plus the reality of God's splendrous love.

Five cases, each one revolving around the same issues of self-validation, self-love, and self-respect, not unlike the hellish cases, really. This need to feel loved and accepted, part of something grander, I found to be the overriding link in every single case of pleasant and/or heaven-like near-death experiences I have investigated (including children's, although many times these issues seemed more for their parents to confront, than the child).

I have observed that once those who have this type of scenario experience what they recognize as *true* love and *true* acceptance, they feel tremendous pressure to pass it on. Not necessarily because they have become a fountain of that love—for certainly many experiencers of what appears to be heaven sense a gross inadequacy in themselves, and some are never quite able to accept any decree of worthiness—but because they now know they are connected to the world at large, members in communion with all life. They have faced the specter of RESPONSIBILITY and returned with a sense of mission.

Just as joy can be as instructive as pain, so too can the heaven-like experience be as much a mechanism the psyche can use for healing and growth as the hellish version. Because I have discovered truth in this concept, I no longer consider one version more important than the other. Rather, I now view near-death experience types as ways of reflecting the progression of an evolving consciousness as it seeks to expand from whatever was original to it, into something more than before.

The idea that consciousness might have the capacity to grow, change, and evolve—individually and en masse—brings me to mention this interesting fact: the word *heaven* comes from the Greek; in the language of the Bible, which is Aramaic, the same word was often referred to as "leaven."

Jesus is quoted in the thirty-third verse of Matthew thirteen as saying, "The kingdom of heaven is like unto leaven." Leaven causes dough to rise, like yeast. Leaven expands, yet the Greeks understood that heaven was that which is *already expanded.*

With that clue from the Greek version of what heaven might be, allow me to conjecture:

The near-death phenomenon may well function as leaven does; expanding the consciousness of its experiencers into the next phase of their growth and learning.

Their consciousness, once expanded, could enlarge to such an extent that it would be capable of accessing other dimensions of reality and connecting with a Greater Source.

Once an individual's consciousness has expanded in this manner, regardless of cause, that individual could become more than before, perhaps permanently.

Sally Leighton, a near-death survivor from Elmhurst, Illinois, has this to say about the overwhelming "otherness" of God that she experienced in dying: "Holiness has an edge to it. You don't bow down because of terror, but because of awe."

FIVE

Transcendent Experience

To find in ourselves what makes life worth
living is risky business, for it means that once
we know we must seek it. It also means that
without it life will be valueless.

—Marsha Sinetar

Transcendent Experience (expansive revelations, alternate realities) *Exposure to otherworldly dimensions and scenes beyond the individual's frame of reference; sometimes includes revelations of greater truths. Seldom personal in content. Usually experienced by those who are ready for a "mind stretching" challenge, and/or individuals who are most apt to utilize (to whatever degree) the truths which are revealed to them.*

Just about everyone who encounters an all-powerful, all knowing, all-loving light during their scenario (no matter which type), equates that light with God. To be in this Light, even for a second, is so overwhelming that simply to have experienced it is tantamount to the glory of transcendence. It leaves a "mark" on your soul, deep and profound.

Still, there are near-death scenarios that are so otherworldly, so unusual in the way individuals are affected by them, they belong in a class by themselves. These I call transcendent experiences, and they are often lengthy and involve complex issues and incredible revelations about life, history, and creation's story.

64

Seldom personal, these episodes stretch an experiencer's mind—sometimes beyond belief. Invariably, the people who have them are inspired to take action, to make a difference in the world. Although hearing claims by near-death survivors that they were privy to all knowledge during their experience is quite common, coming back with that knowledge intact rarely occurs.

History gives us two examples that contrast how a society can be affected by an individual who has had a transcendent experience. Around 300 B.C. the Greek philosopher Plato wrote of Er, the soldier, whose dead body lay in waste beside his fallen comrades for ten days. When at last help came, many were puzzled, for the body of Er had not decayed as had the others. Confused, Er's relatives took him home for burial, but upon the funeral pyre he revived, stood up, and recounted what he had learned while on The Other Side for all to hear. He then set about educating people concerning the spiritual truths that had been revealed to him, teaching them how they could live more fulfilling and satisfying lives. (History leaves in doubt whether the story of Er was created by Plato, or a true report.)

By 1837, Hung Hsiu-ch'uan, a peasant farmer's son, had failed for the third time to pass the official state examination in Canton, China. He fell into a prolonged delirium, his body wasting away as he lay near death for forty days. He revived after having a miraculous vision that portrayed him and an "elder brother" searching out and slaying legions of evil demons in accordance with God's will. Six years later Hsiu-ch'uan came across a Christian missionary pamphlet. He used what he read in the pamphlet to "substantiate" his conviction that his vision was real, and that he, as the younger brother of Jesus Christ and God's Divine Representative, was ready and willing to overthrow the forces of evil (which he saw as the Manchus and Confucianism). With the help of converts to his cause he established the God Worshippers Society, a puritanical and absolutist group that quickly swelled to the ranks of a revolutionary army. Numerous power struggles later, Hsiu-ch'uan declared war against the Manchus and launched a civil uprising—the bloodiest in all history—which lasted fourteen years and cost twenty million lives.

Both men, Er and Hsiu-ch'uan (who changed his name to T'ien Wang, the Heavenly King), were transfigured and transformed by their unusual near-death experiences and became zealous in their desire to "wake up" the deluded of their day. Each man felt the REAL TRUTH had been revealed to him and to him alone, and thus it was his sacred duty to "save" the populace. With Er, many were educated about the secrets of heaven, some becoming as transformed as he from "the good news." With Hsiu-ch'uan, wholesale carnage forged a "Heavenly Dynasty" that ripped asunder the very fabric of China.

Transcendent cases are powerful in both content and consequences, yet they are "risky business" in the way they can affect experiencers' lives... *and* the lives of countless others. This enigma repeats itself each time an individual is so transfigured and transformed. Modern-day cases are no exception.

In 1979, Berkley Carter Mills made history in the Commonwealth of Virginia and the city of Lynchburg by becoming the youngest father ever to win custody of a small child in divorce proceedings. Six months later a massive load of compressed cardboard he was loading slipped out of control, slamming him against a steel pole. He remembers a sharp pain, collapsing, being in a black void, then finding himself floating in a prone position twelve feet above his crumpled body. He saw and heard people running around, yelling for an ambulance and saying "Don't touch him, give him air." His body went from white to blue; there was no breath. The sight filled him with awe. "I'm here, my body is there. How did this happen?"

Not understanding how he could suddenly be airborne, Carter Mills attempted to reenter his body. Crawling downward in swimlike strokes he had almost reached his goal when a gentle but firm hand tugged his right arm. When he looked up, there were two angels replete with robes, wings, bare feet, and streaming hair—no color but opaque white—and no particular gender. "What's going on?" he asked. "We've come to take you to God," they answered. After some confusion on Carter Mills's part the trio left the scene at tremendous speed, leaving the earth behind as if it were a star the size of a pinhead. Their destination was an intensely bright light. Carter Mills questioned, "How come I'm not cold and how come I'm not suffocating this far out in space?" An angel replied, "This is your spiritual body, and these things do not affect it." They took him to a suspended platform, and in the center was a being so powerful Carter Mills thought it was God. The angels bowed and took their places with two others, each with wings outstretched and hands folded in prayer, at the platform's four corners. Male in mannerisms and voice, the clean-shaven being turned out to be Jesus.

Carter Mills could not look Jesus in the face as he perceived himself as naked and unfit for such an audience. After some coaxing from Jesus, he felt more at ease. "I'm going to judge you," Jesus said. Instantly Carter Mills's whole life began to play out, starting at birth. He relived being a tiny spark of light traveling to earth as soon as egg and sperm met and entering his mother's womb. In mere seconds he had to choose hair color and eyes out of the genetic material available to him and any genes that might give him the body he would need. He bypassed the gene for clubfootedness, then watched from a soul's perspective as cells subdivided. He could hear his parents whenever they spoke and feel their emotions, but any knowledge of his past lives dissolved. Birth was a shock: awful lights, giant people, eyes peering over face masks. His only comfort was his mother.

He relived each incident in his life, including killing a mother bird when he was eight. He was so proud of that single shot until he felt the pain the bird's three babies went through when they starved to death without her. "It's not true that only humans have souls," Carter Mills cautions today. "Insects, animals, plants have souls, too. Yes, I still eat meat, for in this plane species eat each other to survive, but I bless my food and say thanks for the gift life gives. If I don't the food sours in my stomach."

He was shown that hell is a black blankness without God. Upset, he yelled back, "How can you sit up here on this throne and allow such misery to happen on Earth?" Gently he was told, "It's your own fault. I gave you the tools to live by. I gave you free will and free choice. And I allow you to be part of my creation. It is your free will and your free choice that is responsible for starvation, war, and hate." Carter Mills felt pangs of guilt when he realized we coexist with God, no one is God's servant or slave.

Jesus, the angels and platform, disintegrated into a giant sphere of light once Carter Mills no longer needed their shape or form to put him at ease. As the sphere grew it absorbed him, infused him with the ecstasy of unconditional love. "Sexual orgasms can't compare. You are so high. Magnify that to infinity!" He zoomed back to his mangled remains as a ball of all-knowing light and crashed into his solar plexus with such force it jolted his body to action. He had been told before leaving The Other Side, "No hospital, no blood, no operation, God will show you how to heal yourself." Thus, when Carter Mills stood, he promptly walked to his car and drove home, on the way passing the ambulance that had been sent to rescue him. Those present verified that he had been dead for twenty minutes. The next morning Carter Mills awoke in a pool of blood.

The doctor he went to for aid committed him to a psychiatric ward as insane when he refused surgery. Since three independent psychiatrists had to confirm the verdict, and one objected, Carter Mills was released. Although his injuries were extensive and severe, he recovered by himself and returned to work. His former wife took advantage of his plight and challenged the custody ruling three times. She lost each try.

> The authorities tried to take my son away. I lost half my friends, my job, almost everything else I had, but I didn't lose God's guidance. I wouldn't talk about my experience for two years. I went from an active social life to that of a cripple before I could change things. I wanted to get a degree in psychology, but had to quit several years later when my money ran out.

Carter Mills's appearance on the *Geraldo* show in 1989 was preceded by an old buddy breaking off their friendship just because he had agreed to discuss his near-death experience on national television. Carter Mills was heartbroken, yet appear he did, there and hundreds of other places, sharing the voluminous knowledge he was given while on The Other Side. For this he has been both hated and thanked, shunned and welcomed. His mind is often flooded with incredibly accurate prophesies that leave him frustrated for want of knowing what to do about them. Sometimes he feels as if he's losing personal control. Light bulbs even blow up in his presence if he flips on/off switches too fast. Nonetheless, he is now healthier than ever, youthful and energetic, and he brags about how his son has turned out in spite of all the problems. "My sacrifices were worth it, for my son knows that God is real. He is drug free and tuned to his own soul."

Berkley Carter Mills created the following sketch in an attempt to picture the five major components of his near-death scenario. His fast scrawl is typical of how many experiencers "lose" themselves and all track of time or space when they engage in remembering.

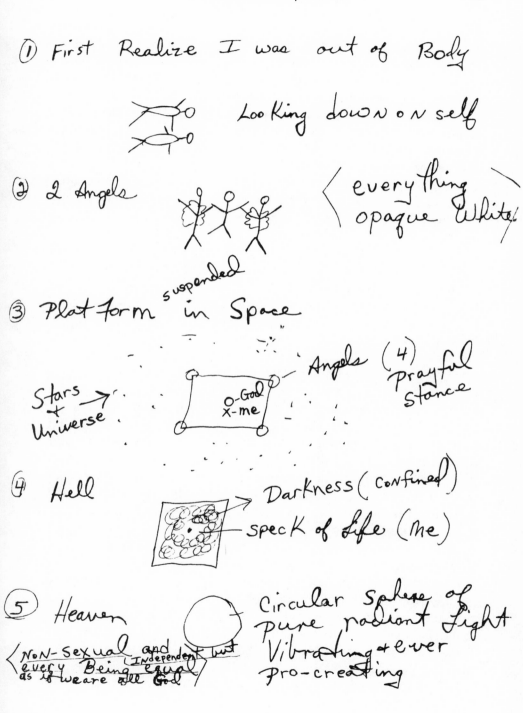

① First Realize I was out of Body

Looking down on self

② 2 Angels

⟨ everything opaque White⟩

③ Platform ˢᵘˢᵖᵉⁿᵈᵉᵈ in Space

Stars + Universe →

O-God
X-me

Angels (4) Prayful Stance

④ Hell

Darkness (confined)

speck of Life (me)

⑤ Heaven

Circular sphere of pure radiant Light Vibrating + ever Pro-creating

⟨ NoN-sexual and Independent but every Being equal as if we are all God ⟩

Keep in mind what happened to Berkley Carter Mills as you consider the case of Mellen-Thomas Benedict. For many years an accomplished lighting/cameraman for feature films on location outside of Hollywood, Benedict had racked up a lifetime of major events before he was thirty.

What may have been a near-death experience occurred several weeks after Benedict's birth when it was discovered that his bowels were ruptured. His body was tossed to one side as a corpse, yet much to everyone's surprise he later revived. As soon as he was big enough to grab hold of crayons, he started what became a compulsive urge to create symbolic renditions of the black/white yin/yang circles of Eastern religious thought. He has no memory of why he drew those particular symbols.

He spent his grade school years in a Catholic boarding school in Vermont, and was baptized in the Salvation Army religion as a youngster. He traveled extensively because of a military step-father until the family finally settled down in Fayetteville, North Carolina.

In 1982 Benedict was diagnosed as having inoperable cancer. He had retired from the frenzy of filmdom by then and was operating his own stained-glass studio. As his condition worsened, he spent more and more time with his art. One morning he awakened knowing he would die the next day, and he did. As the typical heaven-like scenario began to unfold, Benedict recognized what was happening *as it was happening.* The process was familiar to him because he had read many books about the near-death phenomenon previously. Just as he reached the light at the end of the tunnel, he shouted, "Stop a minute. This is my death and I want to think about this!" By consciously intervening, Benedict willfully changed his near-death scenario into an exploration of realms beyond imagining, and a complete overview of history from the Big Bang to four hundred years into the future.

Instantly he was pulled by light away from the tunnel, far away from earth, past stars and galaxies, past imaginery and physical realities, to a multiangled overview of all worlds and all creation, and past even that to the edge of existence where vibrations cease. He saw all wars from their beginnings, race as personality clusters, species operating like cells in a greater whole. By merging into the matrix of his soul, he confronted the "NO THING" from which all things emerge. Benedict saw planetary energy systems in detail and how human thoughts influence these systems in a simultaneous interplay between past, present, and future. He learned that the earth is a great cosmic being.

Benedict was aware of "walking" back into his body after deciding to return from his journey; as near as anyone can determine, his experience took about ninety minutes. His doctor's assessment, though, was the most shocking—the cancer he had once had completely *vanished*.

Because this happened to me my fear is gone, and my perspective has changed. You know, we are a very young species. The violence that formed the earth is in us, too. As the earth is mellowing, so are we as a people. Once pollution slows, we will reach a period of sustained consciousness. We have evolved as life forms from single-celled organisms to complex structures, and finally to a global brain. Employment levels will never again be as they once were, which will force a redefinition of human rights. We will adopt a more nurturing type of consciousness, freeing the mind for exceptional achievement. I now know that all the answers to the world's problems are just beneath the surface in US ALL. Nothing is unsolvable.

Since his experience, Mellen-Thomas Benedict has been flooded with ideas for inventions and the marketing plans necessary to promote them. He has been granted a number of U.S. patents and is actively engaged in developing new types of toys for all age groups, a new type of cellular telephone wristwatch, a new electric power-generating system, a new prototype for self-supporting communities where families can come back together with more control over their lives, and DNA research on the frontiers of science. His first manufacturing project (that of a unique yet simple glass cutter), sold out faster than he could produce the product. "I believe my inventions are channeled psychically because they are beyond my field of expertise," he explained. At my insistence, Benedict participated in an experiment at Baylor University in Texas to identify the cellular makeup of a certain disease pattern, and was able to describe three cellprints a full year before they were verified medically. In 1993, he went on to arrange laboratory experimentation with DNA coding and nerve-cell regeneration that has produced results of far-reaching magnitude [15].

After his near-death experience Berkley Carter Mills felt "directed" to contact and work with political leaders and the political process. Successful at first, he later turned off more people than he turned on, sidestepping his potential to champion a campaign or run for office by giving talks instead of accomplishing tasks. Although he has remained true to his inner guidance, he has been dogged by job losses, misunderstandings, arguments, and, at times, almost irrational paradoxes. The harder he tries to help people the more doors slam in his face. Although he has raised a wonderful son, he has yet to solve the enigma of how to fulfill the guidance he receives.

Mellen-Thomas Benedict was equally affected after his near-death episode, gifted with the same flow of information from The Other Side as Carter Mills and driven by the same need to reach out and assist others. Benedict learned early on, however, that "obeying" inner guidance can be fraught with peril if one is not grounded. This awareness led him to participate in many different classroom and study opportunities where he could learn to tame his own ego before he tackled "the gifts of spirit." His guidance to become an inventor has kept him solidly in the path of practical application, with results that speak louder than preachments or prophesies.

Not that the cases of Benedict and Carter Mills are the same as those of Er and Hsiu-Ch'uan; of course they are not. But they do offer a contemporary rendition of the *same* subtle yet important message the earlier accounts illustrate (a message present in *every* transcendent or impactual near-death experience I have encountered), and that is: setting one's self apart, feeling somehow "chosen," tempts one to pursue *power OVER* others rather than fostering *power TO* others. The difference here is ego, and how it can waylay even the most sincere. "Heavenly" guidance leads to self-deception if one's ego is not redirected from self-satisfaction to service, from self-righteousness to renewal.

The issue of ego domination or ego desire directly impinges upon how a near-death survivor interprets his or her experience, integrates it, and comes to regard that sense of "mission" each is left with. I cannot begin to emphasize strongly enough how powerfully the ego can misdirect even the best of intentions.

Here are two more examples of transcendent near-death experiences, those of George Rodonaia, formerly of Tbilisi, Georgia, USSR (now living in Nederland, Texas), and Margaret Fields Kean, who divides her time between healing centers in South Africa and at Smith Mountain Lake in Virginia. Miraculous as their cases are, the same challenge predominates: Transcendence alone does *not* complete the experience.

You may recall some of Rodonaia's story from Chapter One where I made mention of how he died and that his corpse was frozen and remained without life for three days. This is medically verified. A vocal Soviet dissident, Rodonaia had earned his master's degree in research psychology and was working toward his doctorate when he was assassinated by the KGB. He felt the pain of being crushed beneath car wheels as he was run over twice by the same vehicle. But what bothered him most was the feeling of an unknown darkness that came to envelop him. He thought, I am not what I am. I don't exist in my body, yet I am in my thoughts. Being self-aware outside of his body was confusing at first, until it occurred to him, If I can still think, why don't I think positively? With that, there appeared a pinprick of light, light outside of darkness. He remembered that physics teaches:

We see light because it comes to our eye, hits our eye; light *outside* darkness is impossible. Every experience I have is based on my own intelligence, yet my knowledge is not enough to comprehend light or darkness that is in itself intelligent.

As Rodonaia's sense of logic nullified, he beheld more light, chaos in light, bubbles like balls of molecules and atoms, round, moving, dividing into parts, electrons, protons, dividing into other parts, energy, eternal life-making cells—all moving in spirals. What had seemed chaotic actually had symmetry. He merged with what he saw, living within the living bubbles.

Never have I seen such beauty or felt so warmly caressed. It is important that I experienced such big happiness because I began to learn that light has a kind of power at this higher level. And there are higher and higher levels and the highest is God, and everything is under God's direction. Positive thinking links me to this warmth, this golden spiraling. I obtained my medical doctorate fifteen years before, but I have no words to describe this. All heaviness empties into happiness here. It's better than orgasm, never stops, everlasting unto everlasting.

For a while Rodonaia amused himself by pretending he had never been hit by a car, that he and his family had safely made it to California and he was now high on LSD. Then he thought about his body, and instantly, he was in the morgue viewing for the first time his naked green/blue/black remains, frozen on a slab. "I don't want that thing back," he declared, though an unknown power forced him to linger and look around.

Two little walls separate you from the other bodies. I saw them, all of them. In the darkness I could see. The memory of the car came back. Suddenly I *saw* the thoughts of everyone concerned with the event, as if they were thinking their thoughts *inside of me*. I scanned their thoughts and emotions to find truth. I saw my wife go to the grave where I would be buried and I saw her thinking about herself and what she would do now that I was gone.

He expressed the desire to see and know more, and found himself confronting the idea of being, the beginning of creation. He saw and felt all of history, each molecule and atom of each manifested mass, the thoughts and feelings of each existent form. He reconsidered everything he had ever studied in the schools he had attended, then toured the earth—visiting in London and Moscow.

I could be anywhere instantly, really there. I tried to communicate with the people I saw. Some sensed my presence, but no one did anything about it. I felt it necessary to learn about the Bible and philosophy. You want, you receive. Think and it comes to you. So I participated, I went back and lived in the minds of Jesus and his disciples. I heard their conversations, experienced eating, passing wine, smells, tastes—yet I had no body. I was pure consciousness. If I didn't understand what was happening, an explanation would come. But no teacher spoke. I explored the Roman Empire, Babylon, the times of Noah and Abraham. Any era you can name, I went there.

Rodonaia felt he was able to do as much as he did because time and space, as we know them, do not exist. In the span of mere hours, he could engage millenniums of experience via multi-dimensional simultaneity (being everywhere present all at once). He returned to the morgue and was drawn to the newborn section of the adjacent hospital where a friend's wife had just given birth to a daughter. The baby cried incessantly. As if possessed of X-ray vision, Rodonaia scanned her body and noted that her hip had been broken in birth. He "verbally" addressed her: Don't cry. Nobody will understand you. The infant was so surprised at his presence that she stopped crying. "Children can see and hear spirit beings. That child responded to me because, to her, I was a physical reality." Rodonaia's past-life review came next and it involved reliving his life from birth to death, plus going back several centuries and living *within* the lives of his long-dead relatives, as if he and they were one. The process fascinated him.

After the attending physicians in the autopsy unit quit screaming at the shock of seeing a dead body come back to life, they rushed Rodonaia to emergency surgery. All his ribs were broken, his muscles destroyed, his feet a horrible mess. It took three days before he could finally move his tongue around enough to speak. His first words warned the doctors about the child with the broken hip. X rays of the newborn were taken, and he proved right! Rodonaia remained hospitalized for nine months, during which time he became something of a celebrity.

Many doctors came to see me. In the Soviet Union psychology is a science concerned with the study of life and death. They were interested in what I could tell them about death. The KGB kept an eye on me all the time I was in the hospital, but because I had become so famous they did not touch me again.

George Rodonaia enlisted in a seminary program as soon as he was able and obtained a doctorate in theology, becoming a priest in the Georgian Orthodox Church. "I later earned my Ph.D. in neuro-pathology, what you call psychiatry, and earned my divinity degree as a direct result of my near-death experience. What I learned in dying, you see, enabled me to make sense of religion and science."

For a year afterward, his wife would not sleep in the same room with him. She had great difficulty dealing with his miraculous return and the fact that he had correctly "seen" all of her thoughts. His friends also had to readjust their relationships with him, and for the same reason—his uncanny accuracy about what he had seen in their minds. Years later, the KGB once again became a threat, so Rodonaia and his family secretly slipped away to Moscow and hid from view. They were able to immigrate to the United States in 1989 thanks to political pressure from the American government and through the sponsorship of a friend in Texas. Today, Rodonaia is a Methodist minister in Nederland, Texas. "After my near-death experience, I was doing advanced lab work with brain neurotransmitters while still in Georgia, formulating theories about the source of being. I want to share this knowledge and I want to do more lab experiments." He has visions about setting up a special college where both physics and metaphysics can share equal billing and receive equal support, and is actively working toward achieving that goal.

Margaret Fields Kean almost died in 1978 after being hospitalized for about three weeks with severe phlebitis. An unfortunate turn of events had brought her to a critical state. She had passed a blood clot to her heart and lungs, becoming deathly ill. She was then given injections for nausea which, due to the blood thinners she had received earlier, caused internal hemorrhaging. "There was a lot of commotion in intensive care. The man to my left had suffered a heart attack. The boy to my right was shot through the neck at a massage parlor and his legs were paralyzed. He yelled continuously." She recalls the surgeon telling her that if she could live through six more hours of blood transfusions, he'd be able to perform the surgery that would stop additional blood clots from passing to her heart and lungs. Her vision became blurred, while her hearing became quite acute. Then she began to leave her body and floated up to the ceiling.

Suddenly I could see from a different perspective and noticed that colors were brighter than usual. I saw my daughter's and mother's faces beside my bed. At the same time, I could hear better, much better, than at any time in my life. I could see and hear people in the waiting room down the hall—*right through the walls*—as well as nurses at their station. I not only heard everything anyone said, but knew what everyone was thinking.

She remembers floating "through" the ceiling, then finding herself outside hovering amid an abundance of brilliant green grass.

> I never saw any tunnel or darkness, just this incredible rectangle of green grass bordered on three sides by "a fence row" of swirling pastels. That fence row looked for all the world like opalescent cotton candy. A stream flowed by in front, and there was one tree. I viewed the scene from differing angles and especially noted that the gnarled tree roots were firmly planted in the stream as well as on land. On the other side of the stream, ahead of me, was a great all-encompassing light; blinding yet soft, powerful yet kind and gentle.

Margaret Fields Kean saw herself as a spiral of energy and became aware that she could live on the earthplane and take advantage of the opportunities that existed there, or do the very same thing in this new world where she now found herself. There were no voices, no people assisting in her decision to stay or return, and, above all, no judgment. All that existed in and around her was a sense of unconditional love, peace, and total "knowing." Whatever her choice, it would be okay. Logic was nonexistent. The only question was: "Where could I best be of service?" She decided that being a healer in a human body would be the best service she could perform. This was an extraordinary decision for her to make since she had no background in the subject whatsoever. Her idea of a healer had always been a medical physician. Her idea of herself was that of a super-mom farm wife who excelled in riding horses, teaching Bible classes, leading 4-H and Girl Scout groups, gardening, canning, and baking bread.

Yet all of a sudden she knew everything, instantaneously, including the fact that it was important that she finish raising her daughter. Before returning to earth, she crossed the stream and merged into the Light on the other side. "The Light is God. I anchored in that Light, and in so doing I was shown the evolution of spirit and soul. I knew I was to return to work with people; my mission being to heal." When Fields Kean revived, the nurses were in a state of panic; pure pandemonium reigned. Irritated at first by the abruptness of her reentry, Fields Kean nonetheless took on the role of healer: She spoke softly to the boy shot in the

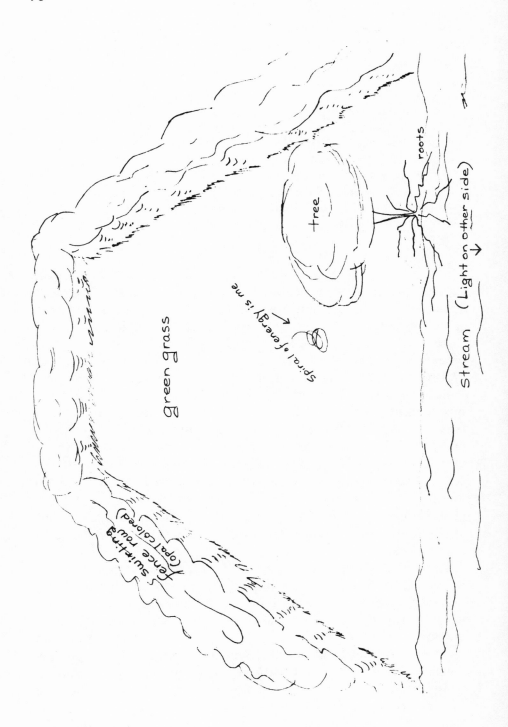

neck and soothed him to sleep (the nurses later thanked her); she "projected" into the isolation room of a white boy charred black by severe burns and counseled him about his purpose in life and told him it was okay if he chose to die, for God was loving and he had nothing to fear.

Months later, while continuing her recovery and still in great pain, Fields Kean was attending a horse show when a couple, hearing the loudspeaker announce her daughter's name as a winner, sought her out. They were the parents of the severely burned boy. Before he had died, he had told them about his meeting with her and relayed all the wonderful truths she had told him about God and about life. The parents were thrilled to have finally located her so they could say thanks for what she had done for their son. The dying boy had identified her by name *even though the two had never physically seen each other or verbally spoken in any manner, nor had any nurse known that the two had ever communicated, nor had it ever been possible that she could have known if the isolation room was even occupied when she "projected" into it.*

She continued to live on pills and was in pain twenty-four hours a day, often drifting into a near hopeless depression, until it finally occurred to her that she could not facilitate another's healing until she first healed herself. Although her doctor had predicted that she would be wheelchair bound within two years and that eventually her legs might have to be amputated, she probed, "Would a change of diet help me?" Her doctor gave a flat No, but she didn't listen. Opting for the natural route, she launched a drive to learn all she could about nutrition and organic gardening. "I was in so much pain, but I grew an organic garden anyway," she explained. Pursuing this path steadily for three years she made some improvement. Then she met a chiropractor/nutritionist who gave her food supplements and worked with the inflamed nerves and veins in her legs. She came to realize the condition of her legs was but a reflection of her attitude: both were as hard as concrete. "It was so confusing living with the dichotomy of, on one hand, being so angry, hostile, and depressed; yet on the other, feeling filled to over-flowing with unconditional love." Her struggle to regain her health wound up being a battle to free her mind and spirit.

It took seven years for Fields Kean to get over the initial shock of the near-death phenomenon. During this time she also ex-

plored psychic and spiritual realities, discovered Thymo-Kinesiology (a healing modality that alters and accelerates
performance by repatterning how the brain interrelates with the
body), and began facilitating the healing of "self" for a steady
stream of people who "happened" to knock at her door. She
taught elementary and high school grades to raise enough extra
money so she could obtain full certification as a Thymo-Kinesiology practitioner.

I tried to change my husband too but, of course, you can't
change anyone but yourself. He wanted a traditional wife
and marriage. Since I could no longer provide either, we
divorced. I took some furniture, an old car, and two thousand dollars. That's it. I signed over the farm and everything
else to him. When I left, I left for good. I was frightened to be
on my own, but God provides. I never turned away a client,
whether the individual could pay or not, and I never suffered
any lack, whatsoever. My fear was groundless.

The story of Margaret Fields Kean's near-death experience is
starkly simple. Yet note what happened to her and the others she
affected afterward. Her case parallels that of Edna in the 1980
movie *Resurrection* (directed by Daniel Petrie, the film tells the
story of a near-death survivor who returned to life with the
ability to heal others, but she first had to learn how to heal
herself). Yet Fields Kean went Edna one better. She went on to
develop The Results System, a technique that enables *anyone* to
access the wisdom of "inner knowing." Currently, Fields Kean
and her second husband operate healing centers on two continents where she regularly trains the interested public and
professionals alike in the fine art of working directly with mind/
body/spirit intelligence. "I once said that I would go anywhere,
any time, even to the darkest jungles of Africa, to heal someone
in need. Well, my husband Leonard is from South Africa, so
guess where I wound up? Right with the *sangomas* (native healers)
of Swaziland and Transkei, teaching them Thymo-Kinesiology
and The Results System. I am now the American representative
of the Traditional Healers of South Africa [16]."

The Results System that Margaret Fields Kean developed has a
spectacular track record as a viable aid in the healing environment. Those who learn it transform as readily as the people they

seek to help. The old adage, "Physician, heal thyself," is primary to how it works.

And so it is with transcendent cases.

Each one is unique, whether possessing an unusual storyline or not, and each instills the potential to make a significant difference in the lives of the many, not just the few.

One could argue that Arthur E. Yensen's experience in the previous chapter was more transcendent than "heavenly" in the way large numbers of people benefited from what he learned in death. And in that regard, the case of Nancy Evans Bush, although unpleasant and hellish, became a source of compassion that enabled her to help countless others as well. My own third episode was certainly transcendent, not only in content but in the way it inspired me to search out and investigate the near-death phenomenon—a labor that has aided many, not just me. My second near-death experience, although heavenly, had several transcendent elements and, as its scenario unfolded, I was able to explore how creation operates.

Obviously, what divides one type of experience from another is little more than a judgment call sometimes; a single incident can encompass several types. The following are the questions I developed that help me make the "transcendent" determination with near-death scenarios:

1. Was the episode primarily impersonal?
2. Was it otherworldly enough to stretch the individual's belief system beyond anything he or she had previously known, been exposed to, or imagined?
3. Was the experiencer radically changed afterward, almost as if he or she had become another person?
4. How compelled was the individual to use his or her experience to make a significant difference in the world? Did the individual do anything about this compulsion?

There are a number of books available now about people who have had transcendent near-death experiences. Some of the better known are Dr. George Ritchie's *Return From Tomorrow* and *My Life After Dying* [17]; Sidney Saylor Farr's rendition of *What Tom Sawyer Learned From Dying* [18]; and Betty J. Eadie's *Embraced by the Light* [19].

What I've presented thus far are the four main types of near-death experiences, as I have observed them. But there are other aspects of the phenomenon we need to examine...cases that occur without death's immediate threat and incidents so bizarre they really can't be categorized.

And that's just for starters.

SIX

Near-Death-like Experience

Spiritual progress demands that every form be
broken, no matter how good it is.
—Joel Goldsmith

The International Association for Near-Death Studies sent out an
unofficial questionnaire to its membership in 1992, inquiring
about those who considered themselves to be near-death survivors. How close had they been to physical death when their
episode occurred? Of the 229 who replied, 23 percent experienced
the phenomenon during actual clinical death, 40 percent at a time
of serious illness or trauma, and 37 percent had theirs in a setting
unrelated to anything that could be construed as life threatening.

The 37-percenters claimed to have had experiences every bit as
real and involved and life changing as those that happened to
people during death or close-brush-with-death crises—and their
reports mimic or match the same spread of scenario types.

Yes, it is true that the closer one is to cessation of vital signs, the
more apt one is to have a near-death episode, yet this large
contingent of near-death-like experiencers indicates that the
occurrence of this phenomenon is not necessarily dependent on
the physical body's possible demise.

Mark McDermott of New York City scaled a wall to rescue a
man who was trying to commit suicide by hanging himself from
a large tree. Police and rescue squads arrived after McDermott
had safely lowered the man and had begun resuscitation. The

whole event, risking his own life to save another, infused McDermott with such surges of energy that it was as if he had skyrocketed through a "barrier" of some kind and was flung into overworldly realms of power and love and ecstatic bliss the likes of which he had never known. Suddenly he was possessed of all knowledge, especially concerning himself and the man he had just rescued. He also experienced merging into a brilliant light and had a past-life review. It took him several weeks to make sense of the earthplane again, as he began to grapple with the typical aftereffects experienced by the near-death survivor.

Mark McDermott "reentered" the workaday world so trans-figured and transformed by his experience that anyone who knew him did a double take; overnight he no longer looked or acted the same. He displayed unusual degrees of wisdom and charisma as well as uncanny psychic abilities (although some-what psychic before, he became more so afterward). Apparently, latent talents surfaced full-blown, and his intelligence increased above and beyond his previous IQ rating. He also found himself filled with a strong sense of being connected to all creation and all humankind. McDermott has since gone out of his way to initiate service-oriented projects.

This man did not simply alter his attitude afterward. He became a new man, completely and totally changed from the individual he once was.

McDermott didn't experience the near-death phenomenon, or did he?

While a freshman at Princeton University, E.G.M. Richie underwent what she describes as a classical spiritual awakening. In the aftermath of this very dramatic event, an ordinary day in May became extraordinary. She explains:

> It was as if all reality were composed of radioactive love and I was being bombarded by waves of love radiation. Every leaf, every tree, every stone in every building was a sun unto itself, emanating love. This was no mere mental perception. It was a physical feeling that penetrated to my very core. Just as the sun's warmth can saturate the sunbather, so too did love saturate my entire body, my Being. Moreover, I knew that every particle of which I was composed vibrated in harmony with this magnificent loving power. Only my thoughts, somehow, stood at a distance, observing. I wan-

dered about dazed, eyes wide. Never had anything living or otherwise shimmered with such a dance of vibrancy. And the blue sky and the sunlight crowned it all. My thoughts screamed with profound joy. My mind exploded, over and over, with this rush of infinitely profound awareness. I could have died then and there, and been gloriously happy. This was truth. All Being was, in the last analysis, composed of the substance of Love. I was beside myself.

Richie eventually chose to major in religion and began an intense exploration of alternative lifestyles. Today, as a wife and mother in Middlebourne, West Virginia, she pursues spiritual mysticism, Native American teachings, and Rudolf Steiner's anthroposophy (a science of spirit developed by Steiner in the late 1800s and now a global movement toward biodynamic agriculture, medicine, architecture, the arts, and social therapies [20]). Richie's only regret is that the vibrancy of her experience has worn thin over the years. In a letter sent to me, she explained:

Somewhere in your past writings, you mentioned that the near-death experience and religious conversions and awakenings are comparable. Speaking from my vantage point and what you describe, particularly in terms of the aftereffects and dealing with them every day, I can wholeheartedly agree. Adjusting to, understanding what happened to me, integrating it into the sociocultural milieus in which I found myself was an immense difficulty. I'm still working at it.

E.G.M. Richie brings to mind a statement I made over a decade ago that has since proven true: Near-death episodes are similar to spiritual transformations (the process of awakening to higher consciousness and developing a personal relationship with God). And the aftereffects of each are more than just similar, they are the same.

To have a better grasp of this, let's consider a few more reports from people who had a near-death-like experience.

Haisley Long of Montreal, Quebec, Canada, was sitting in his living room one day watching television. He got up, walked across the floor, looked out the window, returned to his chair, and was about to sit down when the room lit up and he found

himself "on the outskirts of heaven." The experience was the
most beautiful, brilliant thing that had ever happened to him. As
he walked into this light-filled world, he was overcome by the
power he encountered. He claimed that it was millions of times
more potent than humans can imagine, a power that welcomes
you into it. Waves of unselfish love and unlimited knowledge
nearly blew him away.

I wondered how I was able to withstand this. It was like
standing in front of a huge star, and being amazed at the
power a star can pump out, then having the star go super
nova and the power jump incredibly, but you're not fried. It
was total ecstasy. More and more waves came. You just cry
and cry and cry, while waves wash you and clean you and
remove what little pieces of humanity are left stuck to you, so
that when you go into heaven you are as perfect as the
environment you are in. I became aware that there was
someone standing next to me—Jesus. When I looked at Jesus,
I saw myself. How can this be more me than I am myself? It
was like looking at a big mirror. So I reached out to try and
touch it, and I did. The word that exploded in my mind was
expansion, and I started to fuse, to blend and become part of
the Awareness of Consciousness Himself, Jesus.

I absorbed all the information, all at once. It was as though
Life took the little sentence, "What is beginning and end?"
and fused it into my brain. At first I didn't realize how huge
this phenomenon was. All the information in the world lies
between beginning and end. When I absorbed that little
question it was months, and even years, before I began to
realize that one step in between those questions branches off
into three weeks of speech. It was an incredible experience.
It was not necessary to ask a lot of questions while I was
there. The answers to all my questions were given to me and
locked into my head. Before this experience I had no interest,
and paid no attention to biblical matters whatsoever. For
myself, it took a trip to heaven, and to come into contact with
Life directly, going through the gates of heaven, traveling at
the speed of thought through Life's presence, and coming
into contact with God in His natural state, before I tuned into
biblical matters.

Life's meaning poured into Long, a literal cosmology of creation and darkness and light. He returned to regular living so

radically transformed friends hardly recognized him. The same zeal propels him to share what he learned during his experience as that which one finds with any near-death survivor, and he contends with the same aftereffects and the same questions of worthiness—Why me? What did I do to deserve this? Surprisingly, Long is now able to expound on "the real substance" of biblical scripture in ways that amaze every Bible scholar who has heard him (even though he had never read the Bible before his near-death-like experience).

In 1962, Nancy Clark of Dublin, Ohio, developed toxemia during her pregnancy. She was monitored for a month before delivery since the threat of convulsions and death was very real. She left her body and floated away after thirty-eight hours of difficult labor.

> It was as if I had taken off my overcoat. Below, I saw the nurse pounding on my chest repeatedly shouting, "Come on back, Nancy, you have a son, come back." But that part of me that had separated from my physical form did not want to come back. I felt that I wanted to go toward the light, but once again that darn nurse's voice interrupted my peaceful bliss.

Angry at the nurse, she finally reentered her body, only to discover that she had to peel down a sheet covering her face and hands. She had revived in the morgue!

Seventeen years after her near-death episode, Nancy Clark had a near-death-like experience that was presaged by a vivid dream of her dearest friend dying in a plane crash. The next morning he did. Asked to deliver the eulogy at his funeral service, Clark hedged, offering to write the piece if someone else would give it. About fifteen minutes before the service was to begin, she felt a strange sensation. Starting at the tips of her toes and gradually working its way up her body were gentle waves of a powerful energy the likes of Kundalini. The force exited out the top of her head, replacing her grief with a peaceful acceptance of her friend's death. When asked for the eulogy she had prepared, she surprised everyone by announcing that she would deliver it herself.

> I started to walk toward the podium and just before approaching it, I sensed my friend's "presence" beside me.

He took my right hand in his. I did not see anything with my physical eyes. I saw him through nonphysical eyes. But he was right there beside me holding onto my hand. I told myself that he was dead, lying in a coffin behind me, but that thought made no difference. The fact was he walked to the podium with me. My conviction about this is absolute.

When I reached the podium, I placed the typewritten eulogy upon it and proceeded to read about three sentences when, all of a sudden, my eyes lifted from the paper and were drawn toward the back of the room, at ceiling level and on the left side. I immediately saw a brilliant, pure, radiating, white light. It was unlike any kind of light that you can observe with your physical eyes, nor was it like any kind of light present upon this planet earth. It didn't hurt to look at it, yet it was like seeing a trillion suns merged into one. I knew I was in the presence of God. Every fiber, every cell of my being awakened to the knowledge of who the Light was, joyfully and excitedly welling up to the most incredible feelings of love, gratitude, humbleness, awe, and reverence. I was so enthralled, so filled with ecstasy overflowing that I marveled that a human being could experience this much rapture and still be intact and not explode from the sheer power of the bliss.

Clark recounts an outpouring of unconditional love that was beyond human comparison, and pulsations of luminosity that encircled her in a whirlpool of upward spiraling energy. All knowledge entered her consciousness. In an out-of-body state, she felt sadness for those scientists and researchers who spend their entire lives trying to prove the nonexistence of the dimension she was in. She moved around the room like a sparrow's feather, noticing the radiant white light in everyone who attended, as she observed herself still standing at the podium delivering the eulogy.

The next thing I remember happening is moving upward with the Light through the ceiling, above the building, above the city streets, lifting above the state, the country, the planet and into the dark universe above. We moved faster than an eye blinks. When we stopped, I looked around and was awestruck at the multidimensional cosmos before me. I was aware of at least ten dimensions as opposed to our three-dimensional world. Time and space were nonexistent. Everything was occurring simultaneously. We traveled deeper and deeper into the universe until we reached the beginning of creation. I observed the Light as the Supreme Being and sole creator and starting point of everything ever created. The Light-God was living energy—the sum total and infinite energy of the created and uncreated cosmos.

As she returned to earth, the truth of life permeated Clark's being in such a way that she understood the reason behind social injustices, crime, all chaos and disorder. She was shown that the simplest acts of kindness are of major importance, and that each person is a unique and integral part of some larger plan. She was given a life review that focused on the times she did not love herself so she could realize that her true nature, and everyone else's, was love. She was told by the Light to become a communicator and help people become aware of their true identities and understand that there is life after death. In a "flash-forward" scene, she saw how people would ridicule her and resist anything she said until, eventually, the word would get through that life is a continuum.

Nancy Clark's near-death-like experience was *more* involved and had more impact on her life than her original near-death episode. And it was truly transcendent. *Yet neither her body's health nor its continued existence was at risk or in question at any time.*

In one split second, I was no longer a woman whose life was dominated by a past of fear, guilt, and a belief that God did not love me. I was brand new, energized, and ready to face the future. With God on my side, what do I have to fear? NOTHING!

This realization was put to the supreme test:

In the midst of losing all my earthly possessions when our house burned to the ground a few years ago, the death of my beloved father, family illnesses, pressures of daily living, I have been able to meet life's challenges with God's love, joy, and peace still intact within me. My whole mind and heart changed that blissful day, and a fire of passion burns deep within me to be of service to God and humanity.

Nancy Clark is now researching near-death-like experiences and asks that anyone who has had one, contact her [21].

In looking at her drawing on the next page, start at the upper left where she saw the Light while delivering the eulogy. The nearby angel represents her out-of-body state; the three images on the right depict her speedy trip through the universe; lower right is a mirror reflection of herself as Divine Love. Bottom left, she expresses gratitude upon her return. The central cross illustrates that the Light-God is now central to her new life. (As an aside, Clark has worked in medical research and as a clinical cytologist examining cell structure and function for nearly thirty years. She is married, has two grown sons, and is president of the Columbus, Ohio, chapter of IANDS.)

Vernon Sylvest graduated first in his class from Louisiana State University School of Medicine, New Orleans in 1966. He rotated through various aspects of surgery and medical practice until deciding on pathology for his specialty. For fourteen years he provided pathology services for two hospitals in Richmond, Virginia, earning himself a reputation for excellence and efficiency. His personal life, however, was another matter. After a divorce, he developed a painful and crippling arthritic disease. Overnight, he went from being robustly healthy to walking with crutches. A severe depression set in. He lived with tremendous pain that steadily worsened. Medicine proved ineffectual. In desperation Sylvest turned to prayer, the type his Methodist minister father had taught him. That worked, but it was not enough.

Sylvest was led to a charismatic preacher who asserted that in order to understand disease one must dissect its spiritual nature. The pathologist developed a compulsion to do just that. His quest included researching the Holy Shroud of Turin (believed to have covered Jesus after the crucifixion). Sylvest came to realize that Jesus had really existed, and that the model Jesus left the world for unconditional love and forgiveness was true. By turning to a more spiritual point of view and actively seeking an intimate relationship with God, Sylvest's life seemed to fill with luminous light, his every step seemed orchestrated by a power greater than he. Synchronicity reigned to the point that he was able to be at the right place at the right time, unfailingly. Less than a year after becoming a meditator and mystic and stepping forward into the

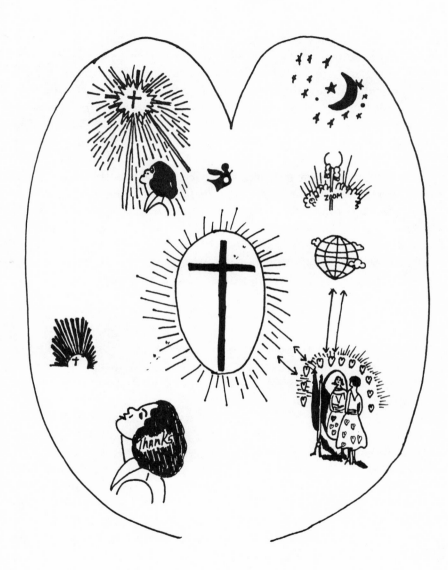

living radiance that enveloped him, the arthritic disease that had
been so painfully crippling disappeared.

Vernon Sylvest remarried and with his wife founded The
Institute for Higher Healing, a holistic healthcare and educational clinic/center that operated for a number of years in Richmond, Virginia, before its two functions split: The healthcare
division evolved into the Richmond Health & Wellness Center; its
educational wing, continuing under the original name, came to
specialize in sponsoring major conferences that celebrate the
coming together of traditional and holistic healthcare practices
[22].

To this day, Sylvest exhibits the aftereffects of the near-death
phenomenon—*even though his light-filled experience spanned an
entire year and directly resulted from his conscious choice to seek a
miracle cure for his physical condition.* Interestingly, the miracle
Sylvest so desperately wanted did not happen until he first
relinguished all ego attachments and ego needs, even his desire
to be cured, and accepted the power of love and forgiveness in his
life.

Unpleasant and/or hellish near-death-like experiences also
happen.

A woman, who asked not to be identified, was attending a
psychic development class at a spiritualist church when she
suddenly bolted out the door after sensing a negative energy that
frightened her. When alone and preparing for bed, she was
overtaken by a dark tunnel that had formed in midair. She was
fully conscious and wide awake, yet the power of the spinning
vortex sucked her in. The tunnel was real and large, and she was
terrified. Inside it there was no light, just suffocating darkness.
The woman fought back, hitting the tunnel sides, demanding
that it release her and leave her alone. After what seemed a fight
for her life, the tunnel disappeared as quickly as it had come.

The woman became convinced later on that the event must
have been a negative near-death experience, because the tunnel
matched everything she had ever read or heard about hellish
episodes. The fact that she was in perfect physical health and the
experience was actually near-death-*like*, seemed unimportant to
her. Then we have the story of Shirley J. Bennett of Indianapolis,
Indiana.

The last thing I said before I went to bed that night was "I don't care whether I live or die." At around two in the morning I was having trouble breathing. My whole body got numb, then a part of me left my body. I was so happy to be free. I can remember flying over treetops at tremendous speeds. Suddenly I was flung inside a van crossing the desert. I asked how I got there; someone said, don't worry, I was just along for the ride. Besides me, there was a driver with brown hair, a teenage boy with a funny suede hat, and an older man we stopped to pick up who needed a shave. We were traveling through the Scenic Valley of Fire when I saw seven steeples of an old building. Something about that building scared me so bad I was back in my body in a flash.

Two weeks after this episode, Bennett went to her sister's for a visit and met a teenage boy wearing a funny suede hat. It was pouring rain, so she offered to give him a ride. As he climbed into her Volkswagen van, she recognized him from her bizarre experience a few nights earlier, and said so. To her surprise, he knew exactly what she was talking about and went on to describe their "trip" across the desert and told her that it had happened in "another dimension." He asked her to name his address. Without thinking, she blurted out "239 on a street that begins with a B." She was right. Shortly afterward the boy moved away, but before he left he called Bennett and asked if she remembered the place called Seven Steeples from their desert trip. She didn't at first. He said she should, because it was a graveyard and it really existed.

This prompted Bennett to do some investigating.

It took me three years before I found someone who had heard of Seven Steeples. I was given its location at Central State Hospital, here in Indianapolis. I called the doctor of pathology there and told him about my experience. He said Central State used to be a mental hospital where patients thought to be possessed by the devil were committed. There was a graveyard right behind the building where patients were supposed to be buried, but because of grave robbers the bodies were gone. Central State was once called Seven Steeples back in the 1800s. It was very old and actually had eight steeples but only seven were visible from the street. That's why it got the name it did.

Bennett said she had asked the teenage boy if he thought someone was trying to tell them something that night, and he had said yes.

I now know what that was—there really is a hell. Every preacher I told my story to said the incident was of Satan. I don't think so. I think it was of God, and God was trying to show me what might happen if I didn't change my life. I once had an abortion, lots of marriage problems, and hadn't yet accepted Christ as my savior. That's the message: Clean up your act. I did.

Glen O. Gabbard, M.D., of the C.F. Menninger Memorial Hospital in Topeka, Kansas, and Stuart W. Twemlow, M.D., of the University of Kansas School of Medicine in Wichita, coauthored an article that asked "Do 'Near-Death Experiences' Occur Only Near Death?" [23]. After ten years of investigating out-of-body experiences and the near-death phenomenon, they confirmed their original supposition that "The *perception* of being near death, independent of the actual reality of the situation, is the key determinant of the classical [near-death experience]." In other words, they found that for such an experience to occur the state of a person's mind is more important than the state of his or her body. They acknowledged near-death scenarios as manifestations of faith and catalysts for the development of faith, and as a remarkably consistent pattern that could be no less than genetic and present throughout the human family.

Gabbard and Twemlow remind us that survival imagery, transcendent scenes that somehow seem to "save" us from the dread of oblivion, can and do occur at any age, under any circumstance (including calm, relaxed states such as meditation), and in any cultural or religious setting.

Their research and that of medical people like them, however, does not take into consideration:

- Vivid and life-changing near-death-*like* experiences, where seldom is there any thought *or* perception of death.
- Cases such as that of George Rodonaia which can hardly be compared with "psychological defenses" of an individual *about* to die.
- Elements and details found in near-death "imagery" that are later verified as *fact*, not fantasy.

When we take a deeper look at the phenomenon we are investigating, it becomes apparent that there is a great deal of information current research does not address. The fact is, we have hardly begun to decipher near-death's many messages.

SEVEN

Anomalies

True fortitude of understanding consists in not
letting what we know be embarrassed by what
we don't know.
                    —Ralph Waldo Emerson

There are exceptions to the universal pattern of the near-death
phenomenon, tantalizing tidbits of the bizarre that stretch cred-
ibility—sometimes beyond reason. These anomalies (that which
does not fit consensual reality) have, for the most part, been
ignored or tossed off as imaginings or discussed only in low
whispers. Since the purpose of this book is to take a straight look
at the *entire* near-death phenomenon, I think it's time to lift the lid
from Pandora's proverbial box and see what else is there. I'll
begin with three examples to give you a sense of what I mean by
"unusual," then I will address more of the "extras," things like
angels, walk-ins, reincarnation, and aliens.

   One of Natalie Rowell's legs was literally cut in half in 1986,
then rotated as part of a surgical procedure, in an effort to put
foot and knee into proper alignment. This was the third of four
such operations that would repair the damage done earlier in her
life, when corrective measures, necessary to create hip joints
missing at birth, had deformed her legs. Surgery was scheduled
in Portland, Oregon. Rowell's mother, unable to afford the flight
from Harrisonburg, Virginia, agreed to come "in spirit." At the
appointed time, she sat down in her Harrisonburg apartment,

relaxed into an altered state of consciousness, and through out-of-body or "astral" traveling arrived via spirit form in time to view her daughter's surgery from above the surgeons' heads looking down. The mother "aided" the surgeons by sending energized currents of divine guidance into their minds and fingers, affirming a positive conclusion to their work. Rowell, expecting her mother's visit, lifted as a spirit being from her anesthetized body. Spying her mother hovering near the ceiling, she floated upward and embraced her mother joyously.

A large swirling tunnel manifested to the right of them. Rowell entered the tunnel, then paused and turned to face her mother, saying: "I have to do this alone, Mother. You cannot come." As she disappeared into the tunnel's swirling depths, her mother felt pangs of remorse combined with a sense of reverence. Years later Rowell's mother recalled that moment:

> The tunnel was so vivid, so real. I'll never forget it, nor will I ever forget the feeling I had to run in and rescue my daughter, pull her back. Yet I knew this was hers to do. She must meet her own destiny herself. I reluctantly returned to Harrisonburg via spirit and reentered my body, telling myself that everything was fine and her recovery would be a total success. It was.

She remembered that her daughter had telephoned the day after surgery.

> Although groggy, she thanked me for coming. Before I could respond, she launched into a description of the event including the tunnel and her last words upon entering it. She didn't give me a chance to say anything. When I could finally get a word in edgewise, I confirmed her story, for it was exactly what I had experienced. Then I took my turn at detailing the surgical room, the staff, and the procedure used. Natalie asked a surgical nurse about this; the nurse verified what I described. The strange thing is, some memory of what happened remains with her today, but not that phone call.

Natalie Rowell left her body during surgery, floated to the ceiling, and was drawn into a large dark tunnel. Yet she only left her body because of a prior agreement with her mother, not because of a spontaneous near-death experience, per se. This I know because Natalie Rowell is my daughter!

Did our meeting as "spirits" cause something to happen that would not have occurred otherwise? Is this why my daughter has so little memory of it? Or, as a result of the particular dynamics involved, maybe, just maybe, I inadvertently witnessed that "tunnels" tend to manifest automatically whenever an individual is forced or propelled into a physical state that separates and/or frees consciousness from its connection to the brain (whether at the brink of death or not). If my hunch is true, the function of tunnels could challenge the interpretive base used in assessing the "imagery" reported by meditators, people who undergo simple anesthesia or head trauma, those who participate in psychic phenomena, and experiencers of near-death and near-death-like states. Tunnel-like vortexes, like the one that manifested for my daughter, might well constitute the initial phase preparatory to a possible brain shift—even if not remembered.

Another challenging "shared" event is what happened when Barbara Ivanova witnessed a brutal murder in Moscow, Russia. Ivanova had a long history of near-death episodes. Her first occurred at the age of six when she drowned in a water barrel, the second at about fourteen when she was carried out to sea by a large wave. On each occasion, she separated from her body, was enveloped by brilliant light, and underwent a life review—starting at the moment of her death and going back to birth. Both of these reviews focused on her "bad" conduct with her mother, instilling in her a desire to do better. She also became more at ease and possessed greater confidence and intelligence after each incident. At eighteen, she collapsed in her mother's apartment and remembers seeing a dark tunnel with a strong light at the end of it and hearing a buzzing sound as if she were being dragged through the tunnel at high speed. She revived only to be consumed in pain, and for several days hovered near death with her doctor giving her only a 10-percent chance of recovery. Ivanova survived clincial death states numerous times after that but never again experienced another near-death scenario... until that fateful day when she was in her early fifties.

I saw on the street a man killing a woman with a knife. I ran across the street and fell down. I was half unconscious, whispering "Help me, help me." I was not next to her body, but some meters away. At the time, I saw myself as a little girl in a strange dress playing with very big toys. My solar plexus hurt, as if my life was being extracted from me. This was no dream. It was very real. I am not so sure but that it was her life review I experienced because my inner pictures were not mine. An ambulance arrived. I still pleaded "Help me," so they would help *her.* I lost consciousness and was carried home by whom I do not know. I regained consciousness some time later and hurt so much in the solar plexus. That is where the woman's wound was, where the knife went in. I was ill for days.

The following sketch, done by Ivanova, is an attempt to give size and dimension to the toys and cubes the little girl in the strange dress was playing with:

little girl — *an oversize Brick. or cube*

Barbara Ivanova seems to have "shared" the life review of the woman who was dying, unwittingly *becoming the woman's surrogate*—even though she had never seen the woman before, nor did she have any way to verify what she witnessed. It was almost as if, in attempting to save the woman, Ivanova rescued the woman's memories instead! She described the review as filled to overflowing with life, light, happiness, and promise. "Perhaps it was a consolation for the dying woman, not for me."

Previous to this event, as a result of her earlier experiences with the near-death phenomenon, Ivanova had begun to recall what she feels were her past lives: an Italian soldier, a German naval officer, a courtesan in Spain, a worker in Brazil, plus others. Learning how to speak the native tongue of each incarnation she remembered was easy for her to do, except with English and Czech. "I never had a past life in those countries, so I have trouble speaking those languages." She went on to become a professional linguist and college instructor of foreign languages.

The ordeal of witnessing the murder shifted her interest to the possible meaning of psychic and mystical states, and she has since distinguished herself in the fields of parapsychology and spiritual healing. She is the subject of the book, *The Golden Chalice: A Collection of Writings by the Famous Soviet Parapsychologist and Healer Barbara Ivanova* [24]. (As a brief aside, in 1973 Ivanova was unexpectedly fired from her job as a Portuguese language instructor at Moscow State Institute for International Relations, where she had been employed for twenty-six years, solely because of her work in parapsychology experiments. Not until the rise of Gorbachev did the state-sponsored persecution against her cease.)

> I am an engineer, and consider myself to be a sane, rational, and analytic person. On August 5, 1983, I attended a horse training clinic in Great Bridge, Virginia. After the clinic my friend and I had dinner, then watched a movie she had previously recorded on her VCR. I left for home at 11:30 P.M. under a light rain. I remember passing through several small towns, then awakening from an unconscious state to find my car hydroplaning out of control at fast speed. I swerved across all four lanes, then crashed into the trees.

The previous quote comes from a woman who asked to remain anonymous. She continues her story:

> The car clipped off several small saplings and headed straight for a large oak tree. As the front end of the car impacted the oak, I could see the hood buckling. The windshield and two side windows shattered. I remember thinking it was only going to be a second before I was splattered all over that tree. I yelled, "Oh God, help me," and then closed my eyes. I felt a searing pain over my ears, which I attributed to my cable temple glasses being pulled off my face due to the impact force. After that, I remember total darkness and quiet. There was no more pain. Suddenly I was standing in the brightest light I have ever seen. It was everywhere. I wasn't standing on anything solid like a floor or the ground. I was standing on light. I squinted because the light was so bright, and said to myself, If this is Heaven, I

need sunglasses. Then a lot of people started laughing, men and women, but I couldn't see them. A man cleared his throat and called for order with the light tapping of a gavel. I sensed I was in something like an English courtroom, with justices at lower benches (which were above me) and above them, the chief judge's bench. I heard voices mumbling, then I felt as if I were on a stage and should do something like tap dance or sing. A deep voice resonated, "She's not ready yet," and I heard what sounded like the closing of a very large book. It was very dark and silent again.

When the woman opened her eyes she had difficulty focusing at first without her glasses. She inventoried her body, but didn't feel anything broken. Her purse was on the car floor with its contents spilled, so she unfastened her seat belt and leaned over the stick shift to pick up everything. She turned to check the saddle in the backseat. As she readjusted forward she noticed that her car was now *facing* the highway—somehow it had rotated one hundred and eighty degrees!

It wasn't possible. There were too many smaller trees very close to both sides of the car. The only way the car could have rotated around was to have been lifted over the treetops, turned, and set back down. Also, the car had been moved away from the oak tree and closer to the road. A large truck stopped and the trucker came running. "Oh my God, are you alright?" I told him I thought so. He said he stopped because the light from my fog lights facing the road at that angle attracted him. He went back to his truck to radio for help, then a number of other people came. The rescue personnel used a crowbar to break my door open. I was able to get out without assistance. My right knee hurt a little and I had a headache, but otherwise I felt fine. If it weren't for the fact that my car was totalled, you would never have known I was involved in an accident. I was taken to a hospital as a precaution.

Come that Monday she was able to view her car in daylight.

I had a year of physics in college, and I couldn't believe what I saw. The car looked more like it had hit a solid wall than a tree, because it was so uniformly compacted from the

front bumper to the windshield. It was a solid eight-inch
block. Also, my saddle and riding gear had remained in place
instead of being thrown to the front. In fact, everything
behind where I was sitting was in perfect order. On my way
home I decided to stop at the accident site. I saw where the
smaller saplings had been broken off or were overturned at
the roots, but there wasn't one dent, not one scratch or
missing chip of wood, on that oak tree. Both police and
rescue crews noticed the impossible positioning of my car at
the time and how it made no sense considering the damage
in the woods—yet no one reported this officially.

Strange dreams and spontaneous out-of-body episodes followed, along with depression and blackouts, until finally...flashbacks of memory...about being abducted by aliens,
a number of times, and again on the night of the crash.

The accident was caused by the fact that I did not regain
consciousness as quickly as I had in earlier abductions. The
aliens, realizing something was wrong, that I did not have
control of the car, used their technology to rescue me, during
which I had a near-death experience.

The inference here is that somehow the "aliens" had levitated
her car, turned it around in midair to face the road, then lowered
it to the ground, thus ensuring that her fog lights would be seen
by passersby.

Whatever you think about the three cases just discussed, each
one did indeed happen.

There are other anomalous phenomena related to the near-
death experience. Let's take a look at some of this "other"
material.

Angels

Adult and child experiencers describe people who have wings
attached to their backs and shoulders: people of grace and beauty,
mostly white skinned, sometimes with bare feet, bare hands and
face, wearing loose-fitting white robes or pale, flowing gar-
ments; males clean-shaven, some males and most females with
long flowing hair; no adornments except for an occasional sash or

belt. In every case, these winged people are called angels. And always the winged ones are said to be without motive or malice, existing only to serve the Divine Will of God.

But the people with wings can be black as well as white, or full colored as with any embodied being. Numerous times, when interviewing near-death survivors, I have been surprised to hear mention of black angels whose job it is to make certain the dying find the Light. Only once have I heard of such an angel who took someone to hell. Black angels appear to be as benevolent and caring as the white ones. But they seem confined to the tunnel or spaces that are dark, as no one has reported seeing them in light realms. White angels apparently can go anywhere, although seldom do they tarry in darkness for any length of time. To my knowledge, no one has seen both white and black angels in the same place at the same time.

Although angels are almost invariably grown adults in appearance, they can be children, too. In fact, there seem to be as many different types of angels as there are people who see them. Near-death survivors often label *anyone* who is made of brilliant light or who manifests as a ball, globe, or cylinder of light, an angel—even if wings or angel-like features are absent. Sometimes normal human types, or black beings devoid of wings, are called angels because of their helpfulness and the great love they emit. I have heard of "black ones" in the tunnel that were disruptive and fearsome, though. Yet their threats evaporated once the individual asserted him or herself, or called upon God for assistance.

The Catholic church and many other religious institutions teach that each and every person is assigned a guardian angel at birth, as a source of guidance and support throughout the individual's life. The catch seems to be: You must ask for your angel's help, then heed it. Ideally, a guardian angel is successful in keeping one on track so one's destiny can be fulfilled—but not always. Remember the catch.

In mystical and esoteric teachings there is a tradition of angel hierarchies connected to and associated with the seven rays of the light spectrum, as regards the spiritual development and evolution of souls. There are also myths about angels guiding the unborn into their bodies before or during birth, and claims of multiple angelic protectors, not just one. (Numerous books are now available on this subject [25]). Regardless of how you may feel about angels, give some thought to the following observation.

Berkley Carter Mills (discussed in Chapter Five) vividly described the angels who led him to a platform out in space so he could attend an audience with Jesus. The minute he felt at ease and bolder with his questions, Jesus, the platform, and all four angels disintegrated into one giant sphere of light that absorbed him in an esctasy of love. I have noticed that what happened to Carter Mills happens to most others who have reported contact with angels: The angels seem to have the form they do *only* for the length of time it takes to quell any discomfort an individual might have during his or her otherworld journey. When no longer needed, angelic-shaped beings dissolve or disappear altogether. This energy mass, or pure sine wave, and that is what I believe an angel is, takes on winged or light-filled or human forms (even during broad daylight) that best complement the present level of an individual's spiritual maturity. At least initially, we seem to encounter whatever shape or form we can recognize and cope with.

I mention this because those who are more familiar with altered states of consciousness and "multidimensional travel" seldom, if ever, report angels as having feature or form. To them, an "angel" is a rarified projection of God's Thought, a pure and powerful presence that interweaves and interconnects creation's story.

Walk-ins

Throughout recorded history and in myth, people who suddenly appeared out of nowhere, aided a human being in trouble, and then vanished, were called walk-ins. Some claimed that angels were also walk-ins, miracle workers who made a difference—like the modern-day report of the man driving a tow truck who rescued a family stranded in a snowbank because their car slid off the road and then disappeared, poof! truck and all, no good-byes, no noise, no tire tracks in the snow to prove he was ever there, even though everyone saw and experienced the exact same event and all were left with the same puzzled looks on their faces.

Incidents like this share equal space with stories of beings who "step" into the earthplane from some parallel or distant dimension, stay for whatever reason however long, and then "walk" out—appearing to enter and exit through some kind of "window" or time aberration. I've seen one of these walk-ins myself. My son has seen several, as have friends of mine. When it happened to me, I felt chills coursing up and down my body. I was really startled. My son Kelly was upset about the carload of people that vanished in front of him as he was bicycling home from a day of swimming, until I relayed my own walk-in encounter and those of other people he knew. Once he realized he wasn't the only one who witnessed such things, he breathed a sigh of relief and was okay about it.

Yes, it is possible that some of these sightings could be of doppelgängers (a German term for the ghostly double or counterpart of a living being that appears and disappears without the person so "pictured" actually being present or even nearby). This phenomenon, and that of "biolocation" (the ability to be in two or more places at the same time), have been part of the human story since time immemorial. However, the scientific premise that "imagery projections from the brain" create all such phantoms does not explain away either the frequency or the complexity or the physicality of such reports.

The term "walk-in" has become part of today's popular lexicon, not because of consistent sightings the likes of which I have just mentioned—but because Ruth Montgomery's "spirit guides" coined the label for other purposes. A former newspaper journalist, Montgomery has done well in the metaphysical marketplace, tempting and tantalizing her readers with abstract concepts and "higher truths."

Her book, *Threshold to Tomorrow* [26], posits walk-ins as supposed "advanced souls" who are somehow "allowed" to walk in and inhabit recently vacated bodies. In order to accomplish this feat, these so-called advanced souls agree to revitalize the recently vacated body and execute whatever remains of the former soul's obligations before they begin their own mission to help humankind. Montgomery claims that the reason for such "switches" is to enable advanced beings to take a shortcut into earthly existence. The soul formerly in residence within the body is apparently "excused" from finishing out the life and is freed to either develop elsewhere in other realms or receive another body through the natural process of birth.

Montgomery goes on to state that these switches occur during extended periods of unconsciousness or during near-death experiences. She has no idea how the switch works, but claims an agreement must be reached between the two souls involved or the switch cannot take place.

Montgomery identified a number of people, both living and dead, as walk-ins, people such as the late Anwar Sadat. One living person so identified is Reverend Carol W. Parrish-Harra, who had believed herself to be "another person" long before Montgomery ever wrote books on the subject. In response to publicity generated when she was so named, Parrish-Harra wrote her own book entitled *Messengers of Hope* [27], *messenger* being her version of Montgomery's term *walk-in*.

Parrish-Harra's near-death experience occurred during childbirth and, of course, changed her life. Her story of struggles and transformation is inspiring, as was her quest to "find herself." I first met her in 1984 and have since spoken with her many times. To say I am impressed with her ability as a teacher and speaker would be an understatement. She is *very* talented! Still, there is nothing in her personal story that would set her apart from any other near-death survivor who had a transcendent experience, or that would indicate she might be a walk-in—except for her belief.

Ruth Montgomery's original description of walk-ins and how to recognize them *mimics the average behavior of the typical near-death survivor or that of someone who has undergone a spiritual transformation.*

It is *normal* for such people to believe themselves new and different.

It is *normal* for such people to even look different and act as if they were "other" than themselves.

It is *normal* for such people to be revitalized, more knowing and able, to possess skills and talents new or expanded from before.

All of this is perfectly normal given the incredible power of true transformations, no matter how they are caused.

There are tens of millions of people throughout the world who fit the pattern of a walk-in as described by Ruth Montgomery, including myself. Are we all advanced souls supplanting our lesser fellows in an attempt to prepare the masses for a new age? I think not. But, since this notion is so confusing to so many people, let's give it a fresh look.

There *are* historical references to Montgomery's walk-in theory in mystical and metaphysical literature and in legends from various cultures, although the terminology differs. *Exchange* was the expression used most often to describe souls who traded places in a given body. Stories about "exchanges" are no different from the current renderings of near-death survivors and those like them.

If you examine the historical material, then compare what you find with modern renditions, you can't help but notice this recurring pattern: Declaring oneself "new" instead of "changed" puts less pressure on the unenlightened and ensures a safer political climate in which to live and work. Socially, it is more acceptable for individuals to grapple with a mystery than to admit that they might have been in need of personal transformation themselves. After all, the public, any public, has always preferred entertainment to embarrassment.

Nonetheless, I have met three people who I think really are the type of walk-ins Montgomery describes in her book. Two are adult women, the other is a very confused young man. All three have unusually bright eyes that intently search what can be seen, rather than just look; and the vibration around them, their presence, does feel at variance to anything I have sensed from an individual before. I cannot explain this, but I can be tolerant. With what I've experienced in my life, I have long since learned that this wonderful world of ours is a treasure trove of miraculous oddities.

I do want to extend a caution, however. Every walk-in Montgomery wrote about went through extensive and lengthy periods of confusion and depression, with little more to offer than disconnected, dreamy ideas. None had the ability to utilize the knowledge they claimed to have or to empower others until after they had engaged in years, and I do mean years, of study and training to learn how. This hardly constitutes "a shortcut" or even a sensible way for "advancements" of the so-called advanced.

Whether people such as these are evolving through more than one incarnation during their present life, or expressing past-life or future-life personalities, or projecting a glamorous fantasy to gain attention (as various researchers have suggested in trying to make sense of the walk-in craze), what I suspect is happening here is that people globally are suddenly becoming *more* of themselves. They are expanding in consciousness and they have no way to explain or understand how that happened or why. Just because someone feels "suddenly new" does not mean he or she is a different soul in the same body. Although I cannot discount Montgomery's ideas about walk-ins, I can affirm that there are many paths to enlightenment—some just involve more detours than others.

Reincarnation

I have encountered near-death survivors whose scenario on the other side of death's curtain involved a review of the lives they had lived *before* their present one, turning their review process into a foray through the corridors of time. I have even interviewed people who described a past-life experience as part of their near-death experience. For example, one woman saw herself marry a certain man as part of a past-life/near-death event, replete with period trappings and medieval music, only to meet the same man several years later and marry him "again." Another case, similar to the storyline in Steven Spielberg's movie *Always*, involved a man who discovered himself to be the disembodied guide for an individual—who happened to be an "old" friend from a previous incarnation who was soon to die in this one.

Besides the occasional interweaving of past-life "threads" within the framework of a near-death scenario, it is fairly common for experiencers to begin remembering existences other than the life they are presently living—even existences that seem alien to their intellects—as part of their aftereffects. Even if nothing like this happens, reincarnation still becomes a favored topic of conversation for the average near-death survivor. Many come to accept it as a fact of life, simply the way things are.

I've heard experiencers state over and over again that the human soul evolves. They speak of cycles and timing and assert that one lifetime is hardly enough to perfect The Self they really are on its journey back to The One True Source of All. They discuss how they think the development of our souls might occur, perhaps happening quickly, but more than likely taking many lifetimes, depending on one's determination to learn and grow. We have the choice, they say, free will, to lengthen or shorten the process. I have never heard any of them use reincarnation as some sort of lame excuse to avoid the responsibility and the effort needed to develop the life at hand.

Personally, none of my three bouts with near-death touched upon previous lives; but during drug therapy to dissolve blood clots after death number two, I did come face to face with a holographic outpicturing of my past incarnations as they paraded across a "misty bridge" that arched over my chest. I was bedfast at the time, and utterly fascinated by these miniature scenes. Although I later tossed off the incident as little more than some drug-induced hallucination, I have had cause since then to reconsider that assessment. I now believe that what I saw was the real thing.

My own journey exploring the theory of reincarnation has been long and disciplined, and it is pertinent that I share some of it with you. I practiced as a professional hypnotherapist for six years after dutifully putting in my three years' apprenticeship, including "on stage" demonstrations. I specialized in past-life regressions, a particular technique where an individual, while under hypnosis, can be regressed or supposedly led "backward in time" to lives lived before birth in this one. My experiences with almost every kind of person and situation imaginable would fill a book by itself. Suffice it to say, I conducted a lot of experiments. Curiosity is a strong suit of mine.

Thanks to several dramatic cases, I learned early on that reincarnation itself, the idea of life-after-life, does not matter one whit. The only significant criterion is the meaningfulness of the "memories" an individual accesses and whether or not these enable him or her to better understand personal character traits and behavior patterns. Regression sessions serve only one purpose, I came to realize, and that is to assist the client in gaining detachment and perspective.

Then I happened upon the human soul. It was most unusual how that occurred. The soul just "popped in" and took over a session one day, surprising me, and changing all the "rules" I thought applicable to hypnosis.

After this first encounter, I discovered that the soul, anyone's soul, is unlike any individual or personality type or supposed incarnation. It is unique unto itself. I came to recognize the soul as an objective and loving source of limitless knowledge. The room temperature would feel warmer when it emerged during a session, and the client would seem to glow. Advice would be given either for the prostrate client, for me, or for another not present. The soul never limited itself or played favorites. Sometimes discourses would issue forth on life and its purpose— gentle, effective discourses that seemed somehow awesome and sacred. The soul's voice, no matter from what client, nearly always sounded the same or similar. It is without identity, eternal, yet personal enough to offer valuable insight about what seems mundane.

Soon after this discovery I closed my practice. Prospective clients preferred finding something to blame their problems on, rather than opening up to the voice of their own soul. I recommended hypnotists willing to accommodate their wishes and shut my door to the experience. Years later, I was reading a professional journal when I saw mention of the Inner Self Helper, or ISH, that was identified in the treatment of multiple personality disorders. Using hypnosis, therapists had at times been able to isolate a peculiar "voice" that was unlike any of the patient's varied personalities. Stating that it was eternal, the voice had no identity, was compassionate and loving, gave objective advice for the patient's best interests, and would guide and instruct the therapist—rather than the other way around. The ISH seemed to be the central organizing "core" of the individual's essence. I smiled when I read that, thinking to myself that professional counselors had at last encountered what had once surprised me so long ago—the very real power of the human soul (or, as they termed it, the ISH).

Now, after dying thrice over, I have found myself questioning the theory of reincarnation once again. Although I remain convinced that the soul evolves through varied life forms, I am no longer so certain of how it accomplishes this feat or even that the idea of progressive lives is valid. It is obvious to me that we reap the consequences of our choices, for that is what seems to create our "heavens" and our "hells." But it is also obvious that the process of how this happens is far more exquisite than what the human mind can fathom. Once you have experienced simultaneity, as I have, anything "linear" loses its logic.

Aliens

A 1991 Roper poll estimated that 3.7 million Americans believe they may have been abducted by alien beings. This staggering number forces each and every one of us to take another look at UFOs and what part they may play in society. As you have already read, at least one near-death survivor had her experience sandwiched between an alien abduction and a miraculous "levitation" of her vehicle (supposedly by the same aliens). It is interesting to note that ample physical evidence was present in this case to indicate that something that defied the laws of physics had happened.

Kenneth Ring has researched what he feels is a connection that links near-death cases with those of the abduction phenomenon. If you haven't read *The Omega Project: Near-Death Experiences, UFO Encounters, and Mind at Large* [28], please do. It will challenge any pet theories you may have. Using a control group to balance out responses, Ring conducted extensive questionnaire samplings of near-death survivors and those who claimed to have been abducted by aliens, and he came up with a provocative conclusion: People who have these kinds of experiences possess an "encounter-prone" personality, a special spiritual, visionary psyche, that may represent a new stage in the evolution of the human mind.

He found, for instance, that experiencers were already oriented that way as children. His study showed that the reason for this was often child abuse or some other type of childhood trauma that forced the child to learn how to dissociate (separate mentally and emotionally from consensual reality) and be absorbed (focusing attention so intently that all else in the external environment is excluded). Specifically then, these two traits, dissociation and absorption, are hallmarks of encounter-prone personalities, people who have the ability to roam "imaginal" realms and have unusual and sometimes otherworldly experiences. These people become "psychological sensitives" who develop extended ranges of perception beyond what is considered normal.

Ring is quick to point out that there is a coherent pattern of how these people change after their near-death or abduction episodes, and that imaginal realms are not fantasy creations but objectively self-existent states every bit as real as our physical world. He affirms that structural changes occur in the brains of these experiencers (something I have been saying since 1981), and he lists a whole compendium of physical aftereffects that will seem familiar to you once you read Chapter Nine in this book. (Ring and I have never compared the findings of our separate research projects, nor have we used the same research methodologies.)

Reading Kenneth Ring's book was a reality check for me. It seemed as if some of my own conclusions were being reflected back to me from the different "mirror" he offered. Along with a confirmation of the things I had observed, his material highlighted how the two of us differ. As an example, I have difficulty believing that child abuse and/or trauma is the deciding factor in the formation of encounter-prone personalities. Yes, his numbers are impressive, his research solid. Yet it is broadly touted these days that well over 70 percent of the population is the product of dysfunctional homes, that trauma of one type or another is endemic to childhood.

Although I cannot submit the kind of figures Ring has, what I noticed during the interviews I conducted was that many near-death survivors (the particular experiencer group I am the most familiar with) were either born with the abilities of dissocation and absorption, or became that way at such a tender age I could not connect the formation of these abilities with any major life challenges. The abuse/trauma link was plainly visible in some cases, but not in enough that, given the current findings on dysfunctional families, I could feel comfortable saying one caused the other. What I did find was that traumatic childhoods seemed to reinforce tendencies that were already present. Amazingly, many adults quite suddenly displayed these abilities as a direct result of their near-death experiences, not because of traits they might have formed while they were young.

Although I applaud Ring's work, I think the time has come for all of us to graduate from an over-reliance on questionnaires to laboratory/biological measurement studies and cross-cultural/cross-discipline research. I know that takes millions of dollars, but we have reached a point when anything less no longer serves the field or the public we inform. (Please note an announcement of such a project at the close of Chapter Fourteen.)

While we're on the subject of aliens, I want to take a moment to talk about extraterrestrials.

I only came across two near-death survivors who described an alien-type being as part of their near-death scenario. Yet, fully one-third of the people I interviewed began to see UFOs afterward, usually in the dream-state but sometimes in broad daylight while wide awake. A small percentage claimed to have seen UFOs land and/or alien beings head their way, a few detailed an abduction. Many started to display the ability to channel, or telepathically communicate, with aliens. Some made this type of communication their life's work; others regarded the whole thing as a novelty and made little of it. Yes, there were those who said they experienced UFO phenomena before their near-death episodes, but this is rare.

What grabs my attention, however, is that after their near-death experiences 20 percent started to have "memories" of arriving on planet Earth as immigrants from another world. They discovered that it was *they* who were the aliens!

I uncovered no particular pattern of who came from where—just the clear and total remembrance each person claimed to have of immigrating to this world from another. Although there was one experiencer who insisted he was a recent arrival, the rest relegated their entry to a time far back in history. Some felt they were here before human habitation had advanced to any real degree, others spoke of visiting the fabled cultures of Sumer, Atlantis, and Mu, then deciding to remain, or having no other choice but to stay. Considering that the vast number of near-death survivors were neither mystically inclined nor metaphysically informed before they had their experiences, this is a startling find. And it caught me off guard.

I say that because I'm one of those with alien memories, too.

For over a decade, I have tried to explain away such remembrances. I have variously insisted that either they are glimmers of my experience in the womb before birth, or the result of the reading I did as a child (I was enthralled with tales of *Buck Rogers in the Twenty-first Century* and the writings of H.G. Wells), or perhaps they're fragments from the exposure I have had since the sixties to mystical and metaphysical material. Yet, try as I may to find an explanation, I cannot deny the utter realness and intensity of what explodes in my mind whenever I recall my life as Arrakkus, a lizardlike being from a water star that went nova in the Sirius system. I have made no mention of this before (except in passing in my first book), because I have no way to confirm or test these memories. It is only because so many other near-death survivors face the same dilemma that I say anything.

After all, who wants to admit they might have once been a tall greenish-gray thing with two-lidded buglike eyes, three hearts, and an intricate arrangement of joints that allowed almost unlimited movement? Look, it was hard enough for me to earn my doctorate in the humanities without having to talk about something like this. Yet I cannot remain faithful to my research if I avoid subjects I find uncomfortable.

The idea of extraterrestrial immigrants seems implausible. Still, refusing to investigate it may be one of many reasons why the "missing link" in our evolution as humans is still missing. Anomalies and myths that suggest a history other than what science assures us is true are numerous and appear throughout the globe. Maybe it is time we took another look at them...and paid more attention to "memories."

II

Aftereffects
and Implications
of Near-Death

EIGHT

Psychological Aftereffects

> There are seasons, in human affairs, when new
> depths seem to be broken up in the soul, when
> new wants are unfolded in multitudes, and a
> new and undefined good is thirsted for. There
> are periods when to dare, is the highest
> wisdom.
>
> —William Ellery Channing

My goal in the first half of this book was to present the many aspects of the near-death phenomenon and of the people who experience it. The second half, which begins here, will be more interpretative, a discussion of the patterns that might somehow give us a better understanding of the experience itself and the vast realm of aftereffects and implications.

My fifteen years of nearly full-time research on this subject have convinced me that it is not the episode itself that is so important, *it is the aftereffects and how the individual responds to them*...what comes next. This is how you determine true value and meaning, not the other way around.

Allow me to illustrate. A man in the audience of a talk I had given in Williamsburg, Virginia, came to the microphone and relayed his own near-death story, one so positive and so inspiring it brought tears to the eyes of the assembled crowd. Yet, much to everyone's surprise, he went on to reveal how cursed he felt to have had such an experience and how difficult his life had been ever since it happened. Then a woman jumped up and excitedly recounted her story. Even though her scenario had centered on a life-or-death struggle in semidarkness at the edge of a whirlpool, while high winds and the presence of evil threatened, she was overjoyed to have experienced anything so inspiring and so reassuring about how life really works and how salvation is guaranteed by our willingness to correct our own mistakes.

Here are two people: One was traumatized by a heaven-like experience, the other uplifted and transformed by a hellish one. *Note the response factor.*

Remember Steven B. Ridenhour from Chapter Four? He spent twenty years trying to re-create his near-death episode through drug use, rather than face the aftereffects and what they might portend. His introduction to heaven became a plunge into hell, until he was laid up flat in bed because of a back injury and had to face what he had tried so long to deny. *Note the response factor.*

And then there was a woman physicist I met who had worked on the space station project. She had spent a lifetime avoiding mention or display of her "differences" until she read my first book. Puzzled, she sat down with her elderly mother and lamented: "Why am I exhibiting the aftereffects of the near-death phenomenon when nothing like a close brush with death has ever happened to me?" Her mother laughed. "Have you forgotten that high fever you had when you were four and how we had to rush you to the hospital? The doctor said you nearly died. After the crisis was over, I stood next to your bed and held your hand, and you told me all about it—about the angels who came and took you to a light-filled city and all the love you felt. We really did lose you that night, for you were never the same again. I'm surprised you've forgotten that incident. I haven't." *Note the response factor.*

You can't fake aftereffects.

Nor can you hide your response to the way they affect you (whether you realize what you are doing or not).

You may be able to delay the onset of them, but you cannot pretend away the complex and life-altering dynamics of the near-death phenomenon. Whoever thinks that experiencers simply undergo a change in attitude as a result of their episode is in for quite an awakening.

Let's begin with psychological aspects here based on what's typical, and then discuss physiological changes in Chapter Nine (including electrical sensitivity).

I was able to isolate a consistent pattern of seven major elements in my original investigation, which has since proven to be universal across the broad spectrum of experience types— regardless of age, race, belief system, or culture of the one involved. This pattern of psychological aftereffects appears in brief form below, along with key positive/negative factors. Additional components and comments follow.

The Psychological Aftereffects of the Near-Death Experience

The inability to personalize love and a sense of belonging. Near-death survivors come to love and accept others without the usual attachments and conditions society expects. They perceive themselves as equally and fully loving of each and all, openly generous, excited about the potential and wonder of each person they see. Their desire is to be a conduit of universal love, God's love, for the rest of their lives. Confused family members tend to regard this sudden switch in behavior as oddly threatening, as if their loved one had become aloof, unresponsive, even uncaring and unloving. Some mistake this "unconditional" way of expressing joy and affection (heart-centered rather than person-centered) as flirtatious misbehavior or disloyalty. Divorces are numerous.

The inability to recognize and comprehend boundaries, rules, limits. One of the biggest reasons life seems so different afterward is because the experiencer now has a basis of comparison unknown before. Familiar codes of conduct can lose relevance or disappear altogether as unlimited avenues of interest and inquiry take priority. This new frame of reference can infuse experiencers with such open acceptance that they can and often do take on childlike naïveté. With the fading of previous norms and standards, basic caution and discernment can also fade. It is not unusual to hear of newly vulnerable near-death survivors being cheated, beaten, robbed, or involved in various mishaps and accidents. This can be misconstrued by healthcare professionals as a sign of encroaching mental instability, when nothing of the kind is true. Family and friends, however, tend to express disgust or embarrassment or insult at what seems to them to be a person indulging in an ego trip.

Difficulty in understanding time sense or references either to the future or the past. Most experiencers come to develop a sense of timelessness, some go as far as to reject watches and refuse to reckon with clocks or schedules. They tend to "flow" with the natural shift of light and dark, and display a more heightened awareness of the present moment and the importance of being "in the now." They use their eyes a lot to search midair for memories of the past, rather than looking directly at anything or anyone, as if to locate something almost forgotten. Making future preparations can seem irrelevant. This behavior is labeled "spaciness" by others, who do their best to ignore the shift in perception, although seldom can they ignore the shift in speech. That's because many individuals refer to their experience as if it were a divider separating one life phase from another.

Sensitivities enhance and expand, the intuitive opens up to the psychic. There is no denying the fact that if not psychic before, the experiencer becomes so afterward; if psychic before, he or she becomes even more so after. Out-of-body episodes can continue, the light beings met in death can become a daily part of life routines, the future is often known before it occurs, extrasensory perception becomes *normal* and *ordinary!* This behavior is not only worrisome to relatives and friends, it can become frightening to them. Unfortunately, near-death survivors are sometimes involuntarily committed to mental wards as insane or charged with witchcraft or demonic possession—just because their faculties and the range of their perception have expanded and been enhanced beyond what was once typical for them. A person's religious beliefs do not alter or prevent the amplification of things psychic, nor do the misconstrued judgments of people who do not understand what is going on.

A changed view of physical reality, with a noticeable reduction in worries and fears. Life paradoxes begin to make sense and a knowing comes, a sense of purpose and meaning. Patience and forgiveness can replace former needs to criticize and condemn. Hard-driving achievers and materialists can transform into easy-going philosophers; but, by the same token, those more relaxed or uncommitted before can become energetic "movers and shakers," determined to make a difference in the world. Actually, personality switches seem to depend more on what is "needed" to round out the individual's inner growth than on any uniform outcome. This is utterly bewildering to family members. Within some households, relatives are so impressed by what they witness that they too change, making the experience a "shared" event. In other families, though, the response is so negative that alienation, separation, or divorce results.

A different feeling of physical self, knowing we live in and "wear" our bodies. The average near-death survivor comes to regard him or herself as an immortal soul currently resident within material form so lessons can be learned while sojourning in the earthplane. They now *know* they are not their body; they are a living soul, a child of God. It may take awhile before experiencers are once again comfortable in physical form and fully accept the importance and specialness of their own bodies, but, eventually, they usually do.

Difficulty with communications and relationships, finding it hard to say what is meant or to understand the words of others. What was once foreign becomes familiar, what was once familiar becomes foreign. Rationale of any kind tends to lose its logic. The world is the same, but the individual isn't. Although many near-death survivors do not experience such extreme change, the majority do, even children. It is commonplace for experiencers to think abstractly and in grandiose terms, rather than to deduce things in the linear mode of sequential thinking. New ways of using language, even whole new vocabularies, emerge. Certainly, communications can improve with patience and effort on everyone's part and life can resume some measure of routine, but not always. The individual sooner or later responds to a "tune" no one else can hear.

I hasten to add that these aftereffects can and do fade with time or disappear altogether in some cases. But with most people, not only do the aftereffects remain, they often enhance and expand even further with each passing year.

It is fascinating to me that as reportings increase so, too, do claims of the aftereffects' impact and intensity. My research illustrates this trend, as well. For instance, when I finished the manuscript for *Coming Back to Life* in 1987, out of the two hundred interviews the book is based upon, 25 percent insisted they were unaffected by aftereffects of any kind, 65 percent claimed major differences in their lives because of what had happened to them, and the remaining 10 percent described radical changes. Presently, using a base of seven hundred interviews, the numbers have shifted: 21 percent report being unaffected, 60 percent report significant changes, and a whopping 19 percent state categorically that "life as always" is now impossible for them.

As a general rule, though, most near-death survivors do not recognize the extent to which they have changed. Often, the most revealing stories come from families, friends, and co-workers, who relate what they observe about the individual's transformation, and their stories invariably differ from the experiencer's version, sometimes drastically. It was my daughter, Natalie Rowell, who first called this to my attention. One day, she asked me to sit down and hear her out. "Well," she began, "you're easier to get along with now, and you're easier to talk to. But you're not Mom and I want Mom back." (We both looked for "her," but neither of us ever found the woman. Years later, I asked each of my three children to write a letter about how what had happened to me had affected them. Natalie's letter was several pages long, ending with, "You have finally become the mother I always wished you would be. You've done a lot of changing, Mom. Now it's my turn.")

There were no gender differences in the near-death phenomenon itself or its aftereffects, but I did find variations in the way males and females interpreted and responded to their experience. Here's what I mean:

- Females generally became more assertive and outspoken afterward; men more thoughtful, caring, and emotionally expressive.
- Men were less willing than women to view an unpleasant and/or hell-like scenario in a positive fashion and take steps to make constructive changes in their lives because of it.
- More men reported lengthy and complex transcendent experiences than women, yet that fact is not representative of the aftereffects nor what the individual did about what had happened to him or her.

I call your attention once again to the case of Margaret Fields Kean in Chapter Five. Her near-death scenario was plain and simple, hardly in the same league as those of the men I discussed. Yet look at her aftereffects and how she was able to develop a technique that *anyone* could use to readily access the healing power of transcendent truth. Thousands of people on two continents have already benefited from her course programs, and that's just the beginning. She is now training teachers and has developed teaching manuals for them. If ever there was an experience that met the criteria for a transcendent episode, it is hers.

What's happening in the way of gender differences, at least what I have seen, leads me to believe that any contrast between male and female experiencers has more to do with cultural programming and expectations than with gender itself.

When a male crime boss or corporate executive suddenly softens and becomes openly loving, philosophical, and compassionate as a direct result of a transformational event like near-death, the contrast before and after is far more noticeable than when a female school teacher or nurse makes the same transition. A woman experiences the shift every bit as acutely as a man, but her journey will not receive the same attention or accolades, either from her family or from the public at large, nor will it be as easy for her to carry out whatever "mission" she feels guided to do. (Transformational, religious, and spiritual domains have always been dominated by men, even though women undergo the same type of enlightenment and are just as changed afterward. History seldom records this, however. Perhaps that's because most historians are men.)

Of those who experienced unpleasant and/or hellish near-death scenarios, a little over 50 percent in my survey had the exact same aftereffects as the universal pattern; the others exhibited traits that ranged from the numbness you find with people who are in a state of shock to avoidance and denial, confusion, and/or occasional bouts with fatigue and depression. (They were able, it seemed to me, to stifle what might have happened next.)

Regardless of aftereffects we focus on, this much I have seen to be true: *The near-death phenomenon enhances and enlarges whatever characteristics or potentials were resident within the experiencer at the time it occurred.*

That means anything suppressed or repressed or ignored surfaces and becomes larger than life, including latent talents and abilities, as well as problems and concerns. Energy accelerates, the mundane is revitalized, a sense of newness permeates routines, materialism/possessiveness fades, long-term gratification replaces a need for short-term pleasure, simple joys outweigh the desire for quick "highs" or fantasy escapes.

And along with this acceleration of energy and what happens because of it, inner-child issues—unfinished business from childhood—come to the forefront. Often exaggerated in content and form, this rush of "old stuff" can interfere with or distort the experiencer's insights and behavior. It's almost as if, in order to facilitate healing in others, one must first heal him- or herself.

The emergence of personal issues that seem unrelated to the phenomenon is so commonplace, I have come to expect it when doing interviews. The impression I get is that the near-death experience tends to operate like a giant washing machine in the way it scrubs up and cleans out one's psyche, freeing anything locked in or held back. As you can well imagine, it often takes years to integrate the aftereffects, which, I believe, accounts for the unusually high divorce rate experiencers have.

Listen to Geraldine F. Berkheimer of Santa Ana, California:

The process of integrating the near-death experience with "normal" life is a continuous, daily one. *Struggle* is an understatement. I often try to explain to groups to whom I speak that the near-death experience is more intimate than sex. Here we are dealing with the very essence of being, with the soul. Beauty and pain go hand in hand in describing the experience, unless one detaches him-herself from it, and few experiencers can, or are willing to do so. My reason for coming back, and perhaps the only reason for any of us, is to share the light which each of us is. It doesn't matter what, where, to whom, or how this is done, if it involves joy or even, on occasion, anger. It just isn't important. The important thing is the sharing.

And from Glenn Patrick Brymer of Houston, Texas:

I cannot tell you how happy I was. For the first time, I was able to read about people who were having problems in dealing with the aftereffects of their near-death experiences. It was such a relief to learn that I was not imagining these things. I was not crazy. I was not hallucinating. This was a big turning point for me, to see my own experience through someone else's eyes.

Brymer, by the way, was the first near-death survivor to contact me after my initial work was published. He tracked me down by phone (which was no easy task, as I was traveling), and was almost in tears describing years of heartbreak in dealing with the Veterans Administration. He was one of those who had to face the specter of being thought mentally ill until he finally found a psychologist who was also an experiencer, and an Army nurse who knew about my first book. (His experience occurred during a military assignment in Europe.)

When I did a guest spot on a radio talk show out of Kentucky, an elderly woman called in and identified herself as one of the initial case studies in *Life After Life* [29], the book by Raymond A. Moody, Jr., M.D., that introduced the world to the near-death phenomenon. "Being in that book was so depressing to me. I didn't fit what Dr. Moody talked about. My life wasn't like that afterward. I felt like a failure, like something was the matter with me, because I wasn't as saintly as he claimed."

Moody's book was, *and still is*, important. A whole new paradigm emerged from its pages, based on a phenomenon occurring at the brink of death that could be medically documented; a phenomenon suggestive of a breakthrough into transcendent states that may exist beyond death's "door." Moody's observation of the aftermath, however, focused on contrasts rather than probing into response factors and the challenge of integration. Other researchers initially followed suit.

Thus, experiencers were left with a conundrum: How does one explain the disparity between research claims and the way things really are?

Some near-death survivors feel as if they were "kicked out of heaven," reviving as they did when they actually wanted to stay. Most of them know they are not as perfect as it seems like they ought to be, considering where they went. None claim sainthood. States of depression can be lengthy, the experience seeming as much a curse as a blessing. Yet, just as many glide through the aftereffects as if riding a "magic flying carpet," with little or no wear and tear, to evidence conflict. Family support is an all-important key.

The fact is that experiencers can and do get angry, frightened, jealous, worried, and impatient just as often as everyone else does. The difference is: They don't stay that way very long. They're more resilient and self-reflective, willing to accept personal responsibility and seek equitable solutions. Small children and those who undergo the phenomenon in infancy simply grow up the different kind of people they are, wondering why everyone else isn't like them. But children who were old enough to compare their lives before with what they are like afterward, can and often do become disruptive in school, or unusually withdrawn. Theirs is the greater challenge, for seldom are they believed by parents, teachers, or counselors.

It is also a fact that experiencers often go on learning binges afterward, craving knowledge like some people crave sweets. Physics and metaphysics are popular subjects, especially the newest quantum theories on light, luminosity, zero-point energy, and the fabric of space. Not only that, merely searching in a dictionary for a word can lead to hours of happy distraction. Decidedly more curious, they enroll in schools and self-development classes, and take as many field trips as their budgets allow for hands-on learning. They automatically gravitate to teaching and counseling roles, or to the areas of religion, spirituality, and healing.

Intelligence and intuition are heightened. One man I know had an unexplainable increase of twenty points on the standard IQ test after his near-death episode. Supposedly an impossible achievement, his case underscores what is so typical of experiencers.

Peggy Adams Raso of St. Louis, Missouri, found her husband awake and awaiting her return from a late-night session in the near-death conference they were both attending.

He said he had some questions for me. So I sat down and listened. He asked, "When did you get so smart?" and then went on, "You weren't this smart when we got married." I asked him what he was talking about, and he said, "I listen to you making speeches and talking to people about NDEs and IANDS and I am just in awe about how you talk to people. I just wondered *when* you got this smart."

Experiencers are infused with a sense of the divine and with boundless joy, which is both wonderful and not so wonderful. Case in point, an incident that happened to me in 1978 when I attended one of the early Death & Dying Intensives put on by Elisabeth Kübler-Ross, M.D., at what was once her center in Escondido, California [30]. It seems my fellow attendees had perceived me as some kind of phony, since, in their opinion, I was just too happy to be real. It wasn't until after I shared my near-death experiences that I learned of their feelings toward me, and they learned of all I had gone through. What they didn't realize was that although they had come to release pain, I had come to *unleash joy*. My needs were just as great as theirs, for joy and love can be every bit as much a catalyst for growth as pain.

And that joy can take on many forms. A prostitute I interviewed in Baltimore, Maryland, described how she altered the way she conducted "business" after her near-death episode.

I became a "celibate prostitute." I now offer a warm, caring voice, excellent full-body massages, a willingness to listen if they care to unload, and lots of laughter. I just know how to counsel men, help them, make them feel good. Sex isn't necessary for that. You'd be surprised at the men who thank me for my service, and the callbacks I receive. Men need love just as much as women, the *real* kind. I've always liked being a prostitute, now I love it!

Dottie Bush of Willow Grove, Pennsylvania, best sums up this chapter:

I never said anything to the doctor or nurses about this special experience while in the hospital, but now I have told many people of my experience. I have gone through some personal trials in recent years, but I know that they are lessons that must be learned here on Earth. I seem to be led to be at certain places or drawn to certain experiences at times, and I look at life differently. Helping people and expressing love for each other, that's what we are here for.

I know and understand things now that seem just impossible to put into words. It is a great frustration to see people running about with a self-centered attitude, pursuing activities that are such a waste of their lives, and to be unable to help them understand. Seeing so much unthinking selfishness in the world today just makes my heart ache. But those of us—and we are many—who have had the benefit of the near-death experience, long to share with everyone the lesson of this higher consciousness and love.

I have no fear of death, actually looking forward to going home when God calls, and yearn to be able to assure others of the reality of the beauty and joy of heaven, for my experience remains as vivid and convincing today as when it happened. I tell others simply: The best is yet to come!

NINE

Physiological Aftereffects

Time and space are modes by which we think,
not conditions in which we live.
—Albert Einstein

Not just the mind is challenged by the near-death phenomenon.
A person's body and the very way life is lived undergo a transformation, too. Mundane chores can take on surrealistic dimensions.

We begin our examination of the physical changes experiencers can and often do encounter by looking at what is typical, at least in around 80 to 90 percent of the people I interviewed who reported aftereffects:

Typical Physiological Aftereffects

- Near-death experiencers tend to look and act younger, are more playful.
- Have brighter skin, eyes that sparkle.
- Have substantial change in energy levels.
- Become more sensitive to light, especially sunlight.
- Become more sensitive to sound and to noise levels.
- Are more open and accepting toward the new and the different.
- Regard things as new even when they're not, boredom levels decrease or disappear.

- Handle stress more easily and heal more quickly.
- Exhibit changes in brain functioning.

Increased sensitivity to light and sound is a major issue, so much so that at near-death conferences sponsored by IANDS, video equipment is now restricted (television crews must do their filming in the halls outside the auditoriums), house lights are kept somewhat more subdued than usual, and sound systems are tuned to decibels lower than for regular conference settings. If these precautionary measures are not taken, the complaint is always the same—pain! It physically hurts, sometimes throughout one's entire body, if the lights are too strong and the sound is too loud or piercing.

Youthfulness is quite apparent. These people appear to age at a slower rate than the general public. Perhaps that is because stress is not as bothersome for them as it once was, nor are they as prone to lengthy bouts of worry. Regardless of the cause, though, near-death survivors look younger longer and maintain a playful vigor that is both innocent and curious. Not only do cuts heal faster, overall health improves—sometimes dramatically.

The following is a compilation of the aftereffects reported by over 50 percent of the near-death experiencers in my research base that seem to be physiological or have a physiological source.

Frequently Experienced Physiological or Physiologically Based Aftereffects

- Metabolic changes
  - It doesn't seem to take as long to digest food; bowel movements often increase in frequency; general health improves.
  - The body seems to assimilate substances more quickly, especially into the bloodstream.
  - It takes less of any substance for full effect.
  - Allergies increase, even to regular pharmaceutical prescriptions that had been taken successfully in the past. Many experiencers cannot handle drugs at all, or may have to take children's dosages. There is a greater sensitivity to household chemicals, the coatings used on fabrics and wood, food preservatives, sprays, and perfumes.

- Experiencers often will forgo pharmaceuticals in favor of homeopathy, herbs, and/or other healing-remedy alternatives.
- Blood pressure lowers and pulse rate can also decrease.
- A reduction in red-meat consumption or complete conversion to vegetarianism occurs.
- With the inability to tolerate loud noises, experiencers find themselves drawn to classical music and to other melodious/ natural sounds. Chimes, bells, and crystal bowl instruments also become very appealing, as they crave the longer, pure sine wave as opposed to short, choppy beats.
- A new preference for open doors, windows, and shades; no locks; few if any curtains.
- An ability to merge into things more easily, to become "one with" them (absorption). It can become difficult to maintain personal boundaries; previous discernments need to be relearned.
- Acquisition of the ability to "hear" plants and animals speak or voice their needs. Experiencers can also "hear" words not spoken and voices and music in the air when no one is nearby.
- Experiencers find they attract animals, birds, and small children to them just by their presence. Plants seem to grow better around them.
- Latent talents tend to surface along with a thirst for knowledge. Experiencers suddenly know more, laugh more.
- Access to memory changes. Old memories seem to take longer to retrieve and are not as meaningful while recent memories are more lively and focused. Experiencers sense a change in brain functioning.
- Thinking processes alter and experiencers may have to retrain themselves how to use their own brains. Cognitive abilities sometimes switch.
- Synchronicity (where unrelated elements suddenly converge in unusually meaningful ways) becomes commonplace.
- Synesthesia, or multiple sensing, occurs frequently.
- Acquisition of the ability to sometimes "see" beings and/or scenes that are not physically present, as well as the ability to see airborne water molecules and movements of energy.
- Experiencers become more orgasmic.
- Reversal of body clocks often occurs (night people become day people and vice versa). Most reject watches.

- Heightened sensations of taste-touch-texture-odors.
- A new awareness of invisible energy fields and a sensitivity to electricity and geomagnetic fields. Sparkles or balls of energy are sometimes seen in the air.
- Increased sensitivity to meteorological factors such as temperature, pressure, air movement, and humidity.
- Experiencers become electrically sensitive. Their body energy interferes with electronic equipment, light sources, security systems, and the like.
- Extrasensory perception and other psychic abilities become a routine part of life and out-of-body episodes may continue to occur. Experiencers often develop "healing hands" and exhibit a charismatic "aura" around them. Noticeably more empathetic, can take on others' problems if not careful.
- An ability to know the future and/or display "Future Memory" (in which one physically and fully "pre-lives" the future before it occurs and remembers doing so when that memory is "triggered").
- Experiencers find they are more creative.
- Whatever has been repressed or suppressed or ignored within the inner psyche surfaces, including "inner child" issues and whatever has not been faced or forgiven from one's past.

Of the three thousand plus experiencers I have spoken with, I have only met one who could tolerate rock music after undergoing the near-death phenomenon, and that was a young woman in Rochester, New York. The rest can't stand the stuff anymore, even if they were aficionados previously. I can't begin to emphasize how tonal people become afterward, and how emotionally affected they are by sounds. To say that music preferences change is an understatement.

Experiencers invariably come to "see" things others don't, for instance, wave forms, sparkling weblike networks, water molecules, or shape-changes in the air. This may seem rather odd or like so much fantasy until you read the latest from science: In January of 1993, the *Washington Post* carried an article about a startling find—the Earth's lower atmosphere is laced with rivers of water vapor rivaling the Amazon River in their flow. The *Post* quoted Reginald E. Newell of the Massachusetts Institute of Technology as saying these rivers, "are the main mechanism by which (atmospheric) water gets transported from the equator to the poles." So don't laugh the next time near-death survivors say they "see" rivers in the sky.... They're right!

And watch those giggles of yours when experiencers describe how they respond to given items, as sensations can and often do tend to come in multiples. Example—seldom will such individuals buy a painting only for how it looks. It must also "taste" and "sound" and "smell" right and fit into the overall "personality" of the room where they intend to hang it. (Notice the different sensations from a single stimulus.) This ability has been medically documented as an elaboration or anomaly of the limbic system in the brain, and is termed synesthesia (multiple sensing).

I also want to call attention to the increased allergies, especially to pharmaceuticals. This is no laughing matter. Near-death survivors are still, even today, being involuntarily committed to psychiatric wards and institutions solely because they are exhibiting the typical aftereffects of the average experiencer... and they are being subjected to large, sometimes mega doses of various chemical medications. At a time when they can *least* handle even *normal* adult dosages, they are given full strengths—or stronger. Not only can this make matters worse (instead of better), it is suspected in causing "multiple chemical sensitivity" (MCS), a particular disorder similar to what seems to be affecting some soldiers who served during the Gulf War. The result? Prolonged psychiatric stays, increased "mental aberrations," deeper depressions, physical trauma, and a mysterious sensitivity to unrelated chemical sources. Supportive environments and better data for professionals are keys to helping reverse this misfortune, for, if experiencers receive even a modicum of positive assistance in dealing with what happened to them, they can flourish in ways that are wonder filled and inspiring and can achieve greater health and stability than ever before. (More information is provided under the heading "Spiritual Emergence/Emergencies" at the close of this book.)

The phenomenon of Future Memory is so important I have already written a book about it as a sequel to this one. In brief, Future Memory occurs when one somehow shifts from the "speed" or vibration of everyday living to that of another "wavelength," while still wide awake and physically active. A future segment of one's life is then lived, replete with physical sensations and details so richly involved that one cannot recognize the difference between the episode and present life activities. Sometimes the memory of this event can fade, only to return when "triggered" by some pre-lived detail that actually manifests. Not to be confused with déjà vu or precognition or clairvoyance, Future Memory is decidedly physical and active and filled with minute specifics that later prove accurate. I believe some near-death researchers have mistakenly labeled this phenomenon "flash fowards," when, if one probes deeper, it seems more indicative of changes in brain structure/functioning than of accessing futuristic information.

Those aftereffects which I have found to be more unusual and/or infrequent, are:

Unusual and/or Infrequent Physiological or Physiologically Based Aftereffects

- Experiencers who become gifted healers, ministers, artists, musicians, intuitives, therapists, and innovative inventors.
- The unexplained ability to "channel" information from The Other Side and/or from nature, the disembodied, other realms, including the ability to converse with the dead (perhaps even to see them).
- The acquisition of a strong force-field. Experiencers can also possess psychokinetic abilities (affecting and/or manipulating matter with the mind).
- An ability to empathize to the point of taking on another's pain or illness; so absorbed they "become" or "merge with" whatever they focus on to the exclusion of a productive life.
- Memories of a previous "alien" existence and of immigrating to planet Earth, UFO dreams, some alien encounters.
- Skin tone changes, skeletal changes such as joints that begin to loosen for unknown reasons, ribs that easily dislocate, hips that occasionally misalign more often than what could be thought of as normal.
- Significant changes in appearance.

Many of the people I interviewed stated that strange incidents began happening in their lives after their near-death experiences, and with increasing frequency. This alarmed some, thrilled others. Three examples follow:

Elizabeth Lynn, Shalimar, Florida:

My spirit guides did not contact me until two months after my NDE, when I first learned to drive. Having no sense of direction and often getting lost, it soon became apparent that if I listened to them I would never be lost again. Success! I worked for IBM and, when I would get off work, I would experience paralyzing fear of traffic and Interstate 35 South. Just getting on the freeway was a nightmare. I would say my prayer of protection and go for it, all the while asking my spirit guides to assist. Well, boy, they did! Often up to a full city block six-lanes wide would clear of traffic. It was like I had the whole freeway to myself. This went on daily for the three years I worked and traveled the freeways of Austin. And it continues today as I move around in my little "Texas Cadillac" (my 1984 truck named Babe). Oh, I forgot to say that Babe does not like anyone else to drive her. She really acts badly if they do. And, once, stones flew out from a gravel truck I was following and struck my windshield, causing two large cracks at eye level on the driver's side. After several weeks of trying to see properly, I "asked" that the cracks move out of my sight. Bingo! The cracks moved to the passenger side and they are still there today. By the way, when driving down the road, I psychically hear other people in their cars talking to themselves or to others with them. The first time this happened, I heard a couple fighting— every word. People ought to be more careful—you never know who will be listening.

Tom Carroll, Encino, California:

The electric typewriter that I am using to write this letter frequently "acts up." On occasion, the machine will lock in upper case, but when I run it through memory, the words come out the right way. Yes, I have had the machine checked several times and no one can explain why this happens. Objects disappear and then reappear around me. It's happened so many times since my near-death experience to keys, photographs, important papers—and for no apparent reason. One morning I had just gotten out of bed, done my bathroom chores, and walked into the kitchen to prepare my coffee. It was a standard routine. However, this morning I could not find my favorite cup. I looked everywhere. Finally I gave up and elected to use another cup. I went to the kitchen cupboard, opened the door, and there it was—my favorite cup—filled with hot, steaming coffee. I was shocked! I had looked there before and the cup was not there. Not only that, I had not made any coffee that morning! I have seen "people" who were there one moment and then gone the next. I have seen doors lock when there was no lock on them. On many occasions, I will hear "voices" of people that I know are not there, and "voices" of people I have known who have died. To be quite honest, until I read your material, I had begun to think I was losing my mind. You can't talk about things like this to anyone but close friends.

From my own life:

I was assigned by my employer to troubleshoot a large, computerized switching system, newly installed as a way to improve phone service in a popular New York City hotel. There had been much fanfare at the beginning, yet two months later the new unit seemed doomed. Not only had it never worked, and none of the engineers could determine why, but the manager threatened—"One more week, fix it or I toss it!" Three days was all I had to size up the situation and write a report. Mind you, I am not now nor have I ever been an engineer. I don't even speak "electronic-ese," but I do know how to "look." I did my observations, checked out every plug and cable, interviewed operators and hotel staff, then, when no one was watching, I'd open the doors to the main cabinets and "merge" with the circuit cards and the power system so I could "sense" and "feel" whatever pulse might be amiss. I handed in a fifty-point report and thought no more of it. Several months later, my boss asked me to come to his office. With head bowed, he muttered, "Thanks to your report we fixed the unit in two days and haven't had a problem with it since. Uh, but promise me you will never ever tell me how you figured out what was wrong." With that said, he jumped up and ran out the door, refusing to look me in the eyes. I worked for this company as a telephone systems analyst for nearly three years, doing field investigations, writing technical manuals, and training switchboard operators—with no prior background whatsoever. I instantly "knew" that equipment as well as if I had been its inventor and I understood circuitry and power flows. I have no explanation. I just KNEW!

Among the many changes that can happen to a near-death survivor after his or her experience is the puzzling and lesser known condition of electrical sensitivity.

Electrical sensitivity is a term near-death researchers use to refer to those people whose energy seems somehow to affect or control electrical and/or electronic equipment, sometimes causing malfunctions, breakage, or other unusual reactions that cannot be rationally explained. It has been established that "electrical sensitives" often have many allergies, report a very high incidence of psychic phenomena, claim to have "healing gifts," are emotionally intense or unstable, and exhibit an abnormal sensitivity to light and sound.

Of the experiencers I have interviewed, 73 percent claimed to have had incidences of electrical sensitivity since their near-death episodes. That figure was so staggering to me, I sent out a questionnaire to check out the breadth and scope of what might be happening here. Out of one hundred queries mailed, forty-six replied. The two-page questionnaire I used marked with the numbers reporting each item appears in Appendix II, Research Methodology. Highlights from that survey follow:

A Survey of Electrical Sensitivity Reported by Near-Death Survivors

Respondents—41 experienced near-death (some several times)
16 of those had additional near-death-like experiences
Light 5 had a near-death-like experience only
Exposure—39 had 50% or more of their episode filled with light
7 encountered 0 to 25% light during their scenario
Light Merge—24 claimed to have merged with The Light/light being
Increased sensitivity to light afterward 80%

Increased sensitivity to sunlight afterward 76%
Wear sunglasses more often 72%
Increased sensitivity to camera flash/video filming lights . . 67%
Occasionally see nonphysical lights 54%
Increased sensitivity to sound and noise levels 67%
More particular to type of sound exposure 74%
Avoid places and programs where sound too loud 96%
Increased sensitivity to radio and television sound levels . . 83%
Occasionally hear nonphysical sounds 57%
Can more accurately sense electrical and magnetic fields . . 57%
Can more accurately feel electrical and magnetic fields 54%
Increased sensitivity to electronic equipment fields 50%
More sensitive to modes of travel, vehicles 61%
Television sets act strangely in their presence 54%
Receive television images on nonexistent channels 33%
Recording equipment acts strangely in their presence 33%
Computer equipment acts strangely in their presence 20%
Other electronic equipment acts up in their presence 35%
Light bulbs blow out, dim, or brighten in their presence . . 35%
Notice a force field around themselves 52%
Other people notice bright glow around them 57%
Animals react strongly (either negatively or positively)
to their presence 63%
Children more docile (or threatened) around them 61%
Experience unusually powerful sweeps of energy 61%

Electrical sensitivity includes, as you can see, more than just an unusual reaction to electronic equipment. Although my questionnaire base is small, it at least gives broader context to the term *electrical sensitivity* and what the phenomenon covers.

Please note: Electrical sensitivity also refers to those who operate electronic equipment better and easier than before. Many are the reports I've received of experiencers who are now able to merge with their electronic "helpers" so completely, they literally *become* the machine they are using. Electronic equipment for them operates as if an extension of their own faculties and their own mind. As you might imagine, their machinery seldom breaks down; in fact, they are often able to elicit from it the kind of performance deemed impossible by manufacturers.

Regardless of what anyone thinks about electrical sensitivity, when given the opportunity to talk about it (or about other anomalous occurrences,) experiencers will often unleash a flood-tide of comments, such as they did for me:

Watches do not keep time for me. But mechanical things seem to work, even for no reason.

Security systems, ultrasonics bother me, also high voltage and power lines.

If I get too close to FM radio frequencies I raise cain with reception.

I feel sounds and hear tastes and smells. I don't have energy to be with people expressing intense feelings, as I often feel their feelings, too. Live more in the present moment.

Recording equipment won't work for me. I can hear energy change on tapes such as a "door opening," frequency shift.

Metallic objects sometimes fall off tables or pop off shelves in my presence.

My energy at times becomes very manic. I'll feel I can do anything I could imagine, and then ground myself to this reality and feel low. I seem to be feeling free of this more as years go by.

I'm extremely sensitive to odors of any kind and to fabric types.

Electronic equipment functions strangely around me.

I called the company hot line about a computer communication software problem I was having. I was hot mad. The long-distance trunk knocked out and the dial tone was lost. It took days to fix it. The company couldn't figure out what happened.

I touch electrical appliances to make them work. They start up with my energy.

I hear dog whistles and alarms in stores. My ears are very sensitive.

If I don't concentrate on what I'm doing, like tell myself "You are turning the light on," I blow them. If I'm angry, they blow, too. With computers, I get so involved in what I'm doing I forget to keep in mind my energy, and computers mess up all the time.

I blew my computer terminal when I got excited. Have burned up three cassette recorders, one overhead projector, and brought

down the power in a ten-block area—all because of my energy.
This is costly!

I start dead car batteries with my energy. But as the years go by,
my energy field has diminished. Things that were once true
are no longer. I lost a lot in order to live in this world.

I wish I could have included all the comments I received from
the questionnaire mailing. Virtually each person who participated spoke of problems and challenges they were having with
electronic equipment, power lines, and magnetic fields; and they
reported possessing a strange charisma or charm they could not
explain.

Every single near-death survivor I have ever met laments in the
same manner about microphones: "The mike fights me"; "It fills
with static"; "The thing goes dead and they have to replace it"; "It
won't work." My personal experience has been the same, almost
to the point of being comical. What I have learned to do over the
years is pray for the equipment, "protect" it with The Light that
has become my constant companion. It works better when I do.

My questionnaire survey *was* large enough, however, to illustrate some things about The Light that appears in near-death
episodes and to enable me to make a few comments:

- 85 percent of the respondents claimed to have had an experience where at least half of their scenario was filled with
  bright, all-consuming etheric light.
- 52 percent said they merged into and joined as one with this
  light or the being of light.
- Of these totals, 80 percent became unusually sensitive to
  physical light afterward.

There does appear to be a correlation between length of exposure
to etheric light and the vivid spread of physical aftereffects—
such as electrical sensitivity, enhanced faculty extensions, devia-
tions in brain function, physical body changes (both external and
internal), and increased intelligence. However, respondents with
shorter exposure rates (1 to 25 percent of the time of the overall
experience) had the same capacity for the full range of physical
aftereffects as those with longer exposures, and some people
with over 50 percent exposure rates declared few if any physical
changes later on.

This suggests to me that *it is the intensity of the light, not length of exposure,* that seems to determine the prevalence of many of the physiological aftereffects.

And this indicates that the etheric light reported by near-death experiencers and others like them might indeed by *real,* thus subject to physical measurement studies and testing.

TEN

The Light of Enlightenment

We understand why children are afraid of darkness, but why are men afraid of light.
—Plato

As a researcher, I can assure you that any type of near-death
experience can be life changing.

But as an experiencer, I can positively affirm that being bathed
in The Light on the other side of death *is more than life changing*.
That light is the very essence, the heart and soul, the all-
consuming consummation of ecstatic ecstasy. It is a million suns
of compressed love dissolving everything unto itself, annihilat-
ing thought and cell, vaporizing humanness and history, into the
one great brilliance of all that is and all that ever was and all that
ever will be.

You know it's God.

No one has to tell you.

You know.

You can no longer believe in God, for belief implies doubt.
There is no more doubt. None. You now *know* God. And you
know that you know. And you're never the same again.

And you know who you are...a child of God, a cell in The
Greater Body, an extension of The One Force, an expression from
The One Mind. No more can you forget your identity, or deny or
ignore or pretend it away.

There is One, and you are of The One.

142

One.

The Light does this to you.

It cradles your soul in the heart of its pulsebeat and fills you with loveshine. And you melt away as the "you" you think you are, reforming as the "YOU" you really are, and you are reborn because at last you "remember."

Although not everyone speaks of God when they return from death's door as I have here, the majority do. And almost to a person they begin to make references to oneness, allness, isness, the directive presence behind and within and beyond all things.

Down through the ages this kind of knowledge has been termed *enlightenment*—literally a waking up to light, an illumination of light, a reunification with The Light. And there are groups, isms and schisms, that decree how one can reach such a state of enlightened knowingness. The rules are many, the pathways numerous, yet the goal is always the same...reunion with the source of your being, God.

This subject concerns the difference between religion and spirituality, a subject of utmost importance to experiencers, a subject we now need to explore. And we'll do that exploration utilizing material from different sources and different viewpoints. To get us started, let's define the territory:

Religion—a systematic approach to enlightenment based on set standards or dogmas, which may or may not alter as the religion evolves. It provides the protection of community support and moral development, and the guidance of metaphors to describe what seems mysterious. Its "Holy of Holies," or mystery teachings, are usually reserved for the elect or chosen. *System oriented.*

Spirituality—a personal, intimate experience of God based on a mystical awakening or sudden enlightenment. There are no standards or dogmas, only precedents, for individual knowing, and/or gnosis, is honored. Usually referred to as "The Inner Journey" deep within the depths of self, it demands a thorough "house cleansing" on every level of being in order to access the holiness of truth. *Process oriented.*

Perspective—At the core of all religions is that moment of enlightenment, that mystical revelation and sacred teaching, from which the religion itself grew and prospered. Sometimes called The Mysteries, Secret Teachings, or the Holy of Holies, this heart and soul of religion is as exquisite and viable today as when first revealed. Yet there is no system of spiritual enlightenment that can guarantee spiritual attainment. The shelter religion offers does not negate the individual's responsibility for his or her own spiritual awakening and spiritual maturity.

Of interest here is that one-third of the people I interviewed continued in a traditional religious setting after their near-death experiences. Though some were members of, or went on to join, fundamentalist or charismatic churches (even becoming evangelists), most expressed a desire to remain where they were and quietly work to uplift and enlighten the ministry of their present church. A number became ordained ministers.

The remaining two-thirds, however, either cast aside religious affiliations or had never been involved in any to begin with. For these people, the spiritual path became paramount, as they shifted from standards and dogmas to a personal, intimate relationship with God. Surprisingly, the greater number came to join or support some type of organized, structured church or philosophy later on, some even originated churches of their own. Popular choices were metaphysical (New Thought) churches and Eastern philosophical religious ideas. Those who continued in a more mystical approach often became involved with shamanism or in ecology-based "return to the basics" movements.

Superficial or overly restrictive teachings turn off most experiencers. Because of this, heartbreaking conflicts can arise. I spoke with several near-death survivors who were spouses of ministers. All of them had withdrawn from attending Sunday sermons and were no longer supportive of their loved ones' messages to the congregation, feeling that the sermons were wrong. Many others came to shun or renounce cherished religious traditions much to the consternation of family members. This turnaround is seldom understood. Labels like "irrational" or "corrupted by the forces of evil" sometimes replace any attempt to seek common ground. Alienation or separation often results.

Previous beliefs, or lack of them, make no difference whatsoever. The near-death phenomenon frees an individual to walk and talk with God without reservation or restriction.

Since the transforming power of near-death is so similar to religious conversions and spiritual awakenings (Christos and Kundalini/Ku), the idea of rebirth, I would like to include this broader spectrum in our exploration. I don't think anyone can understand the near-death phenomenon until he or she gains an appreciation for the spiritual hunger resident within the human heart.

One individual who sought to better understand the enlightenment process was a Canadian psychiatrist by the name of Richard Maurice Bucke. He began a rigorous research project on the subject in the waning years of the last century, narrowing his study to fifty cases he believed to be genuine; people who seemed to possess another type of consciousness and operated on a higher, more spiritual level of mind. He termed this consciousness *cosmic consciousness* (which was also the name of his book, first published in 1901 [31]). In 1902 Bucke accidently slipped on ice and died instantly. His book, however, became the seminal reference work on the universal pattern of aftereffects in the enlightenment process, and remains so today.

The pattern of enlightenment Bucke discovered resembles what you've already read in this book about near-death's aftereffects. Compare for yourself:

The subjective light: A brilliant blinding flash is seen. The individual's surroundings take on colors of unearthly hues and brilliance. Everything expands in size and brightness.

The moral elevation: Afterward, the individual becomes moral and upright, shunning the temptation to judge or criticize another, or be less than honest and fair. A greater duty and service to God and humankind becomes a life priority.

The intellectual illumination: All things are made known, all knowledge is given, all secrets of the universe are revealed. The individual feels no weight as he or she is overwhelmed by total and complete love. Glowing beings give instructions, as the "Word of God" is seen or felt; the oneness of all things shown. A sense of having been "reborn" prevails.

The sense of immortality: Thinking is replaced by knowing. The individual realizes his or her divine identity and the fact that there is only life, which varies by degree of vibration and ascension. This illumination brings the knowledge that salvation is not necessary, that we are all immortal and divine from "The Beginning."

The loss of the fear of death: Death loses all meaning and relevance. The individual now knows death does not end anything, is nothing but a change of awareness.

The loss of the sense of sin: Evil is understood as good misused, that all things are good in God's eyes.

The suddenness, instantaneousness of the awakening: Whether one is actively seeking an Eastern type of enlightenment or what it known in the West as "Baptism of the Holy Spirit," the actual moment of illumination is always unexpected, sudden, and blinding. It can last minutes or hours or days.

The previous character of the person: Most people who experience this are morally upright and intelligent to begin with, and have strong bodies and strong wills. These resident characteristics are expanded and enhanced even further. Latent abilities surface, including genius. Even if the individual is sickly and soon to die, the desire to learn and excel is strong.

The age of illumination: It usually happens when one is more mature and in the middle years, especially around springtime, early summer, or in the first few months of the year.

The added charm of the personality: The individual becomes so magnetic that people and animals are drawn to him or her. The individual seems divinely protected and guided. Other people are affected right away, animals more docile.

The transfiguration: There is a marked change in appearance. The individual seems to glow and have a light around him or her. There are physical changes. The face looks different, and the individual behaves like a "new" person—as if suddenly "more" than before.

I hasten to point out that Bucke did not find any female experiencers or black Africans who fit the pattern, and this puzzled him. (I added feminine pronouns to his rendition above, since it is now acknowledged that women can and do undergo enlightenment.) Nor could he explain the psychic phenomena that were part of the enlightenment process. Bucke's book is definitely worth reading, but keep in mind that he was a reflection of the prejudice encouraged during his lifetime. Remember that before you put too much emphasis on some of his conclusions, such as the previous character of the individual and the time of year experiences were the most likely to occur.

The precedent established by Bucke's work provides us with a useful guide to ascertain the difference between the kind of aftereffects that indicate a "renewal" (a change of attitude), and those that indicate that something far greater and far more transforming has taken place. Bucke cautioned that there are no guarantees during or after a transformation, and that is worth noting.

Libraries of thought have been written about the enlightenment process and what seem to be two distinctly different types of enlightenment—religious conversions and spiritual awakenings. Using the near-death phenomenon to provide the basic elements of the experience, here is a chart that illustrates how semantics can vary from experiencer to experiencer when describing essentially the same event. It is *point of view*, not what happens, that most often decides how an episode will be interpreted.

Basic Element	POINT OF VIEW Religious Conversion	Spiritual Awakening
The experience	Baptism by The Holy Spirit	Light of God
What it represented	A new covenant, being born again	Enlightenment or illumination or awakening
What it was	Heaven	Home
A life force	Angel	Light being
Words spoken	Message from God	Conversations held
Words felt	Gift from God	Telepathy
Opinion of self	Chosen of God	Child of God or Light Worker
The return	Appointed mission to be God's Chosen Messenger	Unfinished business to complete or a job yet to do

Sometimes I think we create our own paradoxes by our refusal to be objective and flexible. We use different words and see through different eyes simply because we are different people possessed of diverse points of view. Unfortunately, we usually see what we want to see rather than what is really there. We can hide just as effectively under the "umbrella" of spirituality as under that of religion (near-death survivors included).

I have come to realize that we color the meaning of our transformations either by a need for attention and love, by a desire to satisfy the opinion of others, or by a choice to remain true to what happened no matter what that means. We have found "home," and we wish somehow to acknowledge that.

Illuminations lead us into structured religions and back out again, as we continue on our journey, carving out our own way along the spiritual path. The need to worship a deity is engrained within all of us, whether we admit it or not. Yet the discovery of God and higher states of consciousness can become a substitute for intimacy, as the subconscious urge to experience the ultimate "orgasm" of enlightenment can take on priority above all else. That is escapism, in my opinion, a copout, an excuse to rationalize life's harsh verities and the uncertainty of change. Since God appears as changeless it is easy to seek haven in anything that seems of God, but that "changeless" image is tricky.

I have noticed that although God never changes, God always changes.

As perceptions and attitudes are never static, how we view God depends entirely on our point of view. As we shift, "The Big Picture" shifts. As we grow or diminish, our concept of God alters accordingly. Escapism offers little but delay and disappointment. Neither the spiritual quest nor religious conversions will "save" us from facing what we have made of our lives. Although forgiveness is very real, an old adage makes clear—"God can do no more for you than *through* you."

Illuminating transformational events, and that includes near-death experiences, revolve around the issue of an awakening. Somehow the individual's level of consciousness changes and, eventually, this can lead to an interest in spiritual matters with the possibility of later enlightenment.

There has always been a steady procession of revelators and avatars (great teachers or messiahs) who have claimed divine authority to reveal Higher Truth. These great ones have often exhibited unusual powers. They have healed, taught, preached, and performed "miracles" for the benefit of those in need. They have assured the multitudes that anyone can do as they have done and have offered to teach how. What they have offered is invariably a course in self-development that involves discipline, sacrifice, virtue, and a lifetime of commitment in service to humankind. *None have taught shortcuts!* Although all have been products of their prevailing cultures, their messages and methods have been similar in principle and can be condensed into two basic themes—Eastern and Western.

Eastern and Western versions of awakening are similar in many ways, yet they are opposite in application, representing mirror reflections of the same goal—the transformation of ordinary consciousness into a higher, more spiritual consciousness. Here is what I believe to be their essence:

Top Down (outside in)

The Western version emphasized descending force, originating from outside a person's body, passing down through the top of the head, or through the chest area, and spreading throughout the body. It is an outward-directed process that seeks outside guidance and looks for God On High. It receives outside energy in. The most familiar teaching of this version is Christos (Descent of The Logos).

Bottom Up (inside out)

The Eastern version emphasizes ascending force, originating from within a person's body, usually from the base of the spine, rising up until it bursts through the top of a person's head. It is an inner process that seeks inner guidance and looks for God within. It projects energy from inside out. The most familiar teaching of this version is Kundalini or Ku (Ascension into The Godhead).

Christos (Kristos) is the Greek word from which *Christ* was derived, and comes as close as possible to translating *messiah* from the ancient phrase that meant the Anointed One. As near as anyone can tell, Jesus rarely if ever accepted *messiah* as applicable to him during his lifetime, preferring instead the title Son of Man. Long after his crucifixion, it was the Western mind that named Jesus "The Christ" and established his identity as the Son of God. Since then, *Christ* has also come to symbolize Christ Consciousness or Christ Mind, which, it is said, anyone can possess. Jesus himself is said to have stated, "All these things I have done, you can do, and more also," thus indicating a state of consciousness others can attain.

The entrance/activation of Christ Consciousness is sometimes called Baptism of The Holy Spirit, and is characterized by descriptions such as: being struck as if by lightning or by a blinding flash; being consumed as if by fire or great heat; being torn as if by an explosion or great wind; being immersed as if by heavy rain or flood swells. The spiritual force seems to enter the individual's body from outside the self, from "heaven," God On High, or through some saintly emissary or angel. The sudden descent or passage of the illuminating force is said to come only when the recipient is ready and worthy. It usually enters through the top of the head or through the heart center and fills the entire body. This activation of divine spirit, energizes and illumines, thus transforming the individual's concerns from mundane to spiritual. This tradition also indicates that the event is *not* the culminating union with God but rather a beginning, a step toward that goal, as various stages or initiations are necessary after illumination before true divinity can be attained.

Kundalini is a Sanskrit word that means "coiled serpent." The term, however, may actually be derived from the much older word *Ku*, meaning "The spirit force of God awaits within each person." (Taken from Mesoamerican traditions that predate the Maya, *Ku* comes from *Hunab-Ku*, "the sacred name of God," and is symbolized by Quetzalcoatl, The Feathered Serpent.) Both Kundalini and Ku refer to the "serpent power" that is said to be coiled in a ball at the base of a person's spine. When stimulated, it is said to uncoil and rise up the spine and brainstem, like a serpent stretching full length, until it bursts through the top of the person's head. While rising, it supposedly ignites or expands seven whirling vortices of energy that are located in or near certain areas of the body trunk, neck, and head. These whirling vortices, called *Chakras* in Sanskrit (meaning "Wheels") or termed *Flowers* in the Mesoamerican tradition, are like spinning energy generators. They relate to each of the seven major glandular centers (endocrine glands). Thus, people are said to have a channel within for spiritual energy to travel (the spine) and power generators to speed it along its way (the endocrine glands). Details of how all this works and which *Chakra* or *Flower* is an extension of which gland depend entirely on what interpretation of which traditional teaching you study. The various versions agree only in principle.

It is claimed that once Kundalini/Ku rises full length, after stimulating, activating, expanding, and enhancing each of the seven major *Chakras/Flowers* and bursting out through the head, enlightenment occurs and reunion with God is possible. In actuality, however, this bursting forth is a signal of a shift from one mode of awareness to another—a shift, if you will, to the spiritual path. Just as mundane life goes through various phases of development in order to spiritualize, the spiritualized life goes through various phases of development before *attainment* is reached. A Kundalini/Ku breakthrough does not guarantee complete or lasting enlightenment.

Both versions of awakening, Kundalini/Ku and Christos, share many commonalities. Both emphasize methodical preparation techniques for experiencing a breakthrough, the aftereffects, plus continued stages of spiritual growth after the awakening is achieved. The two lineages of Kundalini insist a teacher is necessary to insure safe, steady progress and proper guidance en route, but that, once enlightenment is reached, the teacher's job is done and the student must continue on alone. Conversely, the Christos tradition advises the probationer to seek silence and solitude for purifying the self, but that, after illumination is gained, wisdom and guidance from others are recommended. Both systems caution that beginners must be free of negative thoughts and ego desires or else the process could be dangerous, harmful, or it could backfire.

And it is no different with pagan or native societies that utilize hallucinogens or special "brews" (by the way, the word *pagan* simply means "country dweller" in Latin). Their ritualistic and involved processes mimic those of Kundalini/Ku and/or Christos versions with similar and sometimes even identical results. I would not consider the current vogue of drug abuse as having anything to do with these native societies, for they have always put an emphasis on spiritual awakenings. Drug abusers are more interested in quick highs and great escapes, the pleasure of the moment, than on what comes next or the possibility of aftereffects. Awakenings from drug abuse seldom stabilize, often have devastating consequences, and, as time passes, result in aftereffects that debilitate rather than uplift.

Kundalini/Ku and Christos mirror each other. Neither is better or best. They are opposite approaches to the same goal—a spiritual awakening that can lead to the possibility of true enlightenment.

Today, most researchers think the near-death experience is a Kundalini breakthrough. Evidence to support their theory is steadily growing. Among the groups pursuing this and related topics is The Kundalini Research Network in Canada [32]. The Network actively encourages research on a global basis for determining to what extent Kundalini may operate as the creative life force in the evolutionary advancement of humankind, and to what degree medical/psychiatric professionals mistake Kundalini breakthroughs for psychosis. It is known, for instance, that Kundalini is rare among patients who are mentally ill, and that it is distinctly different in character from a psychotic episode. (Kundalini leads to order, not disorder, increased intelligence, not derangement, moral advancement and joy, not despair and despondency. The aftermath of Christos has the same uplifting potential.)

Near-death experiencers can and do exhibit Kundalini characteristics. There's no denying this. But I've noticed more than that, something beyond either Kundalini/Ku (bottom up) or Christos (top down) models of energy patterning.

Allow me to combine Kundalini/Ku and Christos under the heading Spiritual Transformations and compare that with the near-death phenomenon.

Spiritual Transformations and the Near-Death Phenomenon
Comparisons and Parallels

Spiritual Transformations	*The Near-Death Phenomenon*
Setting	
Usually prepared for by following rigid austerity pro-	Usually involves some form of sudden, unexpected, or vio-

cedures and regimens of self-denial, which divorce one from the pleasures and temptations of bodily and worldly environments.

lent physical crisis that results in a close brush with death or actual clinical death. Bodily and worldly environments cease to exist.

Onset

Floating or being flipped out of one's body. Many times a presence of warmth or heat. There can be odors, like perfume or a flat ozone-tinge-of-ammonia smell; and sounds, like popping or snapping or crackling. All faculties are present but heightened. A feeling of being suspended follows, which can be disorienting or confusing at first.

Floating or being propelled out of one's body. Warmth, smells, sounds, sights can be experienced as all faculties are present and heightened. A disorienting sense of suspension is generally followed by a short-lived desire to contact those who are still embodied and/or to explore familiar earthly environments.

Acceleration

Motion is physically felt as vibrations increase. This movement is generally of two types: ascending force (more commonly described by the duo-traditions of Kundalini/ Ku, where energy resident within the body rises up the spine, then bursts out through the top of the head; descending force (held traditional as the Christos effect), where energy outside a person's body enters into the head or heart area, then passes down through the body. With either directional current of force, the individual can sway, jerk, spin, swing or whirl around, or

Motion is physically felt as vibrations increase. Usually one enters a tunnel or dark space, which is sometimes spinning or spiraling. There is a sense of speed, of rushing along. Snapping or popping sounds are present in some cases, but the sound of a wind whizzing or whooshing by is the more common. Directional currents of force can be down (descending) or up (ascending), yet in a strange way both directions often seem to occur simultaneously. Lights can flash, voices can be heard, shadowy beings can be glimpsed, or passage can be silent. (Passage can be in-

Spiritual Transformations   *The Near-Death Phenomenon*

rock back and forth. Colored   stantaneous if there's no
lights may flash.   tunnel.)

Breakthrough

Popping sounds are often   One is drawn to a powerful
heard, even the reverberations   and brilliant light, usually
of an implosion, or a wind   yellow/gold/white. Sound
rushing by, or singing, or mu-   effects increase once the light
sic of some kind. An   is reached. In positive cases, a
overwhelmingly powerful   music not heard on earth is
light, usually yellow/gold/   present along with great
white, draws one to it (some-   warmth and a feeling of ec-
times through a passageway   stasy, euphoria, and total joy.
or vortex). Positive sensations   Unconditional love floods
include: total freedom, the   one's being and all knowledge
ability to fly, ecstasy, eupho-   is suddenly possessed. Every-
ria, loss of body weight,   thing is bright, even
floating, screaming for joy,   translucent, with shimmering
dancing, laughter spasms, a   luminous colors and pleasant
feeling of being engulfed by   smells. There is a feeling of
love-warmth-peace-happiness.   freedom and happiness. In
Negative sensations include: negative cases, sounds are
pain, nausea, fainting, head-   often either dull, deafening,
ache or coma, temporary   or absent. Chilly, cold, or cool
blindness or deafness, sob-   temperatures are reported the
bing, temporary paralysis,   most, along with a pale, dull,
sweating, high fever, the in-   or gray cast to the light. There
ability to eat or drink or   is a sense of anxiety or con-
remember.   fusion or foreboding. Pain and
                                    fear can be felt, or a need to
                                    scream, or a strange paralysis
                                    where all one can do is ob-
                                    serve and listen.

Result

Actual illumination is as sym-   Actual illumination is as symbolic in content as it is literal   bolic in content as it is literal
in message. It can be accom-   in message. Revelations of a
panied by geometric, color,   heaven or a hell are made

and light abstractions and luminosity, as well as by great swells of music. Angels may be present and/or light beings, loved ones, religious figures, and animals. Scenarios range from gorgeous landscapes and instructional gatherings to revelations of creation's story and how life is to be lived.

known and life is explained. In many cases all of creation is viewed. There are usually people present, sometimes even animals. Depending on whether positive or negative, beings can be angelic, of The Light, deceased family members, religious figures, or they can be demonic, gruesome or twisted, zombies, or those who are nude and lifeless. Scenarios also vary: Breathtaking beauty and involved instructional sessions are common with heavenly versions; threatening whirlpools, storms, or denuded landscapes are the most reported with hell-like cases.

Aftermath

The degree of aftereffects depends on the impact of breakthrough. Most common changes are: simple/direct mannerisms that appear childlike; a glow to the skin and a twinkle to the eyes, a charm that attracts; a sense of confidence and control; detached yet loving behavior; the presence of "knowing," and/or gnosis; increased psychic abilities (sometimes called Gifts of the Spirit); loss of relevance for time or space; heightened and expanded senses, lessening of needs and wants, increase in a joyful attitude of

The degree of aftereffects depends on the impact of breakthrough. Most common changes are: a sense of unconditional love for all people; a childlike naïveté and openly curious spontaneity; a sense of timelessness and the loss of any identification with "place"; a disregard for former rules and limitations; the emergence of psychic abilities including the gift of healing and joy-giving; a noticeable reduction in fears and worries; the ability to "see through" problems; a lessening of needs or wants; a

Spiritual Transformations

service to others; increased morality and energy. (For more detail about this, refer to Bucke's material on "Cosmic Consciousness.") There is usually much doubt about what happened and a reluctance to discuss it. Long bouts of depression often follow before understanding and acceptance come. People who go through this process (called "initiation" in spiritual or esoteric traditions) are usually labeled insane by culturally advanced societies, and revered in underdeveloped ones.

The Near-Death Phenomenon

certain detachment from the physical body while becoming more energized and enthusiastic about the ways to serve and help others—including the community; a charmed way of communicating, more inspired, happier, more moral and responsible. Although near-death survivors are accepted and tolerated in today's society, more so than even just five years ago, they are still subject to involuntary commitment to mental hospitals by the medical establishment (as sufferers of "psychosis"), and they can still go through long bouts of depression and confusion as they deal with readjustment complexities and the possible specter of insanity.

Stop for a moment. Be as objective as you possibly can. Doesn't what you have just read remind you of a formula for exposure to strong doses of high-powered energy?

Move past isms and schisms, traditions and dogmas, legends and standards, symbols and revelations. Just look at the topic itself as it exists and as it operates.

It could well be that the path to God revolves around the challenge of how one handles intense power, how one deals with The Force.

If we are completely honest here, the only real difference between Eastern and Western versions of spiritual development is the directional path of the energy currents. That's it. When we are talking about spirituality and religious conversions, I believe what we are really talking about is the force of energy itself, differing by degree and type of voltage, and how this energy force can be accessed and utilized.

We human beings are electromagnetic by nature, stuffed full of water and chemicals with a few added minerals. Any change of flux in electrical or magnetic force fields, which either surround us or exist within us, subtly or significantly alters our behavior, emotions, body coordination, and our ability to think and reason coherently. We are easily "displaced" when environmental impulses do not match those we are used to, and this includes the chemical factor of anything we ingest or absorb. We are like self-contained universes symbiotically connected to and dependent upon the universe at large, yet we are living, breathing transmitter/receivers, multidimensional by nature. We operate more as "nerve cells" than as Children of The Most High until we "wake up" and take charge of our lives and our environments.

During the sessions I had with near-death survivors, rarely was I able to isolate what would show me that a singular path of energy was responsible for either the experience or its impact. Certainly indicators of Kundalini/Ku or Christos directional currents were present but they seemed more auxiliary to me than causal.

What caught my eye were indications of *both* power flows converging together and causing what I would call an implosion. In a way, the condition reminded me of lightning.

Science tells us that the lightning stroke is a huge spark. It equalizes the potential difference between clouds in a thunderstorm and the polarity of soil in the ground. It is, in effect, the culminating result of ascending and descending forces, which in meeting release pressure through a visible charge. Lightning, then, is not some "heaven-borne" bolt of electricity hurled to the ground as many believe. Nor is it only a release valve. Lightning itself helps to produce nitrogen compounds that are essential for healthy plant growth.

Compare what happens with lightning and what I suspect may be happening in major transformational events such as the near-death experience:

In the evolution of the natural world, to equalize pressure differences between clouds in a thunderstorm and polarity of soil in the ground, descending bolts of electricity (from the clouds) and ascending bolts of electricity (from the earth) meet to create a huge lightflash (external explosion/lightning), which stabilizes environmental integrity while stimulating plant growth through the creation of nitrogen compounds.

In the evolution of human consciousness, to equalize pressure differences between latent spiritual potentiality and mundane personality development, descending currents of force (possibly from the soul level, Higher Self, God) and ascending currents of force (perhaps from time/space ego states, lower self, personality level) meet to create a powerful lightflash (internal implosion/illumination), which stabilizes and balances individual bodymind integrity while stimulating human growth through the expansion and enhancement of consciousness.

Think about what this might mean: Whether external or internal, explosion or implosion, a lightflash seems to occur whenever opposing forces of energy current converge to release pressure or radiation.

A lightflash!

Enlightenment by its very definition means an experience of light whereby knowledge and information are imparted for the growth and expansion of human consciousness.

What makes us think that this experience is only symbolic? Or just an exercise? Or merely an attitudinal shift in consciousness? Or the product of wishful thinking?

What if it's literal!?!

I invite you to consider the possibility that all religious and spiritual traditions are but umbrellas of protection to guide us safely along, as we wake up to who we really are, as we prepare to meet and endure and grow through higher and higher frequencies of power on our way back to God.

I invite you to consider the possibility that spiritual development is a physically tangible process, and that true enlightenment is a vibrational shift in the frequencies of our mental processes.

The proof of this I believe lies in the aftereffects, which clearly demonstrate the degree to which an individual has been able to stabilize and maintain the shift that has occurred.

Scientists and engineers have been successful in developing tonal ranges, subliminal cassette-tape recordings, brain-wave machines, special helmets that create vibrational states—all aimed at directing and controlling neural (nerve) firings along the base and sides of the brain and thereby affecting the brain's chemistry in such a way as to create the mystical experience.

Yet none of these attempts at physical manipulation, not one, has managed to replicate true enlightenment or the full extent of its aftereffects. Neither have the hallucinations caused by epileptic seizures or drugs.

You can stimulate the brain and you can drug it. You can caress, tickle, prod, and zap it. You can play with it and you can experiment with it, but you cannot match the richness, depth, variety, and panoramic sweep of naturally occurring spiritual awakenings or their long-term physical aftereffects.

The "orgasm" or "high" of the lightflash constitutes only a small fraction of the awakening process, and in my opinion that's all anyone can induce—the orgasm. As sex is far more than a moment's ecstasy, enlightenment is far more than a lightflash experience.

Most illuminations are partial. But those that are involved, indepth, and impactual (and there are more of those than you think), are making such a difference, not only in the individual's life but in the community at large, that nothing short of Deity could possibly be at work. And why do we doubt this? Is it because we have such a limited or finite concept of what God might be?

Maybe it's not what we think about enlightenment that should be questioned in this regard, but what we think about God.

ELEVEN

Brain/Mind

A mind stretched by a new idea can never go
back to its original dimensions.
—Oliver Wendell Holmes

The typical near-death survivor was dead, that is to say without pulse and breath, for ten to fifteen minutes. Others were "out" for only a few minutes, or five to six at most. It is not uncommon, however, to hear of clinically dead experiencers who revived thirty minutes to an hour, or several hours later. I came across one woman who was dead for twelve hours, another for sixteen. Both "woke up" in a morgue. This is amazing to me since the medical community cautions that without sufficient oxygen, the brain can be permanently damaged in three to five minutes.

I talked with several embalmers about this one day and was surprised to learn that the so-called deceased occasionally move around and assert that they are quite alive once the embalming process begins. A story is told of one such "corpse" who swatted morgue personnel when the syringe was inserted to drain his blood.

History is filled with reports like this. A famous one involves Robert E. Lee's mother. She "succumbed" to an illness, was given a proper funeral, and then interred in the family vault. A relative who arrived too late for the service requested that he be shown the body. When he looked at her, he saw her chest move. After regaining consciousness, a very indignant "corpse" scolded everyone for "jumping to conclusions." Three years later Mrs. Lee gave birth to the child who would someday lead the South during the Civil War.

In 1992, a London newspaper carried a gruesome story about a seventy-one-year-old Romanian man who had been buried alive. Apparently the man had choked on a chicken bone and collapsed, was thought dead of a coronary, given a funeral, and buried. Three days later, gravediggers heard knocking from inside his wooden coffin. Unsealing it, they found the man quite alive. But when he arrived home, his wife refused to see him. It took the poor fellow three weeks to convince priests, bank clerks, doctors, town hall officials, and police to cancel his death certificate.

Because things like this happen on occasion, researchers have been reluctant to associate near-death with full death. One physician who has written several books based on his near-death research is convinced of the phenomenon's genuineness, but not of its link to life's finality. He is quoted as saying: "Give me one documented case of a true corpse that revived, and I'll reconsider what the near-death experience might mean." He now has one—the case of George Rodonaia, a man frozen solid for three days, his body stored in a morgue freezer vault, who revived on the autopsy table as doctors were cutting open the trunk of his body. (The head physician, by the way, had to take an indefinite leave of absence after Rodonaia came back to life.)

Proof of death has never been a clear-cut issue, and it still isn't. Further blurring that edge between life and death is the reality of near-death states. If you think society is challenged by this, imagine what it is like for experiencers...then imagine what happens to their minds.

> Into raw sensations flow things such as memory, imagination, mental habits, feelings, and even our will—in as much as we attend to something. Without the light that we bring to sensations, the world is meaningless and dark.

Thus says Arthur Zajonc in his book, *Catching the Light: The Entwined History of Light and Mind* [33]. Zajonc presents a fascinating historical survey of humankind's emerging scientific and spiritual understandings of the nature of light over the past three millennia. He addresses transformations like near-death when he talks about how "a new light is coming into the world" as more and more people are so changed. His proposal for a "natural philosophy" emphasizes that in order to gain perspective one must strive to see the whole, not just pieces of the whole.

Howard Gardner's latest offering, *Creating Minds* [34], is of equal importance. He profiles the great minds of the twentieth century in an attempt to characterize genius. His discovery? That discarding accepted ideas of what is possible can make it easier to take new ideas seriously, that connecting the unconnected leads to insight, that a tolerance for ambiguity is crucial to creativity. The word *intelligence* literally means "to select among," a reference to one who is smart in detail recognition. But genius "shakes together" or "clusters" information, almost as a child would, so data can be rearranged to form different or larger wholes.

Gardner speaks of Einstein *seeing* a light ray in his mind and *knowing* he was right; of the French composer Olivier Messiaen *seeing* the color of tones; of Picasso *seeing* numbers as patterns of contour. This ability to see what others can't typifies the shaking together and clustering of data common to geniuses, and it raises the possibility that multiple sensing might also be involved. (Both traits are characteristic of near-death aftereffect<)

Scientists now think that genius has more to do with how neurons (nerve cells) are wired than with the neurons themselves. Neuroscientist Arnold Scheibel of UCLA describes it this way: "Smart people have more complex, more efficient, neural highways for transmitting information."

Considering near-death, the average experiencer returns more intelligent than before. He or she is often able to readily detach from previous norms, abstract freely, envision broader perspectives, access latent talents, and display (in some cases) a flowering of genius.

Considering the aftereffects, it could well be that as the brain is restructured from the experience, neural pathways are "rewired" or somehow rerouted or maybe revitalized.

Thanks to PET (positron emission tomography), science has been able to establish that original thinking utilizes a different section of the brain than mundane thinking. To quote Marcus Raichle, a researcher at Washington University: "You can essentially rearrange the brain in fifteen minutes."

What I've mentioned thus far, all of the facts as presented, supports this simple observation: an experiencer's brain is physically changed after a near-death episode—sometimes partially, sometimes radically.

Many claim that individuals become more right-brained afterward. At first glance, this seems true. But I want to challenge that idea. The people who exhibited right-brained dominance as an aftereffect, at least those I was able to interview, were usually left-brained before. Yet there are individuals who became more left-brained as part of their aftereffects. And these people, on closer scrutiny, turned out to have been predominately right-brained previous to their episode.

Move past number crunching for a moment, and take a look at this:

The near-death phenomenon seems to stimulate the brain hemisphere that was not previously dominant. There is also an observable movement in the brain, structurally, toward data clustering and creative invention—as if the experiencer were developing a more synergistic type of neural network— thus advancing the potential of whole-brained behavior (less dependent on any single type of hemispheric dominance, greater flexibility and utilization of the brain itself).

And take another look at multiple sensing. Scientifically, we know that synesthesia is a product of limbic enhancement or variables in the limbic system. We also know that somehow the near-death phenomenon directly affects the limbic system.

For those who have never heard of the limbic system, it is located in a semicircle in the middle of the brain capping off the topmost extension of the brainstem. Consisting of various sections, it is known to be the seat of our basic instincts for sex, hunger, sleep, fear, and survival. The limbic system is often referred to as our "gut," or third brain. In it originates the wide range of emotional perceptions and awarenesses that are elaborated on and refined in the brain's left and right hemispheres. It has a direct neural connection with the heart. Evolution-wise, this small but extremely efficient system has been around for some thirty thousand years or more—yet only recently has it been recognized as the most complicated structure on earth.

Many professionals now believe that if the limbic system does not originate mind, it certainly is the gateway to mind.

Direct or conscious entry into the limbic section of the brain is gained through any type of excitement or heightened stimulation (outwardly expressed emotion). Indirect or subconscious entry is most commonly reached through the blissful openness, even ecstasy, experienced in an altered or flow or meditative state (inwardly experienced emotion). One way or another, some form of emotion is necessary to accelerate and prolong limbic involvement. Parapsychology, that branch of psychology that deals with the investigation of psychic phenomena, has discovered the same link. Example: You cannot conduct accurate and repeatable psychic experiments without some form of excitement or emotion felt or expressed by the subject. No emotion means few or no phenomena. Plenty of excitement means plentiful results. Interestingly, people who are positive and enthusiastic about life consistently report more psychic experiences than people who are not. (*Emotions*, as far as the brain is concerned, means chemicals.)

Here is a chart that correlates patterning in the brain/mind assembly. It may prove helpful to you in keeping this discussion in perspective:

Correlations Within the Brain/Mind Assembly

Left Brain Hemisphere—location of the conscious, objective mode of awareness. It mainly analyzes, clarifies, categorizes, and separates. Intellect and reason are its regions of expertise; science and education its preference.

Right Brain Hemisphere—location of the subconscious, subjective mode of awareness. It mainly collects, absorbs, enhances, abstracts, and connects. Imagination and intuition are its regions of expertise; religion and fantasy its preference.

The Limbic System—location of the superconscious, synergistic mode of awareness. It mainly senses, embraces, and knows that it knows (gut response). The collective whole and memory are its regions of expertise, mystical knowing (gnosis) and convergence with realms beyond self (unification with a Greater Source) its preference.

Use this same chart and substitute brain/mind correlations for modes of awareness:

conscious	normal ego awareness
subconscious	altered state of awareness
superconscious	expanded awareness

Let's do it again, only this time as if the chart referred to states of existence:

objective/physical	wide awake, alert—externalized, outer world
subjective/symbolic	dreamy, subliminal—internalized inner world
convergence/synergy	mystical knowing—unified, collective wholeness

How our mind responds to usage is a reflection of how easily our degree of consciousness operates through the various brain support structures. This alters with each challenge and new opportunity we process and/or integrate. Nothing is static in brain/mind functioning. We either grow or diminish. The limbic system appears to be the key to this, since once stimulated, it seems to direct which section of the brain works on what.

It is my sense that the limbic system is also a key to the near-death phenomenon, not as casual (i.e., the experience), but as the main agent that ensures survival and then, because of the extreme way it was stimulated, "imprints" individuals with the kind of aftereffects that are indicative of limbic enhancement (and most of the physiological aftereffects are).

And when you're talking about the limbic system, you're talking about chemicals, which leads us to another tie-in...chemical yellow.

For those near-death survivors who could recall, the first color encountered during their experience was usually either yellow or yellow-gold. Some described it as just plain gold. Others saw it as more of a yellow-white, gold-white, or radiant white. Invariably, survivors commented on how different that color or light seemed; bright, yet somehow easy on the eyes and not at all like the yellow-gold-white tones of earth. In checking through experiencer files at IANDS, I also noticed the preponderance of people who first saw yellow or shades of yellow-white during the onset of their episodes. Some continued to be surrounded by the color until they revived. Even though other colors or light came next, such as rose, blue, or green, or that of radiant light, the overwhelming majority spoke of yellow. It was fascinating to me that although yellow occurred at onset, many times it changed; first becoming brighter and more mellow as it deepened into gold, and/or then turning lighter and more radiant as it transformed into a glowing white.

The peculiarities of how people perceive yellow has caught my attention numerous times throughout my life. Here is why:

- People who are learning how to have an out-of-body experience go through basically the same range of color hues in the same initial manner as do near-death experiencers. Their first awareness of sight is usually as if through a yellow screen or filter. Yellowish colorations often continue until full separation between consciousness and body connections are made, then bright colored vision is restored. The more advanced the individual, the less yellow tinge to what they see. (For ten years I taught people how to "astral travel." The yellow filtering occurred so often, that I came to depend on it as a signal that some type of genuine separation was taking place.)
- In researching the human eye, I learned that there is no color cone on the retina for yellow. We have cones for red, blue, and green, but not yellow. Yellow is created by a chemical reaction in the brain. The same is true in photography. Color negatives can only imprint red, blue, and green; yellow comes from the chemical reaction that occurs during film development. Yellow exists as a primary color only in paints and dyes. It is *not* primary in the light spectrum. Yellow is actually an illusion, a non-color.
- According to the books I've read on the human eye and the medical physicians I have consulted, it is surmised that the ability to see yellow signaled the crossover in the evolution of eyesight from gray tones (purple-rod development on the retina) to vivid colorations (the development of color cones on

the retina). In the language of symbology, yellow is also considered a cross-over color—the harbinger of change. Tradition has it, for instance, that the sudden preference for yellow signifies that a person's life is about to change, that new, exciting times are ahead, with increased energy, enthusiasm, and upliftment. Yellow has always been thought of as a revitalizing tonic, a sign of spring, vigor, cheerfulness, new birth. As it deepens into gold, yellow is said to symbolize the male or father principle and the beginnings of the wise use of reason and logic. As it lightens into white, spiritual development, intuition, and abstract thinking take precedent. Should it take on silver characteristics, however, it is then said to represent the female or mother principle and the beginnings of the wise use of emotion and feeling.

• Throughout history, halos of light emanating from and surrounding all things were often described as being yellow/white in color. Artists have always painted such halos of light as yellow/white or gold or silver. Drug users, especially those on hallucinogens, report the preponderance of yellow hues as they begin their experience. I've heard of doctors who use a penlight to check the pupils of patients thought to be dead to determine if the soul or animating force is still there: If the retina is yellow, the soul is gone.

No matter from what angle you explore this subject, you wind up back in the same place you started: *Yellow is a chemically created color, a signal of that brain activity that heralds either a mood change or an alteration in brain function.*

A little yellow, a gentle lift. Floods of yellow, significant movement toward change. So what does the brain do during a near-death experience? It floods the limbic system (our survival center) with chemicals that are more than likely perceived in the visual range of experiencers as bright splashes of yellow/white.

Conjecture? Maybe not.

What else are we seeing during our near-death episodes and otherworld journeys, and what might that imagery be telling us?

Throughout the broad spectrum of research findings concerning near-death, it has been noted that child experiencers most often speak of God as a man, usually a grandfatherly type who is loving and reaches out to console and help them. It has also been noted that adults rarely see God as a human figure of any kind, usually more of a light or a presence or a feeling or a voice or an abstract dynamic of some kind. Those who do see God as a man, typically see a wise fatherly type who, if asked what he really looks like, dissolves into a brilliance beyond that which can be described.

Children either have a pleasant and/or heaven-like experience or an initial encounter without much imagery. And they often speak of animal heavens and even visit them. Adults almost never do, although on occasion an adult will be met by a pet previously dead or encounter animals as part of their episode.

No child's case of present record has ever included imagery extremes. Thus, it is *only adults* who report hellish or transcendent scenarios.

With adults who claim to have undergone unpleasant and/or hell-like experiences, I have discovered that those most influenced by Christianity or by similar philosophical doctrines are the ones *most likely* to describe fire and brimstone and red-hot hells. None of the people I interviewed who were not strongly identified with Christian teachings spoke of any such fiery climate; rather, these people described temperatures that were clammy, cold, lifeless, fearful, or somehow void.

The majority of childhood experiencers I came across had their episode before the age of seven (infancy to three years old was the age span I encountered most frequently). I found no such "grouping of ages" with adults. I did find a correlation in physical proximity with older individuals, though. In other words, if two or more teenagers or adults were in close physical proximity to each other when their near-death episode occurred—they tended to have either identical or similar experiences. (Refer to the four hell-like experiences discussed in Chapter Three, Ridenhour's case in Chapter Four.) Only once did I discover an individual who claimed to have had a "shared" episode with someone who was not in close physical proximity, and that was the near-death-like incident of Shirley Bennett discussed in Chapter Six.

In my research, shadowy or black figures were sometimes deemed angelic, sometimes demonic. Light beings were sometimes regarded as splendrous and awesome, or perhaps as threatening or frightening. Interpretative assessments depended entirely on the viewpoint of experiencers. Jazmyne Cidavia-DeRepentigny in Chapter One, for instance, recognized the angelic being at her side as a higher, more perfect version of herself.

Loved ones already dead who greeted the experiencer were *always* described as healthy, glowing, somewhat younger or in their prime, or appearing to be an age at which the experiencer was the most comfortable seeing them. Any infirmity, illness, or handicap was healed. (This was also true with animals).

If you are objective about the cases I have discussed in this book and about any other near-death experiences you've ever been exposed to, including my own, you cannot help but notice the existence of a common denominator between what that person experienced in death and what they had integrated in living. The only exception I've run across is with infants—yet there are connections with them, too...between the expectations their parents harbored at the time and what became important for the child as an individual later on.

Always, I have been able to find common denominators.

And, almost always, I have also been able to find something extra, an element or factor, that I *cannot* pinpoint or associate with the individual or the individual's past.

Thus, there are personal links and there are transpersonal extras—both.

Example: In my second near-death experience I was greeted by Jesus. He was tall, swarthy complexioned, had red-gold hair, and the softest blue eyes I had ever seen. This surprised me, as I did not think Jesus would look like that. The discrepancy in appearance didn't matter at the time, for he was filled with compassion and love and so was I, just being near him. Later on, the incident bothered me enough that I decided my time with him must have been "wish fulfillment" rather than any type of reality. After six years passed, however, I decided to do some research on the historical Jesus. One of the books I picked up was *Portrait of Jesus?* by Frank C. Tribbe [35]. Toward the book's end three communications of Jesus's era are quoted: a letter written by Publius Lentulus, Governor of Judea, to the Roman Senate and to Tiberius Caesar; a report by Gamaliel, teacher of Saul of Tarsus, addressed to the Sanhedrin and quoting the philosopher Massalian; and a report by Pilate to the Emperor. All three stated that

Jesus was quite tall and had a swarthy complexion, hair the color of new wine or sunburned gold, and soft blue or gray eyes. I was stunned!

So what about near-death imagery and that of journeys into other worlds?

The following are the four basic levels of imagery I have found to be consistent in reportings of near-death and otherworld journeys:

The Four Levels of Near-Death and Otherworld Imagery

Levels

PERSONAL	images from one's own life.
MASS MIND	images of a collective nature that reflect the human condition.
MEMORY FIELDS	sometimes called "false images," these are as much archetypal and evolutionary as they are primordial.
TRUTH	that consistent, stable reality which undergirds and transcends creation and all created things.

Explanations

Personal Imagery—landscapes and environments the same or similar to one's own life; loved ones and pets that were once a part of one's world; conversations and dialogue that concern personal matters, family secrets, and intimate revelations. Awareness of physical occurrences during out-of-body states that are later verified as accurate.

Mass Mind—landscapes and environments typical of what one could adjust to or expect from one's culture, an overriding sense of the familiar—even if particular sights seem somehow peculiar or different; interchange with beings about the human condition and how it has evolved and where it might be heading; objectivity about progressions in the human family. Awareness of a mission or a job yet to accomplish for the betterment of one's fellows, and of how every effort counts.

Memory Fields—(sometimes referred to as "phantoms" or "false images") include access to panoramic archetypes/universal symbols of historical appeal such as God as a man, angels as humans with wings, religious figures as loving authorities, globes or cylinders of light as guardians, demons as elements of punishment, satanic figures as the personification of evil. Also covers representative symbology such as a skull for fear, whirlpool for a threat, yin/yang circles for principles of ordered thinking, the tree of life for continuity, the river of no return as a warning, the book of life for accountability, tribunals for judgment. Actual visuals may well harken back to primordial life responses to earth and sky phenomena. These responses antecedent to us could have been imprinted on the evolving consciousness of early humans, and expanded over time through repetition/storytelling/dreamscapes/mimicry. Awareness of wisdom levels, life stages as stairways, layers of thought-forms as differing realms of existence (i.e., the eleven "heavens" and eleven "hells" commonly reported by visionaries regardless of cultural or religious allegiances).

Truth—a sudden "knowing," a strong feeling or sense of higher knowledge and greater sources of that which is true from regions of The Absolute. Seldom is there much in the way of imagery except for vague or indefinite shapes and abstracts. Invariably, one will influence the formation of "overleafs" (thought-forms) to provide the kind of temporary imagery that is familiar or helps one to feel secure, until such time as one can relax—then overleafs dissolve. Recognition of Truth level is accompanied by unbounded joy, complete and unconditional love, all-knowing intelligence, compassion and peace, ecstasy, a communion with oneness. All relationships and interrelationships, connections and interweavings of all creation are instantly known or revealed. There is no sense of doubt with Truth, and no imagery that has permanence. Awareness of having found one's true home, true identity, true purpose follows. Questions cease.

It has been my observation that "false images" build in memory (yours, mine, and the collective) through repetitious thoughts and dreams, and through emotional excitement. As near as I can tell, these images are really the product of emotionally laden thought-forms that coalesce in vibrational density until the matrix they become takes on shape. However false or phantom-like these thought-form shapes might be, they are often "perceived" or "recognized" (either subjectively or objectively) as something from memory or part of the objectified world that is "real and true."

(It is easy to see how this can and does happen. Just notice how quickly people can identify with television "facts" and character- izations to the point that they either lose the will or the ability to discern what is real from what is not, especially if they become emotionally involved in the program. The confusion of hard news with docudramas presented as entertainment is another example of this. Also be aware of how easily adults can be convinced they were abused as children if there is a sudden, unexplainable onslaught of such "memories"—even when no clear evidence exists for this. Certainly, some of these suppressed or forgotten memories are proven true, but just as many others turn out to be emotional fabrications that signal upsets unrelated to what was perceived as "memory.")

There are other ways of regarding false images, though. If you go back in time to prehistory and what can be known of primordial environments, you encounter theories of con- sciousness development that are most intriguing. The earth canopy theory of Issac N. Vail is a case in point. Vail's book, *The Earth's Annular System* [36] was first published in 1902, but his hypothesis that an ice-particle canopy must have once covered most of Earth was originally submitted to professional scrutiny in 1874, one hundred years before the modern-day scientist Bruce Murray discovered the same type of canopy covering Venus.

The upshot of this is that *if* a canopy of ice particles did indeed once cover most of our planet, the underside of that canopy's surface could have appeared as a "molten looking glass." Vail termed it an ice-crystal veil mirror. His research meticulously records relics, early drawings, and historical observations that he thought illustrated what might have been seen by early people in the way of sky phenomena and grandiose sky imagery (i.e., "mirror" reflections). We are talking here about images such as: early zodiac imagery and zodiac glyphs; humanlike forms with huge wings spread out from the shoulders/upper back area; dragons; alien beings/extraterrestrials; mythological giants, gods, and goddesses; large river systems reflected back as if they were enormous sky trees; stairways or pillars leading to "heaven"; and so forth. (Ice crystal mirrors like this *do* exist, and are occasionally seen in both the Arctic and the Antarctic when canopy conditions are present.)

What does this have to do with near-death and otherworld imagery? Perhaps a great deal.

No matter which early dream or visionary symbols you refer to, including those of UFOs and alien beings, you can trace *those same images* back to common roots in the human psyche...and quite possibly to the type of false imagery Vail theorized about. ("False" because the imagery people most likely saw would have been topographical and/or sky phenomena—*not* real angels, real dragons, real stairways to heaven, and so forth.)

What I have just offered *in no way* demeans "imaginal" or near-death imagery, but it does, as far as I'm concerned, help to broaden our perspective of where some of this imagery may have originated. It's almost as if near-death experiences and otherworld journeys enable us to access vast reservoirs of mythological dreamscapes and memory fields—"carriers of truth"—that we, as participants in the human drama, can use to educate ourselves and code data for future retrieval.

Has it not been said that one picture is better than a thousand words?

This statement brings to mind Rupert Sheldrake, the English plant biologist, who in the early eighties came up with the theory of formative causation. In his book, *A New Science of Life* [37], he advanced the idea that primary sources of memory fields reside in nonenergetic currents that permeate existence. He theorized that these "morphogenetic" or M-fields direct the shape, development, and basic behavior of all living species and systems, functioning as invisible blueprints or connecting memories that link any member of a given species or system with its fellows...while supplying a ready bank of accumulated information that members can instinctively and automatically draw from or contribute to.

Although Sheldrake's theory may seem unrelated to our present discussion, I suggest that it sets the stage for a broader examination of memory and memory fields. In much the same way that he describes formative causation as the directing factor in the development of living species and systems, I would advance the idea that primordial imagery (such as Vail detailed), thought-forms, and dreamscapes are the directing factors in the development of consciousness and cognition. *Near-death experiencers tap into these memory wellsprings, and so do the explorers of meditative and visionary states.*

Before we leave this topic, I want to mention the work of Bethe Hagens, Ph.D., an anthropologist who has discovered some striking correlations between ancient artwork/calendar systems and brain shapes. She compared, for instance, the twenty-five-thousand-year-old Venus figurine found in Lespuque, France, with a turtle brain, and found an almost exact match, curve for curve, contour for contour. In fact, *all* of the old goddess figures are interchangeable with depictions of animal brains—many emphasizing the limbic system. Strangely, this same thing is true of older Egyptian scarab (beetle) drawings. (The scarab is said to be a symbol of the superconscious part of the human mind. Refer to the chart on the brain/mind assembly a few pages back, equating this mode of awareness with the limbic.)

Whenever we explore near-death or otherworld imagery, we reconnect on some level with brain function and the limbic system. And what, if not a tube or tunnel or passageway or guardian of the gateway to higher consciousness, could the limbic system be?

Thanks to Melvin Morse, M.D., and his research for *Closer to the Light: Learning From the Near-Death Experiences of Children* [39], we now recognize that electrical stimulation of the right temporal lobe of the brain, above the right ear and specifically in the Sylvan fissure, can produce visions of God, hearing beautiful music, seeing dead friends and relatives, and even having panoramic life reviews. And, thanks to cutting-edge researchers like Robert O. Becker, author of *The Body Electric: Electromagnetism and the Foundation of Life* [40], who have published theories and findings in the newsletter of the International Society for the Study of Subtle Energies and Energy Medicine [41], we now realize that the neurological sciences may be examining only half the brain, concentrating on neurons and missing the glial cells (which are electrically active light receptors), and melanin (the master molecule coating the limbic system and the heart, which absorbs and converts light to sound and back again as it organizes a vast array of biological processes).

This suggests that we humans might be programmed as a species to ever evolve and that we possess the exact apparatus we need, which, when triggered, will advance that growth. Take a look at these fascinating correlations:

There is a universal form of stimulation that enables the brain to be altered and restructured ..... *Kundalini/Ku/Christos power currents*

There is a universal passageway through the brain that leads to pure unadulterated consciousness ..... *the limbic system.*

There is a universal section in the brain that creates patterning (overleafs) so thought-forms can take on familiar shapes for engaging interactions and response ..... *Sylvan fissure.*

There is a universal source of light receptors and light converters in the brain that provides the environment where enough contrast can be generated to promote recognition ..... *glial cells and (neuro)melanin.*

There is a universal condition affecting the brain with enough magnitude and strength to ensure the expansion and enhancement of consciousness itself ..... *a lightflash.*

There is a universal phenomenon that transcends the human experience and reveals the soul's experience ..... *enlightenment.*

A Word of Caution: In an interview with Joseph Chilton Pearce, author of *Evolution's End: Claiming the Potential of Our Intelligence* [42], he is quoted as saying:

> There's something else very important we must understand here. The potential may appear [to evolve], but that doesn't mean it unfolds automatically. One overriding factor in development, an imperative of nature, is that no intelligence or ability will unfold unless the appropriate model environment is present.

That means you either have to be ready for it, or willing to surrender to it.

As long as we are speculating, consider this as well:

Hell-like experience = confrontation with one's own shadow (repressed or denied aspects of self).

Heaven-like experience = reunion with one's authenticity and worthiness (equally denied or repressed).

This implies that:

We have the physical endowments we need to assure the continuance of live—procreation, birth. We also have the physical endowments we need to assure the evolution of life—renewal, rebirth.

I suggest that we use the four types of near-death experiences I introduced in Chapter One as *stages of an evolving consciousness as it passes through the human condition, on its way back to its Source.*

Each stage or experience type is a model of what happens as consciousness begins to awaken to itself (INITIAL EXPERIENCE), untangle false perceptions (UNPLEASANT AND/OR HELL-LIKE EXPERIENCE), recognize true values and priorities (PLEASANT AND/OR HEAVEN-LIKE EXPERIENCE), and embrace its oneness within The All (TRANSCENDENT EXPERIENCE).

I would include full death with near-death in this evolution of consciousness because I have come to regard death as but another stage, another type of experience, in the journey of aliveness that The True Self takes.

*   *   *

At the time of his death in 1992, as he lay on the ground near his mangled car, comedian Sam Kinison talked softly with an unseen presence. He had been yelling, "I don't want to die," until he heard the disembodied voice. He then relaxed and sweetly whispered, "Okay, okay, okay." He died with a smile on his face, and at peace. (The *Las Vegas Sun* newspaper, Nevada)

*   *   *

A terrible car accident occurred around noon on April 4, 1992. Seven people were killed, one survived—a six-year-old child by the name of Ashley. Karen Moore, a children's therapist who worked with Ashley after the accident, said Ashley would often point to the hospital ceiling where she saw her dead mother and brother. "Don't you see them?" she'd ask. "No," said Moore, "what are they doing?" "Oh, they're laughing and eating." "It was eerie," declared Moore. "There was nothing to indicate she was hallucinating. This went on for several weeks, and then they moved her to Rusk Rehabilitation Center, and I remember her saying, 'They're gone; I can't find them anymore.'" (*Wisconsin State Journal*, Madison)

*   *   *

"Frequently throughout 1992, as she sensed the imminent threat to her mortality, she mentioned the names of long-dead friends and relatives and smilingly commented on the pleasure of seeing them again. She looked forward to the pleasures of death, but complained of the pain and the interminable time it took to die, as well as her reluctance to leave me and her many wonderful friends; during much of September in the hospital she lay with eyes open and conversed with interesting spirits—and told me of some of them!" (Personal correspondence from Frank Tribbe in Penn Laird, Virginia, concerning the death of his wife, Audre)

* * *

A young boy asked his parents if he could spend some time alone with his new baby sister. The parents agreed, but without their son's knowledge, they set up an intercom unit next to the crib so they could monitor and record the session. From that recording, here's what the little boy said to his baby sister, "You have to tell me about God. I'm starting to forget." (The family requested anonymity)

* * *

On Friday, October 4, 1991, when six-and-a-half-year-old Katie Thronson got off the school bus, she was beautiful, healthy, and happy. Soon she was drawing and, holding her picture, she bounced to her mother's side and said, "Mommy, am I going to die?" "No," her surprised mother replied. "Never?" "No, Katie, you're not going to die." Three days later Katie died of a cerebral hernia due to primary peritonitis. Two weeks before, she had her school photo taken, but had suddenly changed her mind about what to wear. "Mommy, this isn't my favorite, but I want to wear it for my picture." The night she was pronounced dead, Katie's teacher brought her school picture to the hospital. It showed the young girl dressed in a blue outfit that was covered with stars. Five months after her death, the drawing Katie made before she died was found. One year to the day of her death, her mother gave birth to a baby boy.

Katie's mother, Julie Ann Thronson of Moorhead, Minnesota, has given me permission to show you her last drawing. Notice the angels surrounding her passage into *the tunnel*. Then compare Katie's angelic tunnel with the engraving by Gustave Doré (1832–1883) of Dante and Beatrice as they experience the beatific vision.

It is the same tunnel and the same imagery as that of the near-death phenomenon.

TWELVE

Revelations

I believe that God has a Divine Plan for me. I
believe that this Plan is wrapped in the folds of
my Being, even as the oak is wrapped in the
acorn and the rose is wrapped in the bud.
                                        —Glen Clark

The four levels of near-death and otherworld imagery can be
interpreted literally, symbolically, or as if divinely inspired.
There is tremendous value to be gained for experiencers, significant others, and the general public if all three interpretative
possibilities are applied. Doing this broadens and deepens the
effect of what happened and adds rich layers of value and
meaning. To insist that there is only one way to regard any given
scenario is to limit its power and what can be learned from it.

Each scenario, no matter how it is interpreted or what kind of
imagery it encompassed, is absolutely and totally and completely
real to the one who experienced it. What happened, happened.
No one's belief or disbelief can change that simple fact.

There is no one experiencer and no single experience that is
more important than any other. Nor is there any message or
revelation given to any one person that is more correct or true
than what was revealed to any other. Quoting from holy writ to
validate or legitimize near-death claims accomplishes little or
nothing, and serves no one.

The reason for this is plain enough: All of us glimpsed but a small portion of The Big Picture. *None of us* saw as much as we think we did.

The *real* power that emerges from near-death experiences is a collective one—*not what one person saw or heard, but the sum of the many*. When you have listened to the thousands I have, you take note...for the collective message that emerges speaks with a voice of thunder.

And that's what this chapter is about—revelations assembled from the sum of the many.

The following words reflect a representative composite of experiencer comments:

What It Feels Like to Die

Any pain to be suffered comes first.

Instinctively you fight to live.

That is automatic.

It is inconceivable to the conscious mind that any other reality could possibly exist beside the earth-world of matter bounded by time and space. We are used to it. We have been trained since birth to live and thrive in it. We know ourselves to be ourselves by the external stimuli we receive. Life tells us who we are and we accept its telling. That, too, is automatic and to be expected.

Your body goes limp.

Your heart stops.

No more air flows in or out.

You lose sight, feeling, and movement—although the ability to hear goes last. Identity ceases. The "you" that you once were becomes only a memory.

There is no pain at the moment of death.

Only peaceful silence...calm...quiet.

But you still exist.

It is easy not to breathe. In fact, it is easier, more comfortable, and infinitely more natural not to breathe than to breathe.

The biggest surprise for most people in dying is to realize that dying does not end life. Whether darkness or light comes next, or some kind of event, be it positive, negative, or somewhere in between, expected or unexpected, the biggest surprise of all is to realize you are still you. You can still think, you can still remember, you can still see, hear, move, reason, wonder, feel, question, and tell jokes—if you wish.

You are still alive, very much alive. Actually, you're more alive after death than at any time since you were last born. Only the way of all this is different; different because you no longer wear a dense body to filter and amplify the various sensations you had once regarded as the only valid indicators of what constitutes life. You had always been taught one has to wear a body to live.

If you expect to die when you die you will be disappointed.

The only thing dying does is help you release, slough off, and discard the "jacket" you once wore (more commonly referred to as a body).

When you die you lose your body.

That's all there is to it.

Nothing else is lost.

You are not your body. It is just something you wear for a while, because living in the earthplane is infinitely more meaningful and more involved if you are encased in its trappings and subject to its rules.

What Death Is

There is a step-up of energy at the moment of death, an increase in speed as if you are suddenly vibrating faster than before.

Using radio as an analogy, this speed-up is comparable to having lived all your life at a certain radio frequency when all of a sudden someone or something comes along and flips the dial. That flip shifts you to another, higher wavelength. The original frequency where you once existed is still there. It did not change. Everything is still just the same as it was. Only *you* changed, only *you* speeded up to allow entry into the next radio frequency on the dial.

As is true with all radios and radio stations, there can be bleedovers or distortions of transmission signals due to interference patterns. These can allow or force frequencies to coexist or commingle for indefinite periods of time. Normally, most shifts up the dial are fast and efficient; but, occasionally, one can run into interference, perhaps from a strong emotion, a sense of duty, or a need to fulfill a vow, or keep a promise. This interference could allow coexistence of frequencies for a few seconds, days, or even years (perhaps explaining hauntings); but, sooner or later, eventually, every given vibrational frequency will seek out or be nudged to where it belongs.

You fit your particular spot on the dial by your speed of vibration. You cannot coexist forever where you do not belong.

Who can say how many spots there are on the dial or how many frequencies there are to inhabit? No one knows.

You shift frequencies in dying. You switch over to life on another wavelength. You are still a spot on the dial but you move up or down a notch or two.

You don't die when you die. You shift your consciousness and speed of vibration.

That's all death is . . . a shift.

What Existence Is

Time and space, as we know them, exist only on the earth-plane. When you leave the earthplane, you leave such constraints.

There are realms and dimensions of existence without number, ranging from the slower, more dense vibrations of form to higher, finer streamers of nonenergetic currents. And there is more beyond that, realities that cannot be measured or described in the convenience of mathematics or mind-play.

Hell refers to levels of negative thought-forms that reside in close proximity to the earthplane. It is where we go to work out, or remain within, our hangups, addictions, fears, guilts, angers, rage, regrets, self-pity, arrogance, or whatever else blocks us from the power of our own light. We stay in hell (and there are many divisions to this vibratory level) for however long best serves our development. There is no condemnation here, only the outworking of our own misjudgments, mistakes, misalignments, or misappropriations (what some people call sin). In hell, we have the opportunity to either revel in our folly or come to grips with the reality of consequences—that every action has a reaction, what is inflicted on another can be returned in kind. We experience the "flip side" of our despair or our demands, "living through" the extremes of whatever we dread. This is not a "punishment for our sins" but a confrontation with any distortion of our sense of values and priorities. We do not leave until we have changed our attitudes and perceptions.

Heaven is a term used to describe levels of positive thought-forms that reside in close proximity to the earthplane. It is where we go to recognize or enjoy our worth, talents, abilities, joys, courage, generosity, caring, empathy, givingness, virtue, cheer, diligence, thoughtfulness, patience, loving kindness, or whatever else reveals the power of our own light. We stay in heaven (and there are many divisions to this vibratory level) for however long best serves our development. There is a sense of benefit here, as if one has found one's true home and all is well (what some people call "recess," or a time of rewards). In heaven, we have the opportunity to assess our progress as a soul, to evaluate pros and cons and outcomes, to remember all truths including that of our *real* identity. We experience the glory of love and the power of forgiveness. This is not an end point, but, rather, the realization of our purpose in creation's story, how we fit, and what possibilities for future growth and learning exist. We do not leave until we are ready for our next advancement either in the world of form or beyond it.

No one knows how vast creation is... only that it has always been and will always be. Shapes and embodiments change and alter, substance is recycled, but existence exists, as does energy.

Existence is life, never ending and ongoing, forever and ever eternal. Yet its only true movement (without the distortion time and space give) is expansion and contraction, as if the existence that exists were capable of breathing. What appears as a progression, a time-line of starts and stops and ever-changing variations, is but an overleaf, an illusion, that helps us to focus on whatever spot on the dial we currently inhabit so we will accomplish what we set out to do (or at least have an opportunity to), and not be distracted by The Truth that undergirds reality.

Using television as an analogy, the picture we enjoy seeing, the progression of a storyline with characters acting out a script, is but a trick of perception. What exists, what is really there, is quite literally one electron at a time (with black and white, and three at a time with color) fired from the back of the television tube to the screen to be illuminated once it hits the screen as a tiny dot. The continuous barrage of electrons-turned-into-dots creates the appearance of images, as scanning lines (raster bars) roll from top to bottom separating information coming in (new dots) from information fading out (old dots). You adjust the vertical hold on your set, not to remove strange bars appearing in the picture, but to place all screen activity within the range of your own perceptual preference. A television picture tube is nothing more than a "gun" that fires electrons at a screen. Your mind connects the electrons/dots into the picture images you think you see, while it totally ignores the true reality of what actually undergirds the operation. The way television operates, at least in our daily experience of it, is an illusion.

Existence is a lot like television. What exists, what really exists, can't be fathomed by how it appears to operate or what it seems to be.

The Realness of God

God is.

God is the one presence, the one power, the one force and source of all. There are no competitors to God, no reality existent outside of God. God is omnipotent (all powerful), omniscient (all knowing), and omnipresent (present everywhere). There is no place where God is not, simply because nothing exists without God.

God is neither a man nor a woman nor a thing.

God is no one's father or mother or benefactor. These terms are used only to help us understand relationships—ours to God—not to establish a more human type of parentage. We use such terms as a matter of convenience or because it is comforting to do so. We call ourselves Children of God because we do not know what else to call ourselves, and it seems as good a term as any to use. We are made in the image of God, not in the sense of physical appearance, but with respect to the power of our souls and the potential of our minds. God is Creator; we are co-creators. It would be more appropriate and more in line with Truth, if we called ourselves Extensions of God or, perhaps, Thoughts in The Mind of God. It would even be appropriate to use another name for God, like The Force, The One, The All, The Isness, The One Mind, The Source, or whatever conveys that sense of deity that is without limitation or boundary, beyond what can be comprehended.

While God is more than any name, protocol, hierarchy, concept, or grandiosity could describe or define; God truly is as near as our next breath—as close as our next thought. We are part of God and existent within God. A belief in separation, that we could possibly exist and have our being apart from God, is the only real sin. This belief is of our own making. God has not decreed separation; this we did ourselves by our own perception that somehow, some way, we could transcend That Which Cannot Be Transcended.

God is not dependent on our belief, for our belief or disbelief in God does not affect God—only us.

God is not a member of any church or religion. It is the churches and the religions that are members within the vastness and the glory that is God. There is no one religion just as there is no "chosen" people or person, nor any single way of regarding what cannot be fully comprehended. We are all "Sons" of God in the sense that we are all souls of God's creation, without gender, without form, without nationality, complete and whole and perfect as we explore the never-endingness of God's wonderment. A spark from the essence of All God Is resides in each and every one of us as an unbreakable connection, that thread or cord that ensures we remain a part of That Which We Could Never Leave.

The splendorous joy of recognizing and acknowledging our specialness, our greatness, as creations of God and as co-creators with God, is akin to being engulfed by overwhelming floodtides of God's Glorious Love.

The Big Picture

There is no sense of "crime and punishment" in God's Light, only the clear, complete, and total knowing that you are loved unconditionally and fully—right now and forever more.

Truth in this light, God's Light, is so powerful and so piercing, there is no way you could lie, exaggerate, avoid, or deny what you have done with God's gift to you, the gift of an embodied life in the earthplane replete with abundant opportunities to learn and develop and grow—be the best that you can be. This gift, the earthlife God gives us, comes with a catch: We are to give the gift back.

We cannot keep the life we have on the earthplane, not our possessions or attachments or relationships. What we *can* keep is our memories and our feelings of what we have integrated into our heart of hearts from the experience of being here, plus the love we have shared with others. This that we can keep enriches God's experience of us as well as enriching our experience of ourselves and one another. How joyful this is depends on what we did about who we are.

Each gain or loss anyone makes affects everyone else to some degree. That's because we are connected, somehow, as sparks from The Mind of God. Everything created either has a soul (independent power mass) or is capable of being ensouled (from out of the group power mass). Because human forms contain larger portions of a soul mass than many other types of form, they represent opportunities of greater diversity, challenge, and involvement. Yet even animals, minerals, plants, and planets, enfold degrees of ensoulment replete with intelligence, feeling, and volition. Density of structure or shape may seem to deny this, but the creative fire is ever-present, nonetheless.

All souls are holy in God's Light, and all souls are loved.

And all souls have a purpose for their existence and a reason for being who or what they are. Whatever form a soul empowers "fits" in creation's story, for each soul has a job to do, a position to fill in the greater scheme of things.

And all souls evolve. Nothing stays as it is because nothing is static, regardless of how "otherwise" conditions may appear to be.

Evolution is not restricted to linear progression. It only seems so.

Thus, the drama of creation's story is unbounded—neither limited by our perception of it, nor by our ability or lack of ability to comprehend it. This drama is as stupendous as it is terrifying, as awesome as it is wonderful, as miraculous as it is mysterious, as beautiful as it is the ultimate act of all-consuming love. To witness even a glimpse of such glory, to know The Real Truth of it, leaves a mark so deep and so profound you are forever uplifted and transformed.

You return from your near-death experience *knowing* we affect each other because we are all part of each other, and that we affect all parts of creation because all parts of creation interweave and interrelate with all other parts. Any sense of aloneness or separation dissolves in The Light of such knowing.

We each matter. And we are each challenged to "wake up" and realize that we matter. Once we so awaken, our task is to act accordingly.

To know is not enough. We must express that knowing. How we do that is up to us.

Although we are each connected to the other and to all others, we are individual in our choices, in the power of our will, and in the product or result or consequence of our ever having breathed a breath in the earthplane. The responsibility we have for this totality of our beingness is as freeing and exciting as it is humbling. And it represents high adventure.

The greatest fear we have in living out our earth life is not what might happen to us, but what might be expected from us if we recognized who we are.

Priorities and Values

We glorify God just by existing.

Our mission or our purpose in life reveals itself as we go along. It is not something we have to know in advance; it is simply an urge of "rightness" we follow or associate with or are open to, when we are receptive enough.

Whatever brings us closer to God or wholeness is of value. And what does that for us is love, charity, patience, joy, faith, wisdom, knowledge, healing, laughter, sharing, cooperation, upliftment, doing for another, service, discipline, kindness, constructive effort, using our talents, lending a hand, giving a blessing, grace, forgiveness, meditation, prayer, respecting ourself, happiness, harmony, melody, the pleasure of satisfaction in a job well done.

Thus, what is positive and life-affirming is desirable.

Yet, negatives are not undesirable.

Fear is positive in that it protects us from harm. It fosters the gifts of caution and discernment and discrimination. Fear is only negative when we allow it to paralyze or cripple or restrict, suffocating us with "phantom enemies" of our own dread.

Anger is positive in that it motivates us and "sets the record straight." It fosters the gifts of creative force, drama, inner cleansing, and truthtelling. Anger is only negative when we allow our ego to let surface on its fiery currents whatever is repressed or suppressed within the inner depths of our own psyche.

Our priorities in life depend on the choices we make and what we empower by our presence and our personality. Literally, wherever we put our attention is where we put our power.

We walk by faith, not by sight.

We live by grace, not by effort.

We exist in love, not in time or space.

The Small Stuff

What I have just shared with you is a consensus of the countless messages that have emerged from near-death accounts. This offering, hopefully, will introduce you to a broader view of life and its living. No "gospel" is intended here; rather, a type of wisdom that simply "sings a new song"—from a chorus of millions.

Many experiencers say, "Don't sweat the small stuff," and then they add, "It's all small stuff." (There's a lot of laughter among near-death survivors.)

During my interviews I did ask some topical questions, just to see what responses I would get. On the question of suicide, nearly everyone said it was not an option—yet most were quick to say that artificial extensions of life were not necessarily desirable either. When I broached the subject of abortion, over three-fourths disapproved. They seemed to respect a woman's right to choose, but felt that through proper counseling and appropriate alternatives, a woman could find ways to respect and honor God's gift of life—whether the child was kept or given for adoption.

As you can see, experiencers usually support "the life urge."

And most claim that it is their thoughts, their attitudes, and their beliefs that are the major cause of any troubles they might have had in their lives. They come to emphasize personal responsibility over blame, conflict resolution over revenge, creative problem solving over dictatorial threats or demands. They are more at ease with diversity, and they display a greater tolerance for ambiguity and change.

The majority accept psychic abilities as soul abilities, feeling that these faculty extensions enliven their lives, save them time and money, and add a "grace note" to relationships. Since science has established that 99 percent of the universe is either infra or ultra to our perception as humans, these psychic "extras" are regarded as a way to access more of the electromagnetic spectrum—a way to expand the range of what is typical.

It is true that near-death survivors smile often and give great hugs. Wouldn't you, if you were no longer controlled by the tyranny of time?

THIRTEEN

Making the Adjustment

Sometimes, I lie awake at night, and I ask,
"Why me?" Then a voice answers, "Nothing
personal...your name just happened to come
up."

—Charlie Brown
(by Charles Schulz)

Approximately one-third of the adults who brush death have a
near-death experience. With children, the number is in excess of
75 percent! Every type of experiencer you can imagine is repre-
sented in those figures, along with every conceivable and inconceivable life challenge.

Kimberly Clark Sharp, MSW, president of Seattle IANDS, an
experiencer and a social worker who has interviewed over a
thousand near-death survivors, many in intensive-care and cancer wards, gave a presentation in St. Louis, Missouri (at the North
American Conference of IANDS), geared toward intervention
techniques for professional health-care givers [43].

With Clark Sharp's permission, here are some of her recommendations. I think you will find them helpful and thought
provoking.

The Near-Death Phenomenon

Immediate Intervention Techniques Developed By
Kimberly Clark Sharp, MSW

During Cardiopulmonary Resuscitation (CPR): Assume,
rather than dismiss, that the patient may be having a near-

death experience. At the very least, the patient will be able to hear what you say, even if he or she is unconscious.

It is disorienting to be out-of-body, so orient the patient as to date and time, his or her location, the patient's name, and all activities related to the patient's body.

Talk the patient through CPR either aloud or silently. Often patients report being able to "read the minds" of those in attendance and can "hear" your thoughts regarding the activities around their physical bodies. It is additionally helpful to brush the patient's body lightly with your hands, naming the parts as you touch them, so the individual can find his or her way back into the body when the out-of-body episode is over. Simply put, physical contact can act as a "beacon" to guide the patient "back in."

For the Unconscious Patient:
- Use the recommendations as previously stated, i.e., orient the patient and provide light touch while naming corresponding body parts.
- As a courtesy, introduce yourself to the patient and let him or her know what you are doing.
- Tell the patient about the near-death phenomenon. Briefly mention several elements of the near-death experience while reassuring him or her that what is happening is *normal*. This will validate the near-death experience before the individual revives.

For the Conscious Patient Who Cannot Verbalize:
- For the patient on a ventilator or otherwise physically restrained, remember to give your name as a courtesy and state your purpose. Verbally educate the patient about the universal elements of the near-death phenomenon, and validate for him or her that the experience is *normal*. Establish a method of nonverbal communication, such as hand squeezes or head nods and ask if he or she remembers any near-death element.
- Promise to return when the patient can verbalize so that he or she can discuss the experience. If you cannot return, let the patient know that someone else will come in your stead to hear the story, if he or she desires.

For the Fully Conscious and Verbal Patient:
- Introduce yourself. Maintain eye contact and give your full uninterrupted attention.

- Ask the patient if anything unusual or different happened to him or her during CPR or a close brush with death. If there is hesitation and fumbling for words, tears, and lot of "ohs" and "ahs" and "wells," that person probably had a near-death experience.
- Begin interviewing by asking the patient to describe his or her memory of events. Be nonjudgmental. Be honest about yourself and your values. Don't patronize. Near-death experiencers are *very* sensitive and they will know a lot about you just by looking at you. Stop your interview at any sign of discomfort.
- Avoid pressure or probing. Assure the patient that you will be there to listen if wanted. Lend authority to the patient's account, as he or she (and others) will tend to discount or disbelieve. Begin to plan how the patient will integrate the near-death experience with recovery and "normalcy."
- Put the patient in touch with appropriate resources of where to obtain emotional support and more information about the near-death phenomenon.

After the patient has recovered, there is often depression or anger—either because the event happened in the first place, or because it was not possible to stay in the dimension of the near-death experience. There can even be feelings of rejection that he or she was "kicked out of heaven," or a great relief that somehow he or she was "saved from hell." Invariably, there is amazement and puzzlement: Was it real? What does it mean? Why did it happen? Will anyone else believe the story? There come a million questions with no ready answers. That's why it is so important to have an empathetic listener available. The experiencer *needs* to talk. And the experiencer *needs* to have information about the near-death phenomenon—lots of it.

Children usually have the same or less complicated experiences than adults, with similar aftereffects. But there is a *big* difference in how they communicate. Children often lack words to describe what they went through and cannot explain their confusion or anger or joy. This is obviously more problematic for infants, since they must wait several years before they speak well enough to verbalize their stories. Allowing children to paint or draw their experiences, rather than describe them, is not only revealing, but therapeutic. Acting them out or using puppets is also a helpful activity for the younger set.

A word of caution here, though, for anyone involved with a near-death survivor: They may not want your help.

Regardless of how much it is needed, help may be refused. I have yet to meet an experiencer who could adequately assess his or her situation with any real discernment or clarity during the first three years after reviving. (I was no exception.)

You cannot help experiencers who are convinced they can handle their own situations themselves.

Sometimes patience is the greatest gift you can give. Sometimes only the passage of time makes any difference. Survivors need some assistance, all of them do, at one time or another; but it is not always accepted, nor is it necessarily welcomed.

The Most Common Negative Reactions
From Near-Death Experiencers Are:

Angered, for having been revived and forced to leave wherever they were.

Guiltridden, for not missing or even being concerned about their loved ones.

Disappointed, at discovering they are once again encased in their physical bodies and they will have to breathe, eat, and use the toilet.

Horrified, if their experience was frightening or hellish or unpleasant.

Dumbfounded, if they want to talk but can't or are afraid to.

Depressed, at realizing they must now resume their former lives, that they must find a way to go on with regular living regardless of what happened to them.

The Most Common Positive Reactions
From Near-Death Experiencers

Ecstatic, at the wonder and beauty and glory of it all.

Thrilled, because they feel so privileged to have experienced such a miracle.

Grateful, that anything so incredible could have happened to them.

In Awe, possibly unable to speak or to find words.
Evangelistic, immediately desirous of telling others the good news about death and God and the power of love.
Humbled, by the magnitude of the incident and what it may portend.

After a near-death experience you want to talk about it, you want to tell the whole world that death ends nothing but the physical body, that God exists and love is God revealed. You want to scream this news from the highest rooftop. You want to shake up a deluded world. God is real, life is ongoing and never ending and worth its living. And the life we have is multidimensional, limited only by the prejudice of our own misperceptions and the folly of blind belief. You want to say this; you need to say this.

But I honestly don't know who does more to silence experiencers: the interested or the disinterested. Allow me to share a few examples from my own life.

I drove to the post office in Falls Church, Virginia, one Saturday to mail a letter. As I returned to my car, the largest man I have ever seen, nearly as wide as he was tall, stood in my way. He threw open his arms, and bellowed: "There's a white glow all around you. I know what that means. You're a Messenger of God and you have come here to deliver a message about God's word."

Well, I froze in my tracks and listened. He went on like this for several minutes until I began to wonder if he knew something I didn't. After he quieted down and the crowd around us dispersed, he explained that he was a "born-again" Christian and he needed to know the message I had come to deliver so he could help me fulfill my mission.

I stammered a few things about my near-death experiences, then, before I could say another word, his eyes flashed and he began another volley of shouting and screaming. "My God, woman, I knew it. I knew you were special. Just leave it to me. I'll make you famous. I'll make you rich. Every country on this planet is going to know about you." Needless to say, I shut my mouth and ran. His passionate pronouncements struck me as funny the next day, but at the time they horrified me. His version of "sainthood" I could do without.

Yet the disinterested can be just as vocal.

During my original quest to seek out others like myself, I

responded to a request by a psychologist who lived near Winona, Minnesota, to stop by and visit. While I was there, he arranged for me to speak about my near-death experiences to a grief group that met in a funeral home. Midway through my description of death number two, a pastor sitting opposite me in the large room jumped to his feet and yelled, "You have not been washed in the blood of the Lamb!" With that, he stomped out the door followed by half the audience. I affirmed his and everyone else's right to leave, sharing with them that I knew exactly how the pastor felt. When my three experiences had happened to me, I couldn't believe them at first either.

After I finished my talk to the audience that remained, the funeral director came over to me and said: "There's no reason for the pastor to have behaved like that. You must have touched a nerve. But I want you to know I found what you had to say one of the most inspiring messages of hope I have ever heard."

Not only do near-death survivors and others so transformed become more interested in things spiritual, they also become more psychic. And that's a fact! Yet no one wants to talk about it, at least not in public. And I can't say that I blame them, for being psychic can represent a double-edged sword. What comes to make perfect sense in the psychic world isn't always sensible, nor is it even desirable. With marketing-blitz techniques and television talk shows being what they are, it is difficult if not almost impossible to separate that which helps from that which doesn't. Really good material is now readily available on psychism and psychic abilities—but so is a lot of trash. Since this subject is so important and so rarely addressed, I want to express some of my thoughts about the psychic.

My experience has been that, although appearing as different abilities and manifestations, psychism is really just differing expressions of *one* mechanism—the extension of faculties normal to us. It functions as a basic talent that can be developed, directed, and controlled. Call it a skill, if you will; and, just as with any other skill, it can be ignored, used as is, enhanced and improved with practice, or it can emerge seemingly full-blown at birth. Using piano playing as an analogy, occasionally child prodigies are born, but, for the most part, people do not master great concertos until first pounding out "Chopsticks" and then spending years in dedicated study and practice.

Psychic ability is no different than piano playing in the sense of skill development. Yet its components are vague and subtle, its effects all too often elusive and unpredictable, hinging more on superstition and ignorance than on practical results. Since the psychic world is outcast, it is wide open for anything, from the serious to the ridiculous. It often appears more negative than positive, its practitioners more as jealous backbiters than dependable professionals.

Perhaps we expect too much of what we call *psychic*. We are so conditioned by tales of magic and trickery that anything less is boring. When the expected is received from "tuning in" it is called a confirmation. When the unexpected is received it is called a revelation. Predictions that come true excite us; those that don't are forgotten. When an entity from The Other Side suddenly manifests before us we are shocked and surprised, forgetting that we as humans regularly attract all manner of phenomena, visible and invisible. Greeting a disincarnate or a light being is not as unusual as some would have us believe. Since we humans are electromagnetic by nature and natural transmitters/receivers of signals, it is no wonder we are dubbed "psychic" when we become increasingly sensitive to higher, faster frequencies.

Developing psychic abilities out of the context of a balanced and healthy life is not wise. Perhaps the reason there are so many warnings against psychism is because the price for misuse and abuse is so high.

Psychic ability is easily perverted—but it is just as easily converted into helpful, constructive abilities that can enliven and enrich life. Psychic abilities are not by nature positive or negative, destructive or constructive, spiritual or demonic. They simply are. How they are used and for what purpose determines their worth.

As extensions of faculties native to our existence, psychic abilities provide us with wonderful "extras." Direct those extensions toward the spiritual and the exact same abilities can become Gifts of the Spirit, treasured components to spiritual discipleship. By the way, the word *psychic* literally translates as "of the soul," the inference being that psychic abilities are really soul abilities, part of our inheritance as Children of God.

There is nothing wrong with psychic ability. It is neither

supernatural, abnormal, or paranormal. But neither is it a key to any kind of Golden Door. There is no magic in its use, only skill.

Carl Gustav Jung, the famous Swiss psychiatrist, acknowledged in his later years that his experience with the field of psychism "was the one great experience [that] wiped out all my earlier philosophy and made it possible for me to achieve a psychological point of view." After admitting this, he went on to detail a fascination with the subject that had spanned his entire life.

It is interesting to note that, of those psychics who have been able to maintain the most successful careers and long-standing reputations of selfless service, *the majority had at least one near-death experience* at some point in their lives (many had several).

It is also of interest to realize that most clergy during seminary training are taught breathing exercises to control psychic phenomena and their own burgeoning psychic abilities. Yet never is any mention made of this to their congregations, nor do they offer to pass on these skills to those in need. Many condemn psychism out of hand rather than admit that the emergence of things psychic is a natural component of spiritual growth.

I handled this dilemma for myself by taking up the practice of rune casting. My introduction to this ancient divinatory art form was in the feminine or yin style of free-form casting without benefit of formats or layouts. Because the feminine system is illustrative and based on the energy of the moment, it is unlimited in its use and in the realms of information that can be accessed. Since fortune-telling is a waste of time, as there are no fixed futures, rune casting is actually an objective and detached way of tapping into one's own subconscious mind and being of service to others. Its practice stimulates synergistic or whole-brain development. And it's fun. You become four years old again and engage in sacred "play."

Thus, rune casting became the method I used to retrain my brain after my three near-death experiences. It helped me to stabilize and ground the faculty extensions I had, while returning me to an appreciation of manifested form and the wonders life on earth. I wrote *The Magical Language of Runes* [44] as a way of giving thanks and passing on the skill. Because Barbara Hand Clow, my copublisher at the time, suggested that I rename the rune set and expand the book, it is now titled *Goddess Runes*.

Whether you choose to develop and express your new or enhanced psychic abilities as I did, or to follow a different path, it is helpful to select some avenue with which to direct our skills; study, control, and understand them. I have found the faculty extensions I gained a wonderful godsend and a practical adjunct to my daily life. I know you can achieve a similar level of comfort with yours, if you desire, and are willing to apply the necessary effort to do so.

We need to remember something here, though. Near-death survivors do not lose their individuality just because they have expanded into a more universal type of awareness. If anything, each of their given traits becomes more pronounced. Whatever existed before, becomes more noticeable after. This means weaknesses as well as strengths. Because of this, experiencers can be difficult to deal with; their lack of clarity can be frustrating.

It takes time to make the adjustment from the dimensions of near-death to the confines of earthplane living. And it takes patience. As an aid in the process of "coming back," I recommend this five-point plan as the best way to assist near-death survivors of any age get started:

1. **Active participation of empathetic listeners** who exhibit interest instead of scorn. Give the experiencer plenty of time to talk. If he or she is a child, encourage drawing or playacting or storytelling. *Be certain to notify the class teacher if the child is of school age.* Encourage the teacher to read up on the phenomenon so interactions with the child can be handled in clear yet supportive ways.

2. **Absence of pressure** to resume everyday life routines. Let them ease back. For a while, do not expect them to be the same people they once were, and do not be too surprised if they want to make sudden or unusual changes in their lifestyles.

3. **Freedom to explore ideas and ask questions** without shame, ridicule, or guilt. Many display an absolute thirst for knowledge afterward, so encourage classes or study or experimentation or the adventure of exploration.

4. **Supportive therapy of some kind,** even if it is just a family rap session conducted in a nonjudgmental manner. Group therapy with fellow near-death survivors is ideal, but *only* if professional or caring strangers are also present to offer clarity

and feedback. Experiencers need other viewpoints and opinions besides their own, but not to the point of being overwhelmed by others.

5. **Exposure to as much information** about the near-death phenomenon and its aftereffects as possible, including scientific findings, personal accounts, books, and articles.

> The sooner near-death survivors realize how normal and typical their feelings and concerns for what they went through are, the faster they will stabilize their aftereffects and the easier it will be for them to integrate their experience.

I found that it takes the average near-death survivor *seven years* to even begin to integrate the experience. This if often true of children as well.

Even if individuals seem completely adjusted during this time period, they seldom are. They are still detached from the rest of society. No matter what they claim or how they act, that first seven-year period is disconnected. Family and friends can see this, but experiencers usually do not.

Of these seven years, the first three are the most challenging, and for all concerned, since it is during this early phase that the average near-death survivor is the most disoriented and significant others are the most confused as to why. Their behavior centers primarily around self and the newness of everything, even though they might appear to be aglow with love and infinitely more courteous. They can become so absorbed in whatever they are doing or thinking that the rest of the world ceases to exist for them, and other people are ignored. Schedules become unimportant. For this reason, they may appear to be selfish and unreasonable. Former goals and interests diminish or fade in importance. All that matters is *experiencing newness*, and learning everything they possibly can, and "following" what they sense as "guidance from on high." Thus, they often offend or insult others without meaning to, or come across as zealots or overly idealistic dreamers.

At about the fourth year, the average near-death survivor's behavior begins to alter significantly. They become easier to deal with. It's as if the experiencer has finally discovered other people and the wisdom of addressing the needs of others. They reach out more during the four-year timespan that follows and become keenly aware of society and the pressures of work and lifestyle. Former goals and interests can resurface during this phase, but each will have a different priority and value than before. The experiencer is still detached but, by now, he or she is much more involved in earthplane living and more sensitive to relationships.

It takes the full seven years (and sometimes longer) before the average experiencer regains true comprehension skills and discernment, and finds comfort in being back "on Earth." Using the seventh year as a benchmark, before and after differences are remarkable. Even the individual involved usually recognizes the change and is amazed to realize how disconnected he or she had been. Although few are those who are ever "the same" again (and some never make the adjustment), the majority are surprised and even amused at how much more "normal" they and their life become after the seventh year.

I doubt if all aftereffects ever fade, but they do alter as time passes. The biggest change I noticed in myself and others like me after our "seventh birthday" was the return of clarity and discrimination, precious gifts I have learned to honor.

It takes time to make the adjustment. No matter how hard the individual tries to hurry up the process or pretend everything is under control, he or she is still visibly affected. There seems no way to shortcut the first seven years, even with the most understanding and supportive of environments. *It takes time.*

Challenges of the first seven years, however, have an interesting side effect. When these years have passed, depending on how successful the experiencer was in adjusting, life gets noticeably easier. It's almost as if the individual has joined "in sync" with the natural rhythms of life itself, the flow of seasons and cycles, of synchronicity and "right" timing. Health improves and so do attitudes. From then on, miracles become daily fare (not that they weren't before), as the individual gets "in gear" and gets busy.

I have observed that the near-death phenomenon seems to enhance, enlarge, accelerate, and expand whatever was present or existed as potential within the individual at the time it occurred. Keep this observation in mind as I list the most common negative and positive adjustments after the phenomenon is over:

The Most Common Negative Adjustments
After the Near-Death Experience

Initial confusion and disorientation. What happened? Can you believe your own instincts? Can you trust yourself?

Disappointment with the unresponsive or uncaring attitudes of others. Who do you tell? What do you say? Where do you turn?

Depression and the inability to integrate the experience into daily life. Is this incident applicable on the earthplane? Who really cares? Is it worth the effort to integrate it?

Behavior threatening to others. What does it take to make this practical? How can I honor what I now know without alarming everyone else around me? How do I rebuild relationships?

Seen as arrogant and unloving. Am I capable of intimacy? How do I express myself without being misunderstood?

The know-it-all syndrome. How do I convince other people I know what I am doing? Why can't people be more cooperative instead of competitive? Why do I feel as if I am being manipulated by some unseen force?

The Most Common Positive Adjustments
After the Near-Death Experience

Unconditionally loving and generous. Still capable of intimacy but no longer as needful of the kind of ego-driven role playing society considers typical in relationships.

Unhindered, detached, childlike. More adjustable and flexible in dealings with others. Happier and more joyful. Spontaneous.

A heightened sense of the present moment. A shift in priorities and values. Knowing what is really important in life and what is not.

Enhanced sensitivities and a greater awareness of the needs of others. Knowing what might work and what might not. Sensitive to subtle impressions, energy vibrations and the true power of one's own mind.

Expanded worldview, fewer worries and fears. No longer afraid of death. Comfortable with diversity. More tolerant and at peace with the unknown and with challenge and change.

Knowledgeable of spiritual identity. No longer restricted by religious dogmas. Aware and responsive to the sacredness of life and the importance of personal responsibility/accountability.

Accepting of a greater reality and the existence of God. Convinced of God's realness, our divinity as souls, and of a reason and purpose in and behind all creation.

Berkley Carter Mills's son has grown up unafraid of death, knowing, positively knowing, that God is real and that he is important in God's sight. This young man is bright, exuberant, intelligent, and curious; keenly in touch with the nuances of otherworldly dimensions. And all because he, as a youngster, grew up with a father who was totally transformed by the near-death phenomenon. The son grew up not knowing there was any other way people could behave or believe.

How are other families affected by their experiencer parents?

Listen to the words of Tonia Hugus, formerly of New York City, and now residing in Charlottesville, Virginia:

My mother had become severely depressed from my father's activities, the lack of money, her many pregnancies, and a miscarriage. She saw no way out, so she decided to commit suicide and kill her four children and her unborn child (my brother Christopher). She herded us into the kitchen. She shut the door and sealed it with towels. She then turned on the gas stove and oven, but did not light it. It was her idea to gas herself and her children.

The next thing my mother experienced, as she later told me, was that she could be wherever she decided to be. From the tiny kitchen window she saw a tree in full bloom, and in a split second she had gone into one of the flowers. She saw the flower and its network of veins and then she saw even beyond that, and felt what she called God. "I knew what God was," she said. "I understood life and its meaning."

She came back to her physical senses, immediately shut off the gas, and ushered us children out. She went back to one of the small bedrooms, got on her knees and prayed to God. She told God that she would love Him, serve Him, and obey all His Commandments. She also mentioned to me, which I found strange, that she understood from God that she would have to do this on her own—she was responsible for herself and her own development and life.

This near-death experience and the subsequent decisions of my mother had both a profoundly negative and positive effect upon all her children. On the one hand, we all developed a sense of "otherness." My mother taught us that there was a very thin veil between this earthly existence and a "heavenly existence," and most importantly that all it took was a simple act of faith to plug into that Source and get help. I completely believed that, as surely as I have two eyes, a nose, and a mouth. This belief has gotten me through two almost fatal degenerative illnesses, from which I was able to come back healthier than I was before. It has carried me through some very serious life crises, such as the illness of children, divorce, and horrific incest issues from which I could have been rendered insane. I am most grateful to my mother for this spiritual legacy.

On the other hand, she chose to believe that God must be embodied in the orthodox Catholic tradition. She became fanatically Catholic. She despised sexuality and made all of us feel ashamed. She stayed married to my father and went on to have six more children, even though our financial situation devolved into hopeless poverty. She also turned her head away from the serious abuse of myself and my two other sisters by our father.

I would have to say that the good and bad were equally extreme because of my mother's near-death experience. In many ways, my brothers and sisters and myself are remarkable people. We are good parents, even though we were horrifically treated. But, also, thanks to mother, we learned to be impractical when it comes to earthly matters, the use of money, being on time to anything, feeling really "here."

Hugus spoke through many tears as she related being utterly fascinated by her mother, yet feeling absolutely abandoned by her.

She was too detached from the awful reality going on around her. She lived her life to get back to God; that determined her every action. She wanted to be "good" and she would sacrifice anything including her children to do it. She had ten babies in fourteen years. To me, this was complete arrogance on her part.

Hugus acknowledged how much her mother had taught all her children from what she had gained from her near-death experience. "She gave us a faith that could move mountains. But it was a mixed bag. I will probably be sorting it out for the rest of my life."

Once the near-death experience is over, none of us has the

innate tools or skills with which to understand or evaluate our new awareness and how we feel. We struggle and stumble, sometimes alienating when we mean to inspire, confusing when we mean to clarify, threatening when we mean to soften, frightening when we mean to enlighten.

We are not perceived by others as we perceive ourselves. The message we seek to deliver is sometimes lost in the translation.

Hugus said her life with her mother was a "mixed bag," and that exactly describes the aftereffects and how experiencers respond to them. For those who are successful in integrating their experience, and many are, life becomes so wonderful and so joyful you honestly begin to wonder how you could have ever lived any other way.

But the truth is, the legacy of near-death's phenomenon is often bittersweet.

At a meeting of Seattle IANDS last year, a tearful paramedic asked the group why he should resuscitate people if the procedure he used pulled people away from such a beautiful experience. A near-death survivor answered him by saying how grateful she was to be alive now and how, without the paramedic who saved her life, she would not be here with the people she loves. I would add to her reply that, no matter how wonderful The Other Side is, the real curriculum is right here, right now, wearing the bodies we have and doing the work we do.

Life *is* worth living!

I am overjoyed at the people, regardless of who or where, who find inspiration from reportings of the near-death phenomenon *and* from the experiencers who talk about it. There are a number of counselors now who use the pattern of the experience as a model to help their clients move past restricting fears and feelings of loss to reconnect with their own innate potential for positive life fulfillment. Also, people in the process of dying often find encouragement and peace when they come to realize that the light described by millions of experiencers, adults and children, might well be The Light of God.

Near-death themes are popping up in movies, on television shows, in novels, and in children's literature. And, would you believe it? in commercial advertising.

Thanks to Giro, a leading manufacturer of special bike helmets for the discriminating biker (purple, no less), I have this offering to give you. Turn the page...and have a good laugh!

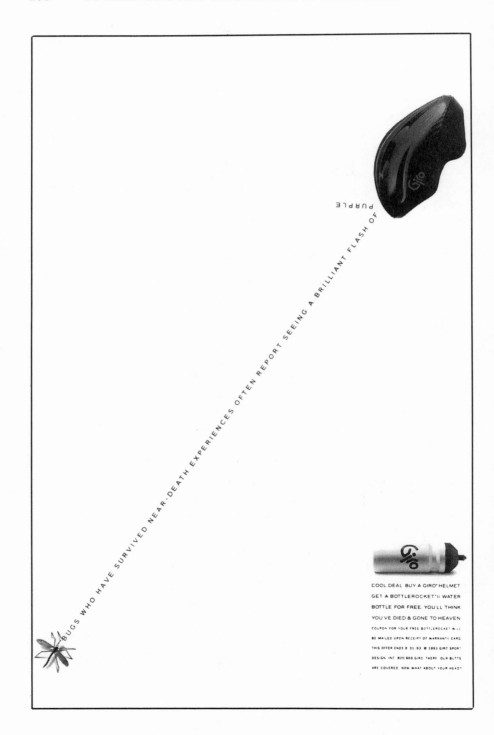

FOURTEEN

Let's Get Personal

I long to accomplish a great and noble task, but
it is my chief duty to accomplish small tasks as
if they were great and noble.

—Helen Keller

I felt possessed of God and filled with the sum of all knowledge
after my three near-death experiences. And I was propelled by an
almost messianic need to preach the new gospel as revealed to
me—one of love and life, eternal and ongoing.

As I preached this gospel, unsettling discrepancies began to
appear. What I felt inside me, the passion I was charged with,
didn't translate into the work-a-day world. Audiences everywhere were absolutely enthralled with my story and what I
learned from beyond death's door; but, once the applause faded
and my "cheering section" paraded home, I was left with an
empty sinking feeling that the talks I gave were simply entertainment. Being a good speaker uplifted people, but little else
resulted. This was untenable to me.

Admittedly, there were many forces at work that drove me to
research near-death. What became primary though was not only
a desire to understand my own experiences and explore the
greater phenomenon through outreach to others, but to establish
value. What good is all this, I asked myself, if in the end all that
remains are preachments and prophesies? A haunting memory
from my childhood resurfaced—the specter of *self-deception*.

207

That memory concerned the long walk I made to school each morning as a first-grader, a walk filled with the horror of death. That's because there were large gold stars on the front windows of people's houses. I knew what those stars meant, they meant someone in that home had died during the war effort. One morning there were six new gold stars on a person's window. When I saw them, I just stood there... sobbing. Seldom did I begin a day of school without first having to wipe away my tears and quiet my shudders. World War II had a tremendous impact on me, and I was acutely aware of how Hitler had fooled the world, cleverly disguising the Holocaust with persuasive rhetoric and the passion of his "sincerity." The gold stars that haunted me as a youngster became a reminder to me as an adult: Don't be deceived by appearances or anyone's truth, including your own—test, retest, verify.

Thus my own experiences were not enough. I had to be certain of the dimensions and the scope of that which seemed so miraculous, so otherworldly, before I would share what death had taught me. It wasn't God that I didn't trust, it was me—my perception.

This driving need of mine was totally misunderstood by the near-death community and by other researchers, nor did they believe me when I tried to explain. The more I defended my findings, the more I was shunned or ignored or attacked. I had neither a knowledge nor an understanding of the proper protocol researchers were expected to follow, nor could I appreciate why my peer group quailed when I barraged them with the same type of "dumb" questions I had asked of the experiencers I had interviewed. Double-blind studies, controlled questionnaires, statistical analysis, although necessary tools in research, are not complete without field observations—the footwork of a "cop on the beat." And that's what I did, footwork.

One of the big myths in the near-death community is that everyone involved is a saintly person, unselfish in their devotion to their work and in their support of one another. As within any segment of society, ours has its disasters and tragedies, jealous feuds, and petty politics. I should know, I have experienced more than my share.

Here's a sampling: The original publisher of *Coming Back to Life* folded, the victim of a corporate raid, just as the book had sold through two printings. Promotions and publicity peaked when there were no more books to be had. I lost all my royalties, as well as most of my advance money—stolen by the agent I had at the time. Another near-death survivor began a campaign to vilify me and slander my work. When I sat down with her to find out why, she was nice enough at first but then launched into an irrational tirade, shouting "If you ever speak to a near-death group I will have you publicly censured. And don't think I can't. People will do anything I tell them to." Not believing my ears, I called her back a half hour later to inquire if I had heard her correctly. She exploded.

The woman was as good as her word. She tried to cancel my appearance on the *Sally Jesse Raphael* show, and instigated a vote against me throughout the near-death community. She said, quite politely, to anyone who inquired about me through the office where she worked—"You don't have to talk with her. I know all about the aftereffects. I can help you." (I learned about this a year later when several media people finally tracked me down and complained about her.) As a result of this campaign, I was effectively shut out. The only opportunities I received from the heavy book promotions I did in 1988 and 1989 were two offers to give a talk, made by people who happened to know friends of mine. My husband and I almost went bankrupt.

I want to publicly thank Jay Wolfman, a stranger who knocked on my door one day and said, "You're being blacklisted by the near-death community, and I want to know why." I let him read copies of every letter I had written or received. His assessment: "There's nothing wrong here. You haven't said or done anything to provoke the treatment you're getting."

I also want to thank Laurie Schwartz and Patricia Fenske, who came to my defense and gave me a chance to prove myself.

How did I handle all of this?

I became a cynic.

In my grief, I had destroyed my original research notes and vowed to quit my involvement with the field. As far as I was concerned, any notion that researchers were impartial or that experiencers were capable of unconditional love was pure fiction. My attempts at forgiveness and understanding had only served to make matters worse. When I had asked the woman who slandered me for an apology, I was ignored. Although my personal life was steadily becoming more and more joyous and loving, my marriage a wondrous gift, the work I thought I was doing for humankind was in a shambles. I cried an entire winter.

1995 marks the twentieth year since Raymond Moody, Jr., first published *Life After Life*. Millions of people throughout the world have benefited from what he did and have been challenged and changed by the idea he advanced that death does not end life.

From the very start, many people have sacrificed greatly and given much to the field. And there has been incredible caring freely offered from many others. Without question, all of us have tried to do our best even when our best wasn't always that helpful.

And we have all been deeply affected, just by having participated, and every one of us has had to face "the dark side" as well as The Light. For instance: A researcher who wrote the most marvelous book about the love near-death survivors meet on The Other Side of death killed himself in a violent suicide after terrorizing his entire family; a medical doctor was denied tenure at a major university just because he had dared to research the phenomenon and write a book about his findings; there have been threatened lawsuits, name-calling, and accusations galore as standard fare in the field, with little or no money going to IANDS, the very organization created to provide leadership and public education on the near-death experience.

Yet, it's been a wild twenty years. And to quote Tonia Hugus, "It's been a mixed bag."

Yet no one wants to talk about any of this, and that's the real problem. If we don't acknowledge our mistakes, how can anyone do better? If we don't admit our stupidity, how can we recognize the wisdom we could share?

The near-death experience expands and enhances and enlarges and accelerates any trait or any issue *anyone who comes in contact with it has*, whether or not that person is an experiencer. That's why so many benefit, and that's why so many are hurt. And that's why I'm breaking the "code of silence" that seems to exist by admitting my walk on "the dark side." None of us will learn as much as we hope to if we don't compare notes.

As for me, my cynicism turned out to be a smokescreen I had erected to mask my own disappointment with myself; my losses were but a reflection of a deep-seated fear of success. My attacker eventually became a "prod" I used to ensure that I would work harder and do better. I thank her for being in my life. She did me a favor.

Forgiveness didn't work in my case because I was too busy wallowing around being a "victim" to face this question: In order to experience peace, was I willing to give up my anger?

I had been so busy giving love that I had forgotten to *be* love. I had been so busy helping others that I had forgotten to respect and honor myself and my own needs.

In a nutshell, I was so infused with The Divine I forgot my humanness. That means I denied my dark side. When you do that you block your growth, for only in darkness can seeds germinate and ideas take root; only in darkness do we each face all that we are and all that we have ever been. It is that quiet place where we feel the pulse of our own soul. Darkness isn't hellish any more than light is heavenly. They are just opposite poles of the same energy. On the earthplane *we need them both* for balance and stability. On The Other Side, we don't.

With compassion, I name my three near-death experiences "The Heavenly Sledgehammer Effect," since it took dying thrice over to "crack" the tough nut I can sometimes be. My three experiences illuminated for me my true relationship to The Source of My Being. My near-death aftereffects revealed to me my true relationship with *myself*.

Yes, we have an anniversary coming...twenty years of near-death research. And you may be interested to know that although most of the female researchers in the field are experiencers, *none* of the males are. It is the women who have probed the deepest into the aftereffects, developing how-to techniques and manuals, and seeking ways to create positive, new relationships. The men have been more concerned with contrasts and with what that might mean scientifically. As the women have pointed out the negatives, the men have spoken almost entirely of the positives. And, of course, it is the men who have published more and been paid larger royalty checks, even though the women have conducted more interviews with more people and worked in greater depth for longer periods of time with less reward. Male researchers are more inclined toward number crunching and the phenomenal aspects of the experience. Female researchers get more into feelings, adjustments, and the human angle.

Yes, we have an anniversary coming. There are over eighty researchers of the near-death phenomenon today, and that's just in the United States alone, it doesn't include dozens in other countries—and their numbers are growing. From this effort is emerging a neutral model anyone can study that may indeed be representative of a breakthrough into higher consciousness and the next stage of human evolution.

Yet, I wonder about that.

It seems to me that what's really going on is—*species adaptation*.

All species of life on this planet either adapt to changing environments or die out. Every biology student knows that, so consider this:

- Most people today recognize not only the color blue but can distinguish fine gradations of varied colors and hues. This was rare before 1850.
- Most people can now dream in Technicolor; many are lucid dreamers (self-aware while dreaming)—an aspect of the dreamstate thought impossible for anyone to achieve at the turn of this century.
- Females today begin their menses earlier than either their mothers or their grandmothers. Males are having wet dreams at an earlier age, as well. (It is thought that artificial light, vitamin supplements, and better health care are responsible for this.)

And now, when people *need* to be more flexible, to be able to thrive on change, to have brains that can reason and intuit with equal skill, to have bodies that can adjust to fickle climates, and to have energy levels that can mix and merge efficiently with technological equipment... at this exact moment in history when we *need* people who can increase their intelligence and extend their faculties and enhance their perception without lengthy training... what happens? Milions are going through transformations of consciousness that prepare them physically as well as psychologically to successfully adapt to the demands of our new global society.

Forget New Age buzzwords for a moment and look again. Our species, us, we're *adapting*, and we're doing it now because our world, our environment, is changing so quickly and so radically that either we adapt or we're out.

Einstein was a lousy student, nearly failing in school, yet he could think creatively. Our challenge is to develop Einsteinian creativity, and we can and we are. And it won't take another hundred years, unless we reject the opportunity at hand.

What prepares us for a global society will be a worldwide revamping of the role of education, the place of women, and the need for political leadership. And with the pressure this change will bring, along comes a global phenomenon, not just of the near-death experience, but of a whole potpourri of spiritually transforming episodes to feed our hungry souls . . . and just in the nick of time for millennium fever.

Conditions are now ripe for anyone to be grist for a great "God-pitch." David Koresh and his Rancho Apocalypse were just the beginning. Self-appointed "messengers of God" are popping up everywhere, even in Russia, to wave a banner of "truth" in these, the so-called latter days. And not only because a millennium is ending, but because of something much bigger: One hundred ninety-nine centuries ago Jesus came to plant a seed which is now, in the decade of the 1990s, beginning to sprout. His words went something like this, "All these things I do, you can do too, and more also." He wasn't kidding.

So here we have a grass-roots movement, unplanned and without leadership, of people discovering who they really are and responding to the need for change. And they're doing it on their own because it "feels" right. And their numbers are awesome.

To understand this, study the near-death experience, for it reveals more about life than it does about death and what it reveals is staggering.

Don't forget, though, that the experience is merely *STEP ONE*. After the initial lightshow and the illumination that follows, there comes inspiring upliftment and enthusiastic vigor; then a letdown at the frustration of trying to apply new wisdom atop old prejudices, depression, the surfacing of repressed or suppressed guilts and fears, confusion and disorientation followed by feelings of being overwhelmed or abandoned. Eventually, there is a surrender to The Truth one gained during the experience. This comes about through the reidentification of one's place in the scheme of things; reeducation; healing; acceptance of personal responsibility/accountability; experimentation; and, at last, the realization of what is worthwhile in life and what is not. Then there is renewal and the conscious choice to live in accordance with Higher Laws.

The Berlin Wall fell and so did the Iron Curtain, leaving the exhilaration from freedom's cry echoing around the world. Our prayers for peace have been answered, or have they? Nationalism and the surfacing of repressed and suppressed anger and hatred is now on the rise, and there is depression and confusion and disorientation and fear. What began as a miracle has become a nightmare.

Does this pattern sound familiar? It should. That's why The Myth of Amazing Grace has a place in the human psyche, because myths educate and empower and help us to heal.

I hope every near-death experiencer in the world comes forward and speaks out. This is the time we have been waiting for and sharing our stories is what most of us feel led to do. I hope the marketplace of books and ideas is flooded, literally flooded, with first-hand accounts and research findings. But I also hope that near-death survivors will refrain from one-upmanship, as there is *no single experiencer* who qualifies as a "super star" or as a revelator of "the real truth." Each has a valuable contribution to make that is well worth considering. If individuals tell their *whole* stories—the challenges as well as the miracles—the world's people will truly have a model of transformation to learn from that *can* make a tremendous difference for each and every person no matter where located.

We are leaving the age of believing (which fosters suffering), and coming into the age of knowing (which fosters restoration and renewal). It is the Age of Flowers...when the creative fire of our souls is freed.

John in Chapter 13, Verse 35 of the Christian Bible said it best: "By this shall all men know that ye are my disciples, if ye have love one to another."

The two questions most asked of individuals when they reach The Other Side of death are: "Whom have you served? Whom have you loved?"

Stop right now.

Pretend it's your turn.

How will you answer those two questions?

You do not have to go through a near-death experience to be transformed. There are as many different ways to do it as there are stars in the sky. The following four people went through such a change, and met their own souls in the process. I highly recommend the books they wrote that share what they discovered:

MARLO MORGAN, *Mutant Message Downunder*, available from MM Co., P.O. Box 100, Lees Summit, MO, 64063; (816) 246-6365.

MICHAEL J. ROADS, *Talking With Nature*, available in bookstores from H J Kramer Inc., Tiburon, CA, came out in 1985.

JENNIFER BORCHERS, *Facing Myself*, available from A.R.E. Press, P.O. Box 656, Virginia Beach, VA, 23451-0656; 1-800-723-1112.

DAN MILLMAN, *Way of the Peaceful Warrior*, available in bookstores from H J Kramer Inc., Tiburon, CA, came out in 1980.

A N N O U N C E M E N T
A Near-Death Measurement Study Research Fund
Has Been Established
Your Contribution Is Solicited

Current methods of researching the near-death phenomenon are no longer adequate to address the growing needs in the field. A central computer database, international protocols, and tested psychological measurement studies must now be undertaken.

To accomplish this, the International Association for Near-Death Studies has agreed to establish a special fund and solicit contributions. Bruce Greyson, M.D., Research Director of IANDS and editor of the *The Journal for Near-Death Studies*, will help to oversee organization and direction of the project. Five million dollars is projected for startup costs. Moneys are to be spent for:

Establishing a central working committee of professionals from varied disciplines.

The investigation of current near-death research; identification of accomplishments, problem areas, and future needs pursuant to launching expanded field-interview programs.

The establishment of international research methodologies, creation and testing of laboratory controls for physical-measurement studies of aftereffects and electrical sensitivity.

The design and implementation of kits for researchers, educators, experiencers, and the general public, plus a centralized computer database to be available for access nationally and internationally.

No contribution is too large or too small. The project will begin when sufficient moneys are received. If moneys fall short, IANDS will utilize whatever funds are raised for work approved by its Board of Directors. Contributions are tax deductible.

Send your personal check or money order in U.S. dollars to:

NDE Research Fund, c/o IANDS
P.O. Box 502
East Windsor Hill, CT 06028
(203) 528-5144

III

Steps Beyond

APPENDIX I

Spiritual Emergence/ Emergencies

Every mystic born has been a specimen of the man to come. His self-imposed penances and his religious beliefs were the creation of his culture, faith, and the environment around him. But his vivid descriptions of the new visions gained, the new worlds unfolded, and his basic teachings about the way to be followed to reach the same state of perception were the outcome of knowledge gained in the new dimension of consciousness to which he had attained.

—Gopi Krishna

Some of My Experiences

During the first year and a half after my near-death episodes, three strangers came forward to help me and we became close friends. These people were Terry and Elizabeth Macinata, and Tom Huber (he has since changed his name to Thomas Shawnodese Wind). The four of us would hold "sessions" whereby we would gather to test out different psychological counseling techniques, explore "other" dimensions, role-play, or do whatever it took to probe deeper into the depths of the mind.

219

We became "soul travelers." I called us "cousins." I am forever grateful for the companionship they offered, and for all we did together. Those sessions helped me to gain clarity and objectivity about myself and what happened to me.

While involved with my "cousins," I launched a campaign to relearn everything I could get my hands on. Thus, I became a student in a multitude of beginner classes on varied subjects, including cooking and homemaking.

I also went on veritable binges of experimentation, examining and reexamining what was in my environment. Everything from pots and pans to underarm deodorant was suspect. I even wrote to commercial manufacturers for research reports about varied substances and production processes, and then had these checked out in a private laboratory. I called people and met with them in my self-styled investigation of truth-in-packaging. I questioned every manufacturer's label and challenged every claim. To say I was obsessed about this would be an understatement.

When I moved from Boise, Idaho, to the Washington, D.C., area, this driving quest intensified. That's because, within three months of moving, although I ate the same kinds of food at the same time of day cooked in the same manner as I had back in Idaho, I lost substantial weight, my monthly menses went from a healthy, bright-red flow to a sickly greenish-yellow trickle, I could not maintain body warmth, and, finally, I passed out on the subway. Three doctors confirmed the problem—I was starving to death!

It took awhile and cost me a small fortune to regain the health I had lost. Part of the problem was the fact that, at the age of forty-one, I was for the first time in my life relying entirely on a grocery store for all my food needs. Another part of the problem was the food itself and the soil that food came from. As you can well guess, I traced the food I had eaten, drove out and interviewed what farmers I could, and participated in soil analysis. What I discovered was that the degree of damage that has been done to soils in the eastern part of this country from acid rain, overreliance on chemicals, and other unhealthy farming practices, is far greater than admitted or reported. Needless to say, I made immediate changes in what I consumed.

But my biggest problem, as I later learned, was the extent to which my own physical body had altered after my near-death experiences. Not only had I become more sensitive to stimuli, I had also become ultrasensitive to food and drink, and chemicals.

I mention this to you—all the relearning I put myself through—for a reason, and that reason is this: Anyone who undergoes an impactual transformative experience changes to some degree throughout *all* levels of his or her being—physical, mental, emotional, and spiritual. It is a fallacy to think that such an event merely alters your attitude. Far from it. Certainly, not everyone goes through what I did; but for the majority, the aftermath of a consciousness shift can be disorienting...and the aftereffects can change you more than you realize.

Here is a brief list of some of my own changes:

Hair and nails now grow faster, blood pressure is lower.

Muscle strength decreased while energy levels increased.

Sun tolerance decreased. The first seven years I would turn bright orange and become nauseated and dizzy if exposed to direct sunlight for over fifteen minutes. The orange coloration finally ceased, but sun sensitivity remains, although I can now handle longer exposure time.

Both temporal lobe areas of head thicker and more spongy than before, and so sensitive even finger pressure cannot be tolerated.

Body clock reversed to mornings (was a night person).

No awareness of tiring at first, would suddenly collapse with the onset of sleep. It took several years before I could adequately control sleep urges and withstand longer hours awake and active.

Food flushes out of digestive system within fifteen to twenty minutes if in disagreement with my body or tainted.

Jaws and teeth hurt if I say an untruth or hear a falsehood.

Hearing range has increased and I have become more tonal. Example: I now hear pain (not just feel it), hear paintings (not just see them), and follow tones when traveling. But can no longer handle "mixed" sounds, like having both the television set and the radio on at the same time.

Taste and smell more acute, can also taste words and feelings. Regularly display synesthesia (multiple sensing).

Developed allergies to chemical medications to the degree that I switched to homeopathy, herbs, and natural remedies. I can no longer tolerate most pharmaceuticals.

Would suddenly quit breathing for no reason whatsoever. Body would continue to operate as if nothing was amiss, with the longest such episode lasting eight minutes. Lasted one year. I have no idea what caused or ended it.

Had difficulty at first handling the great sweeps of joy that would suddenly overwhelm me. Meditation and prayer enabled me to redirect this ecstatic energy into modes of healing and help for other people.

Memory seemed disconnected and hard to access at first, as if it belonged to someone else or somewhere else, and energy flows were fragmented. Exercises and effort corrected this.

Much more sensitive now to any fluctuations in air pressure and electromagnetic fields. Can no longer wear a wristwatch.

Look younger, feel younger. Eyes and skin brighter.

No longer store stress in my body in the same manner as before. Can become "stressed," but it's easier now to release tension.

Cognitive abilities reversed. Where once analytical, now intuitive. Where once intuitive, now analytical.

Intelligence increased and I developed an insatiable hunger for knowledge. Once memory disconnection and energy fragmentation were corrected, my ability to concentrate increased significantly. My mind now works like a laser beam and I can completely lose myself in whatever I am thinking about or doing.

The "newness" of life doesn't wear off. No matter how many times I do something, hear or see it, I find myself caught up in a childlike sense of wonder and curiosity. Absorption levels have reached such a high degree that I have learned to be very selective about what movies and television shows I watch. Nothing is mundane anymore.

Am now more in tune with soul levels than with human levels.

Had to quit going to funerals. Could see the "dearly departed" enjoying his or her funeral and couldn't stop laughing.

Some of What I've Learned

Just because you have changed does not mean anything is "wrong" with you. Remember that. But if you have changed to any extent, also remember that it is now your responsibility to stabilize and integrate those changes. You begin to do this as I did by looking around and asking questions, then taking action. Positives and negatives are determined by your response, *not* by what happened to you. You can change your life at *any* stage of its living—and very much for the better. Anyone can.

Validation becomes an overriding issue after one has shifted consciousness, though, and I want to admit that. There are endless questions with no ready answers: Was it true? Did it really happen? Can I believe it? Can I trust the experience and what it reveals? Can I trust myself?

There are no signposts along the pathway to transformation, but there are precedents, stories, legends, and a few teachers here and there. Yet, no one and nothing can make much difference until you finally come to realize that the only person who can ever validate you *is you, yourself*. No one else can do it for you. Once you know this, the question switches from Is it real? to What am I going to do about this?

I learned that there is a tremendous difference between the challenge to LET GO AND FLOW and the invitation to LET GO LET GOD, and that difference is worth noting:

LET GO AND FLOW denotes a time when you allow yourself to be swept away on unseen tides, bereft of landmarks or guides, and subject to ever-changing floods of emotion and thought. It can be healthy to experience this type of immersion into the cosmic breath, the unbridled flow of pure energy and complete detachment, but too much of it can lead to excessive disorientation and confusion, destroying anything constructive that might result.

LET GO LET GOD is an equal time of detachment and disorientation, but putting God in charge invariably leads you to specific places, people, and events that offer a balanced and wholesome way to change and grow. Yes, landmarks alter here, too, sometimes radically, but there is a sense of direction and purpose, a steady knowing and faith, also the aftereffects are easier to stabilize.

Neither focus will save you from yourself, but while the former discards all structure as meaningless, the latter embraces whatever might be meaningful. With LET GO AND FLOW no one and nothing is in charge. With LET GO LET GOD there is direct or indirect guidance. Life structures alter with either focus, and the individual is never the same again.

Another way to consider the transformational process and the surrender one finally comes to make to A Higher Power is presented in the following chart that compares the psychological approach to that of the spiritual. Diane K. Pike of the Teleos Institute arrived at this comparison and published the chart in the Institute's Summer/Fall 1991 issue of *Emerging* magazine. I am grateful to Diane for allowing me to reprint her comparison here. (The chart title is my attempt to identify the chart's contents.)

The Transformational Process
Psychological/Spiritual Profiles of Self

In Psychological Work

1. You are identified with the personality. You feel/know: I am my feelings, my thoughts, my beliefs, my memories.

2. You approach things subjectively, from your own point of view. You may recognize that others see your situation differently, but that seems irrelevant to your dilemma.

3. You work problems through from the inside of them. You reenter memories of experiences, recapture your experi-

In Spiritual Work

1. You are identified with the observer, the witness, the power-to-be-conscious. You feel/know: When I am conscious, I have creative jurisdiction over my life. You embrace the personality as your vehicle of expression, but do not feel limited to it.

2. You approach things impersonally. You are not totally identified with your personality even when very involved in life circumstances. You view your personality as one among others.

3. You view problems as opportunities to learn and grow. You seek to see them in the light of an expanded picture of your life

ences, relive them, and seek to find a way through them to the new.

and the world around you. You do not find it helpful to dwell on your feelings and thoughts, but rather you look for creative action you can take.

4. Feelings are important in and of themselves. You seek to identify feelings and to give them expression by talking about them or acting them out.

4. You use your feelings to guide you into action. You do not talk about them to others. Rather, you act upon them.

5. You believe your feelings are evoked by the persons and circumstances with which you interact. You get caught in reactions.

5. You know that your feelings are internal messages, from you to you. You know you have choices about what to feel and that your feelings are not caused by any external circumstance. You do not allow reactions or habit patterns to govern.

6. You need and want to be heard and understood right where you are, and until you are, you cannot move on.

6. You are eager to see things from a wider perspective than the one you first experienced. You welcome other points of view in order to put your own into proper perspective.

7. You believe your choices are limited by both the past and the present.

7. You know you are free to make new choices in every new moment of awareness.

8. When you ask for help, you rely on the other to fulfill the observer role: that is, to be objective. This frees you to go deeper into your subjective experience.

8. When you ask for help, you do not abdicate your observer position. You retain creative jurisdiction over your life and take in the help as a supplement.

In Psychological Work	In Spiritual Work
9. You are not able to let go of a dynamic until the energy of it finishes in you and through you.	9. You are able to withdraw your energy at will from relationships, situations, and interactions. You call this "letting go" or "surrender to what is."
10. You view spiritual insights and solutions as coming from "outside" your life circumstances, from "beyond" you.	10. You are aware that spiritual insights and help come from within. You open to recognize, receive, and act upon them. You know that the pattern working within you brings your life into being, and you seek to align yourself with that Will.

Adjusting to the aftereffects of the transformative process is similar to the culture shock one feels when moving to a foreign country. Some people adjust readily and enjoy the trip. Others are traumatized. Because I intimately understand what is involved here, I offer the rest of this section to those individuals who could use a little help.

A Crisis Arising from Rigid Attitudes and Beliefs

Fundamentalists of any type or persuasion are usually people who cannot or will not tolerate ambiguity and uncertainty in life. Their way of coping with change is often based on a need to retreat behind fantasy models of good and evil, quick fixes, dogmatism, and flat-out denials of any viewpoint different from their own. As in the children's story *The Emperor's New Clothes*, once a contradictory undeniable truth is revealed to them a crisis of belief frequently follows. Spiritual emergencies result more often from this type of situation than from the brainshift associated with a new emerging consciousness. Richard Yao, a former Wall Street attorney, founded the support group Fundamentalists Anonymous in 1985 to help people break away from the rigidity of fixed religious beliefs. His book about this is well worth reading: *There Is a Way Out,* published by F.A. Communications, New York City, 1987.

A Crisis Arising from a New Emerging Consciousness

Since modern psychiatry does not officially recognize the difference between a psychotic breakdown and a spiritual breakthrough, here are some excellent books on the subject to help you deal with this situation and find personal solutions.

Avalanche: Heretical Reflections on the Dark and the Light, W. Brugh Joy, M.D. New York, NY; Ballantine Books, 1990.
Call of Spiritual Emergency, The, Emma Bragdon, Ph.D. New York, NY; Harper & Row, 1990.
Coming Into Our Own: Understanding the Adult Metamorphosis, Mark Gerzon. New York, NY; Delacorte Press, 1992.
Sourcebook for Helping People in Spiritual Emergency, A, Emma Bragdon, Ph.D. Soquel, CA; Lightening Up Press, 1988.
Spiritual Emergency: When a Personal Transformation Becomes a Crisis, edited by Stanislav Grof, M.D. and Christina Grof. Los Angeles, CA; J.P. Tarcher, 1989.

Here are some other books that may be helpful. Notice that the last two in the adult section are "home-grown" editions, published by the authors. I have found that sometimes less commercial books are remarkably practical and to-the-point.

Adults

Art of Being Yourself, The, Frank E. Richelieu. Available from Science of Mind Communications, P.O. Box 75127, Los Angeles, CA 90075.
Embracing Ourselves: The Voice Dialogue Manual, Hal Stone, Ph.D. and Sidra Winkelman, Ph.D. San Rafael, CA; New World Library.
Four-Fold Way, The: Walking the Paths of the Warrior, Teacher, Healer, and Visionary, Angeles Arrien. San Francisco, CA; Harper, 1993.
Helping Heaven Happen, Donald Curtis. York Beach, ME; Samuel Weiser, Inc., 1992.

Homecoming: Reclaiming and Championing Your Inner Child, John Bradshaw. New York, NY; Bantam Books, 1992.

Instead of Therapy: Help Yourself Change and Change the Help You're Getting, Tom Rusk, M.D. Carson, CA; Hay House, 1991.

Power of Positive Attitudes, The, written and published by Ernie Panza, Jr., D.O., 804 Merrimac Trail, Williamsburg, VA 23185.

Seeing Through Your Illusions, Paul K. Chivington. Denver, CO; G-L Publications, 1983.

Self-Esteem or Self-Abuse? and *Take Charge! A Guide to Feeling Good*, both books written and published by W.V. Johnston, Ed.D., P.O. Box 3336, Gresham, OR 97030.

Thirst for Wholeness, The, Christina Grof. San Francisco, CA; Harper, 1993.

Where Two Worlds Touch: Spiritual Rites of Passage, Gloria D. Karpinski. New York, NY; Ballantine Books, 1990.

Your Life: Why It Is the Way It Is and What You Can Do About It, Bruce McArthur. Virginia Beach, VA; A.R.E. Press, 1993.

Children

Positive Self-Talk for Children, Douglas Bloch. New York, NY; Bantam Books, 1993.

Spiritual Emergence Network (SEN)

SEN operates an information and referral service, answering calls and letters from people throughout the world who are interested in, or who are experiencing, nonordinary states of consciousness. Most of the volunteers who staff the phone line have themselves experienced intense periods of nonordinary states or "spiritual emergence/emergencies." They are uniquely able to convey a sense of trust and offer referrals to books and periodicals, and to practicing therapists who will be sensitive to the needs of the caller. Whether you are someone who wants help, or a professional desiring to become a part of the Network, you can call or write:

The Spiritual Emergence Network
5905 Soquel Drive, Suite 650
Soquel, CA 95073
1-800-788-4084, and/or (408) 688-4745

or

The Spiritual Emergence Network
1010 Doyle, Suite 10
Menlo Park, CA 94025
(415) 327-2776

Other Organizations Able to Facilitate
the Transformation Process

A.R.E. Clinic
A division of the Association for Research and Enlightenment, this clinic utilizes only holistic measures to enhance healing, growth, and change. Their Temple Beautiful program is outstanding. Write or call: A.R.E. Clinic, 4018 North 40th Street, Phoenix, AZ 85018; (602) 955-7729 or (602) 955-0551. Inquiries are welcome.

Smith Mountain Lake Retreat Center
Operated by Margaret Fields Kean (herself a near-death survivor) and staffed by a number of professional health-care practitioners, this center offers many services for individuals or groups through a balanced program of healing and learning opportunities. Their Results System is especially geared to help those in the process of transformation integrate the aftereffects constructively. Their program of repatterning left and right brain hemispheres so each can work more harmoniously with the other is excellent. Medical supervision is available through the Richmond Health & Wellness Center if needed. Write or call: Smith Mountain Lake Healing and Retreat Center, Route 1, Box 77A, Huddleston, VA 24104; (703) 297-1828.

Sun Valley Institute
Directed by near-death experiencer R. Lia Newsome, Ph.D., Sun Valley Institute provides a safe environment where integration can be facilitated following a transformational episode. Week-long workshops are held in a setting of small cabins next to geothermal springs. A healthy diet of live foods combined with Spiritual Emergence Balancing Programs give total purifying and cleansing of body, mind, and spirit. Newsome and her staff are personally and professionally experienced in helping individuals move through the tears, humor, and awe of

what happened to them so new wisdom for everyday living can be gained. Workshop schedules are geared to demand, so contact well in advance. Write or call: Sun Valley Institute, P.O. Box 2553, Sun Valley, ID 83353; (208) 726-2121.

Teleos Institute

Two programs offered by Teleos Institute are especially helpful in grounding and centering individuals undergoing the transformational process. Life As A Waking Dream™ is an introspective method for recognizing meaning in everyday events. Based on ageless wisdom teachings and modern dream interpretation, this reflective process helps an individual to see overall life patterns and define life purpose. The Theatre of Life™ is a dynamic experiential program designed to give a person practice in exercising creative jurisdiction over his or her life. During sixteen-day intensives in a small-group setting with two facilitators, participants come to know the real Self as The Player (Higher Self). Operated by Arleen Lorrance and Diane K. Pike (both authors and teachers of long-standing repute), the Teleos Institute recently moved from San Diego to Scottsdale. Write or call: Teleos Institute, P.O. Box 12009-418, Scottsdale, AZ 85267; (602) 948-1800.

The Monroe Institute

The Monroe Institute is a nonprofit educational and research organization devoted to the following premise: Focused consciousness contains all solutions to the questions of human existence. Internationally known for its work on the effects of sound wave forms on human behavior, the institute discovered that nonverbal audio patterns have dramatic effects on stages of consciousness. With that established, they offer an incredible range of classroom and participatory programs—all supervised and all based on solid professional ethics and experience. Programs cover sleep-restorative training, psychotherapy, pain control, music therapy, expanded awareness, out-of-body traveling, and Gateway Voyages. Individuals dealing with the transformational process will benefit from their programs, and the availability of a large selection of audio-cassette tapes. Write or call: The Monroe Institute, Route 1, Box 175, Faber, VA 22938; (804) 361-1252.

Specials

A Holistic Resources Directory—A comprehensive directory of alternative health-care professionals can be obtained from Holistic Resources, Inc., P.O. Box 25450, Seattle, WA 98125-2350; (206) 523-2101. Contact them directly.

An Individual Practitioner of Note—Kathy Forti (Powers), author of the only children's book yet written on the near-death experience (*The Door to the Secret City*), is more than qualified to address the special needs of individuals who have had a spiritual emergence/emergency, especially if they are near-death survivors. And she is very good with children. She is a licensed psychotherapist in the state of Virginia. You may contact her through: Virginia Psychology Services, 328 Office Square Lane, Suite 204, Virginia Beach, VA 23462; (804) 456-5527.

Kundalini/Ku Breakthroughs

Kundalini/Ku energies transform the nervous system and the endocrine glands. They promote the rising of the creative life force within the individual. Since physical sensations can sometimes be confusing, here's a list of what is traditional to the experience (given so you won't think you're crazy):

muscles twitching, cramping, or spasms
tremors, shaking, convulsions
prickly, itching, tingling, or vibrating sensations under the skin
rhythmic, spasmodic, or graceful involuntary movements
sensations of intense heat or cold
blockages in the back, throat, base of skull, or head
surges of tremendous high vibrational energy in the spine or throughout the system.

Don't let this list scare you, but do be informed. To slow these energies down until you can either obtain assistance or learn how to manage them yourself, try the following:

Either stop meditating for a while, or redirect your energy after a meditative session to others in the form of healing prayer. Always affirm that these prayers are for the highest good of all concerned in accordance with Divine Order. (This puts God in charge, not your ego.)

Eat meat (and that includes red meat on a temporary basis, if you can), grain dishes, solid vegetables (especially if below-ground varieties), and dairy products. Avoid salads and incomplete proteins until your energies are under control. Eat less, more often.

Stop using sugar. If you need sweeteners, use limited quantities of honey and fruit.

No spices, stimulants, alcohol, or tobacco.

Engage in manual labor and/or exercise programs. Housecleaning, gardening, digging ditches, scrubbing walls—all are wonderful ways to redirect and manage this kind of energy.

Give yourself ample time to think, take walks, contemplate, relax. Get plenty of rest and drink a lot of water.

Avoid stressful demands and/or environments for as long as possible.

Don't resist the changes that are happening to you; flow with them for awhile.

Ask in prayer for positive guidance, knowing that you will receive it, and you will.

Adopt an attitude of gratitude, and laugh more. Humor is an amazing healer and balancer.

Take up some type of creative endeavor, craft, or hobby—and enjoy!

Elements in the Process of Awakening

In brief, here are the elements natural to a mystical awakening and/or the beginning steps to the process of transformation. These were given to me by Tricia Nickel, M.A., a family counselor at 3702 Mt. Diablo Blvd., Lafayette, CA 94549; (510) 283-3940. She is also an astrologer and has found a correlation between these elements and what happens when an individual deals with what is known in the trade as The Neptune Factor.

Alterations of thinking
Disturbed time sense

Loss of control
Change in emotional expression
Body image change
Perceptual distortions
Change in the meaning of one's life

All this is absolutely normal, and, if they are signs of a true awakening, will lead to things wondrous and exciting and joyful and uplifting. I call awakenings growth events.

Growth events come in all shapes and sizes. They can be negative or positive or both. We can have repeats if we miss one, or we can receive a whole series of them, one right after another. Some examples of growth events are: losing when we were certain we would win, or winning when we were certain we would lose; being forced to slow down in life when we wanted to go faster, or being speeded up when we wanted to go slowly; suffering when we wanted to prosper, or prospering when we were unprepared or even unwilling.

Growth events, all of them, give us an opportunity to face our inner selves and "clean house," to glimpse the collective mind and higher realities, to expand beyond limiting ideas, to discover the impossible and experience the "paranormal," to become in some way transformed. As lightning fertilizes plant growth, enlightenment "fertilizes" human growth.

Life insists on growth and change. If we block these urges, something will happen to unblock them. If we forget common sense and balance, something will happen to help us remember. You can count on it!

Some Tips About Natural Lithium

Everyone needs lithium, absolutely everyone. Most of us obtain enough from our food and environment to give this trace mineral nary a thought. However, with extensive computer use, overly stressed lives, pollution, and transformations like the near-death experience, one of the first elements lost in our physical bodies is the lithium necessary for us to function healthfully and think clearly. There is a tendency among medical professionals to use the pharmaceutical version of lithium in ways that may not always be in the best interests of near-death survivors. (Remember how sensitive experiencers often become.)

Because of this, and because we could all benefit from some fresh viewpoints on the subject, I want to focus on a more holistic approach to lithium and how it appears to function in the natural world.

Natural lithium is a nonmetallic mineral, a cell salt. There have been twelve cell salts used in the past as homeopathic remedies. Lithium has recently been recognized as the thirteenth. According to the older traditions of natural healers, the task of lithium is to bond spirit in matter. Without sufficient lithium, it is said that spirit does not balance properly in manifestation. Animals, plants, soil, humans—all must have lithium to maintain their infusion of light (spirit). Do not mistake natural lithium for the pharmaceutical product, as the manufactured substance is bonded to sodium carbonate.

Natural lithium is a common part of everyday life and is readily found in the diet of most people. Should lithium levels deplete for any reason, they are usually easy to replace. For instance, in the plant kingdom, it is known that lemons and limes are rich sources of the trace mineral: Squeeze a little fresh lemon or lime into your drinking water from time to time—once every day should be plenty—and/or use it in cooking and food preparation. In the mineral kingdom, lepidolite is a rich source, followed by kunzite and rosy tourmaline. Wear lepidolite as you would jewelry, or just have it around—perhaps in your pocket as a "worry stone" you can touch on occasion. (I have mine near where I sit at my computer.)

According to research on odors released in 1989 by Shimizu, a large architectural, engineering, and construction firm and the developer of Aromatherapeutic Environmental Fragrancing Systems, they found that if lemon scent is pumped into business and manufacturing environments, human errors are reduced over fifty percent. (Lemon is the only scent they have discovered that influences workers to this degree.) The reason for such a remarkable drop in errors, as least in my opinion, is that *any* form of real lemon or lemon scent contains lithium. Even in small doses, I have observed that lithium perks up the brain and centers and balances the human energy systems and emotions. It is subtle but effective.

(Of interest here is the medical fact that only the sense of smell directly accesses the limbic system—affecting memory and brain function. The others are indirect. Hence, people respond quickly to odors. This is especially true with near-death survivors since it is typical for them to have enhanced senses of smell after they revive. It seems to me that the correlation between natural lithium and the limbic system and the near-death experience is obvious.)

But there is more to know about what seems to be the behavior of lithium in its natural state.

According to Haroldine in her book *Lithium, Nature In Harmony* [45], if an individual is in a negative mood, angry or fearful, the lithium in his or her body transmutes mainly into potassium. Since potassium has an odor, she conjectures that the old adage, "Dogs smell fear," may have a basis in fact; the dogs most likely smell the potassium. If an individual is in a positive, joyful mood, or is meditating, she states that the lithium in that person's body transmutes into the mineral beryllium—recognized by some researchers as the "fuel" of higher consciousness and higher brain development.

(There is a type of crystal available now, and it is quite expensive, called phenacite. It is touted as "the" stone to use for developing higher consciousness. Simply said, phenacite is a rich source of beryllium. Numbers of people are buying and using this crystal without proper guidance or preparation, and many of them are having problems with it. Phenacite supposedly expands and accelerates higher brain development; but without the "bridge" of grounding and balance the lithium offers, the "short-cut" it seems to offer can be more delusional than constructive. Care in its use is recommended.)

To my way of thinking, *lithium is the key*, the "bridge" spirit appears to utilize in bonding with matter, and magenta is its color. Symbolically, magenta represents the phase shift that separates one advancement through the various phases of spiritual development from the next of a higher vibration. Magenta, then, as a color frequency, helps energy to balance (cohere) before it shifts from one growth phase to another. (Wear clothes accented with magenta or use it in decorations, on occasion, and see if it makes any difference in how you feel.)

Regardless of how you view it, the trace mineral *lithium is essential and necessary*. And there are easy, inexpensive ways to augment its effectiveness in our lives for better health.

Storytelling as an Aid in the Transformational Process

Mythology, legends, and lore comprise some of the most helpful sources that chronicle the transformation process. Storytelling not only makes this immense font of wisdoms more available and immediate, it often becomes an invaluable tool with aiding in the challenge of integration as we each share our own stories . Here are some practical and enjoyable ways to utilize this skill:

Awakening the Hidden Storyteller: How to Build a Storytelling Tradition in Your Family, Robin Moore. Boston, MA; Shambhala, 1991.

Sacred Stories: A Celebration of the Power of Stories to Transform and Heal, edited by Charles Simpkinson and Anne Simpkinson. San Francisco, CA; Harper, 1993.

Semiannual Newsletter—*Heart and Soul, Storytelling for Spiritual Growth and Healing*. For more information, contact: Carol McCormick, 625 Windemere Drive, Plymouth, MN 55441.

Answering the Call to Be of Service

The Call of Service, Robert Coles. New York, NY; Houghton Mifflin, 1993.

Quarterly Magazine—*Who Cares*. For information or to subscribe, contact: Who Cares, 1511 K Street, NW, Suite 1042, Washington, DC 20005.

Answering the Call to Learn More

If you are interested in where you can go to attend graduate schools that teach dream interpretation or spiritual philosophies, or want specialized training in the use of spiritual disciplines in psychotherapy, there is a directory now available listing such schools. It is called the *Directory to Alternate Graduate Schools*. To obtain one, write to the magazine *Common Boundary*, 4304 East-West Highway, Bethesda, MD 20814, and request information.

If you are interested in pursuing scholarship outside of academe, look for the book *The Independent Scholar's Handbook* by Ronald Gross, published by Ten Speed Press. You should have no difficulty finding it at your favorite bookstore, or placing an order for it.

Answering the Call for an Ecumenical Ministry

In 1981, Gelberman (a Jewish rabbi), Jon Mundy (a Methodist minister), and Giles Spoonhour (a Catholic priest) began what has become a growing international ecumenical movement. It is nondenominational and embraces all the world's great religious traditions. Seminary training and ordination are offered. If you are interested in pursuing this, contact: Rabbi Gelberman, Interfaith Fellowship, 7 West 96th Street, New York, NY 10025; (212) 866-7395. Inquiries are welcome.

Should you wish to attend an Interfaith Fellowship service and are visiting in New York City, stop by at 165 West 57th Street (across from Carnegie Hall) at 11:00 A.M. on Sundays. The services, operated by Reverends Diane Berke and Jon Mundy, are some of the most inspiring I have ever attended. Mundy is a near-death-like experiencer. For more information, contact them at: Interfaith Ministries, 459 Carol Drive, Monroe, NY 10950-9565; (914) 783-0383.

For Additional Material on Reincarnation

Since the majority of those who undergo a transformational episode come to accept reincarnation as fact, not theory, here are some sources and resources that may prove helpful with the subject:

Beyond the Ashes: Cases of Reincarnation From the Holocaust, Rabbi Yonassan Gershom. Virginia Beach, VA; A.R.E. Press, 1992.

Driving Your Own Karma, a book of humor about reincarnation by Swami Beyondananda. Rochester, VT; Destiny Books, 1989.

Eye of the Centaur: A Visionary Guide Into Past Lives, Barbara Hand Clow. St. Paul, MN; Llewellyn Publications, 1986.

Initiation, Elisabeth Haich. Palo Alto, CA; Seed Center, 1974.

In My Next Life I'm Gonna Be the Princess, a book of cartoons by Chuck Vadun. Available from Valley of the Sun Publishing, Box 38, Malibu, CA 90265.

Many Lives, Many Masters, Brian Weiss, M.D. New York, NY; Simon & Schuster, 1988.

Search for Omm Sety, The, Jonathan Cott. New York, NY; Doubleday, 1987.

The Journey Within, Your Adventure Into Time is the name given to workshops conducted by the hypnotherapist, Henry Leo Bolduc. Filled with sensitivity and good humor, Bolduc's techniques are among the best I have encountered for helping people to explore possible past life "memories," activate hidden creative potentials, and facilitate the pathway to spiritual development. His gift is in enabling people to do this by themselves in a healthy, positive way. For more information, write: Adventures Into Time, P.O. Box 88, Independence, VA 24348.

The Association for Past-Life Research and Therapies is a professional organization with over eight hundred members. Anyone can join but the emphasis is on using past-life regression techniques in the therapeutic environment. Hypnosis is really an altered state of consciousness that enables an individual to deepen his or her awareness. Whether or not reincarnational memories are true, the psychological benefit of the regression experience is remarkable. Contact the association at P.O. Box 20151, Riverside, CA 92516-0151; (909) 784-1570.

Research Methodology

The growth of the human mind is still high
adventure, in many ways the highest adventure
on earth.

—Norman Cousins

So many people have asked me to be more specific about my
research, how I do it, the questions I ask, statistical findings, etc.,
that I have created this section for those who are curious.

My interviewing style with near-death survivors changed
quickly once I realized that none of them, including me, could
recognize the extent of their changes—unless someone else
pointed this out for them, as my daughter Natalie Rowell did for
me. Thus, I began to interview significant others whenever I
could, especially within the home setting. This proved to be a
wise decision. Attempting to view the phenomenon from as
many different angles as possible not only enlarged my findings
considerably, but it enabled me to see myself "reflected back"
from the many eyes who studied me as I studied them. This was
extremely therapeutic—and then some!

Knowing that personal bias could jeopardize anything I did, I
dealt with that issue by playing dumb a lot. That is to say, I asked
as many open-ended and unstructured questions as possible,
trying not to reveal my identity or intent any more than necessary. If I did reveal myself, individuals would say, "Well, you
know how it is." Then I'd have to stand my ground: Maybe yes,

maybe no, but tell me anyway. Give me all the details and don't leave a thing out. Don't assume I know what you're talking about. With most experiencers, I simply used phrases like—"oh really" or "tell me more" or that wonderful all-purpose lead "and...?" In fact, the more details people would give me the more I would say "and...?"

In my case, I found that voice intonation and inflection, along with nonthreatening body language, gained me more information than complex or "scientific" questions. All I had to do was "leave the door open" and the experiencer would more than willingly "walk through." With a nonjudgmental and sincerely interested listener, most near-death survivors will jump at the chance to express themselves.

I did experiment with interview styles, though, and here is what I discovered:

Interviewing Styles

Formal	Informal
Measured replies, as if individuals were trying, at least subconsciously, to either please me *or* them.	Conversational dialogue, and an easy ambience, where no one felt more important than the other.
Less material given, beginnings and endings were more pronounced—time seemed of importance.	Unlimited material given, as more of a "flow" was established whereby clocks and schedules ceased to exist.
Material was almost always one-sided, emphasizing either how positive it was or how negative (depending on type).	Material was almost always two-sided, with a more in—depth and free interchange between positives and negatives (regardless of type).

I began interviewing near-death survivors in 1978, and started publishing my findings in 1981. My first round of sending out questionnaires was in 1983. Unfortunately I destroyed all the questionnaire materials and notes that I had kept during the time after my first book came out when I was feeling sorry for myself.

Hence, I cannot convey to you the questions I used with certainty—except to say that I sent out a balanced mailing, half to people picked at random from the IANDS archives and the other half to people whose homes I had been in. Both groups filled out their questionnaires exactly the same way, effusive in their descriptions about how wonderful their lives were now... even though I knew from having been in some of their homes and interviewing their families that what they claimed was not the way their situation was at all.

And always, no matter where I was, I learned more by watching experiencers, and their significant others, and by studying their nonverbal cues, than I did by listening to what they had to say. (It is amazing to me how "loud" unspoken language is.)

How did I find so many people to interview? Lucky, I guess.

Honestly, I have no other way to explain it. Yes, I was constantly on the road during the time as a telephone switchboard trainer and systems analyst on large computerized telephone installations, and always around people, but, no kidding, whomever I spoke with, wherever I was, invariably, that individual would be a near-death survivor. How did I know? Their eyes. Experiencers' eyes sparkle with a childlike curiosity and innocence, and there's a certain tilt to the upper body—almost as if they are looking for someone to talk to. I learned to "bait" them, let a word or two slide by that inferred a certain otherworldliness to the way I regarded life, and that's all it ever took, one or two words. They'd do the rest. It's almost as if they had been waiting for someone like me to come along.

Sixty percent of my interviews were like this, "accidentally" meeting people as I traveled around the country. They didn't know me and I didn't know them, there was no advance contact of any kind. Another 30 percent occurred because of talks I gave. Experiencers would be in the audience, come up afterward to share their stories, and I'd start in (sometimes grilling them the way my father had once grilled me). It was rare for me to just "visit" or be "friendly." (I'm not like that anymore, thank goodness. That kind of intensity wears thin after fifteen years.) The final 10 percent were the result of the questionnaires I had sent out or from phone calls and letters I had received after requesting volunteers for my research.

Caucasian Americans, Europeans, and Arabic people constituted 80 percent of my interviews. Although I did not encounter experiencers who were Asian, 20 percent of my interviews were with people of the Negro race (15 percent African American, the other 5 percent divided between Kenya, Haiti, and Canada. Haisley Long in Chapter Six is an African Canadian.)

I did find regionalisms in near-death imagery: People from the Northwest, Southwest, and from Haiti had more animals in their scenarios; people in the Southeast, Midwest, and central states had more overall themes of good and evil (notice I did *not* say "hellish" experiences). I did not find the heavy concentrations of hell-like scenarios among Bible Belt Christians that some researchers claim, but I did find that *only* fundamentalist religious types ever reported hell as hot and fiery. The greater majority spoke of how cold or clammy or void of temperature the "place" where they went was. Other regionalisms were less pronounced. I did find a lot of superstition, however, among the less educated *and* among the most devout (regardless of religion). And with those from the former Soviet Union, I couldn't help but notice an overwhelmingly emotional gratitude for having been in what they felt was God's presence during their episodes.

What really surprised me, though, was the pattern I discovered with *how* adults and teenagers died who experienced the phenomenon. A whopping 70 percent of the females had their experiences either during childbirth or somehow connected with miscarriages, hemorrhaging, or hysterectomies. Over 50 percent of the males had theirs because of heart-related conditions, and about 25 percent because of acts of violence or accidents.

If viewed symbolically, one could conjecture that the males might have had challenges in dealing with issues of the heart (emotions), aggression, and stress, versus being able to "lay back," relax, and not take life so seriously. With the females, one could say that childbirth, as a rite of passage, is still just as important today and just as "dangerous" as it ever was— dangerous in the sense of how the experience forces a woman to draw deep from within and discover parts of herself she never knew were there. I offer this brief exercise in conjecture because, afterward, experiencers tend to shift around in ways that make me think that the symbolism involved in how they died may be a valid interpretative tool.

On the following two pages are reproductions of the recent questionnaire I used to investigate electrical sensitivity. Forty-six out of the one hundred people contacted replied. The numbers you see in the various columns are the total sum of experiencers who checked that particular item.

This questionnaire was not meant to establish electrical sensitivity as an aftereffect. I had already done that, with 73 percent of my research base reporting it. What I wanted to know was how it spread out; what types of electrical sensitivity might these people be experiencing and how pervasive it was. Anything I forgot to ask about, respondents let me know, and in no uncertain terms! These people were rarin' to go on this one, almost as if they had been holding this kind of information back for a long time. They seemed quite excited that, at last, someone cared enough to ask.

Notice the "vagueness of the frequency" that I headed each column with: (F) Frequently, (O) Often, (W) Once in a While, (S) Seldom, and (N) Never. I did this on purpose because I was looking for subjective values. In other words, I wanted most of all to have some sense of how this phenomenon affected experiencers, what they felt about it, what meaning it had for them. For instance, one person had a computer monitor blow up only once in her presence (hence she checked "S" for Seldom); yet to her this was such an impossible event that it made a tremendous impression on her, which she so noted in the remarks. The fact that I even asked the question, made her think about it and reflect on any possible connection the explosion might have had to her energy field. The more she thought the more she remembered how this type of thing was actually happening rather frequently, only at different times with different equipment. She was one of many who reacted this way. Thus, on many of the questions, you could easily add up the first four columns (F, O, W, S) for a more revealing picture of what was really going on.

Do that. Take question 40. The spread looks rather thin, doesn't it? But read the question: Do people/beings disappear/appear when you are around? That's an incredible thing to have happen to anyone at any time, whether frequently or just once. If you do the percentage by adding up the first four columns, you get an unbelievable 54 percent. How about question 25: Do you receive images on (television) channels that don't exist? Once again, if

NEAR-DEATH AFTEREFFECTS - ELECTRICAL SENSITIVITY

QUESTIONNAIRE

Fill out and return to the Central Desk at the Conference, or mail to P. M. H. Atwater, P. O. Box 7691, Charlottesville, VA 22906-7691. Thank you in advance for filling out this questionnaire!!!!!!

YOUR EXPERIENCE (Check Yes or No)

	Yes	No
1. Did you have a near-death experience?	41 did	
2. Did you have an experience like near-death?	21 did	
3. Regardless of NDE or Like an NDE, did you see or experience a bright, all-pervading, radiant Light?	37	
4. Were you in or near the Light?	35	
5. Did you merge with or go into the Light?	24	
6. Did your experience happen in a light-filled world?	27	
7. Did light predominate in your experience?	30	
8. Did you see, meet, or converse with beings of light?	30	
9. Estimate what percentage of your experience involved light or was in light or was light-filled? (give %)	50% or above predominated %	

PHYSICAL AFTEREFFECTS (Check proper column: F=Frequently, O=Fairly Often, W=Once in Awhile, S=Seldom, N=Never.

(Please mark out that which doesn't apply or add more)

	F	O	W	S	N
1. Are you more sensitive to light now?	23	4	7	1	8
2. Does sunlight bother you?	20	8	6	4	7
3. Have you experienced sun-sensitivity (sun stroke, rapid skin burning, dizziness, different skin colorations, or other_____?	13	7	2	13	6
4. Do you wear sunglasses more often now?	29	4	0	3	7
5. Does camera and/or video filming light bother you?	15	6	10	5	10
6. Do you see lights that have no physical cause?	9	5	6	5	12
7. Are you more sensitive to sound/noise levels now?	21	8	2	3	7
8. Does certain sounds or noise bother you?	22	8	4	7	3
9. Do you avoid places or programs where sound is too loud?	25	11	8	1	1
10. Does radio or television bother your ears/hearing?	10	15	13	5	3
11. Do other parts of your body hear besides your ears?	13	7	8	1	15
12. Do you hear sounds that have no physical cause?	6	10	10	6	10
13. Are you able to sense electrical or magnetic fields?	13	5	8	7	10
14. Are you able to feel electrical or magnetic fields?	10	8	7	7	12
15. Do electrical fields bother you?	8	8	7	6	17
16. Do magnetic fields bother you?	7	8	8	4	15
17. Are you sensitive to energy fields around hi-tech equipment such as computers, video, television, microwave ovens, or other_____?	9	4	10	3	14
18. Are you sensitive to energy fields around regular household appliances such as coffee-maker, stove, frig, mixmaster, can opener, or other_____?	5	4	10	6	18
19. Are you sensitive to energy fields around power lines?	7	6	11	2	18
20. Are you sensitive to energy fields around telephone lines?	5	4	8	4	21
21. Are you sensitive to energy fields around generators, engines, air conditioners, furnace units, or_____ other_____?	5	2	7	5	19
22. Are you sensitive to elevators or escalators in any way? Explain:_____	5	1	5	7	21

	F	O	W	S	N
23. Are you sensitive to modes of travel such as to cars, trucks, buses, trains, airplanes, motorbikes, recreational vehicles, or other_____? Does exhaust bother you more than usual?	20	6	2	4	8
24. Have you noticed television reception acting strangely in your presence such as channels switching by themselves, raster bars rolling rapidly, lots of "snow," or other_____?	8	5	12	7	14
25. Do you receive images on channels that don't exist?	2	5	3	5	30
26. Does strange programming override the channel you are on?	2	0	6	7	28
27. Have you noticed video equipment acting strangely in your presence such as won't record, fuzzy pictures, raster bars showing, recording wrong channel, or other_____?	3	1	5	7	27
28. Have you noticed audio recording equipment acting strangely in your presence such as cutting off, blowing fuses, smoking, tape blank after recording, or other_____?	3	5	7	2	25
29. Do you get strange voices when recording, extra voices?	1	2	6	2	30
30. Have you noticed computer equipment acting strangely in your presence such as losing imagery, unusual images, connections jumping, memory loss, smoking, blowing fuses, computer screen (monitor) blowing up, or other_____?	3	2	4	8	25
31. Have you noticed any other equipment acting strangely in your presence, such as projectors, telephones, cash registers, gaming devices, cameras, or other_____?	5	6	5	7	21
32. Have you noticed light bulbs or yard lights or street lights acting strangely in your presence such as popping, blowing out, diming, becoming brighter, or other_____?	8	1	7	7	21
33. Have you noticed security systems, electronic locks, or security beams acting strangely in your presence such as becoming ineffective, breaking down, fuse blown, alarms set off quicker, or other_____?	1	3	2	8	28
34. Have you noticed a force field around your own body, like an additional or enhanced energy shield?	11	8	5	5	17
35. Have other people commented on a bright glow around you, like an aura or energy field?	11	9	6	3	13
36. Have you noticed glass or metal objects behaving strangely in your presence such as glass breaking or popping, stoves turning off or on, metal bending or twisting, hanging lights beginning to move or spin, other_____?	3	0	5	8	27
37. Have you noticed animals behaving differently around you such as becoming suddenly docile, threatened, attracted, trying to communicate, or other_____?	13	8	8	3	11
38. Have you noticed children behaving differently around you such as becoming at ease, wanting to snuggle, attracted, threatened, frightened, or other_____?	15	9	4	6	8
39. Do objects disappear/appear when you are around?	8	5	7	5	18
40. Do people/beings disappear/appear when you are around?	5	2	8	5	23
41. Do you have more energy than before?	10	8	6	5	12
42. Do you have great sweeps of energy?	10	9	9	4	8
43. Do you have less energy than before?	3	9	5	8	12
44. Are you easily drained of energy?	13	11	5	7	4
45. Do you wear a wristwatch? * (most said they had trouble with their watch)	21	7	3	1	11
46. Do you use a cellular phone or car phone?	0	2	2	1	34

47. List any other changes or happenings, or use this space to explain previous answers or make comments: (give your name and address if you would like)

you add up the first four columns you get 33 percent. Certainly not a very high figure until you stop and think about it. How can anyone receive images on television channels that don't even exist?

See how this questionnaire makes you think?

By being somewhat vague about how often, yet probing on what might be entailed, I opened the door for my respondents to make connections I don't think they would have made otherwise. That's what I wanted. In studying the previous pages, I hope the questionnaire makes you think, too. Read past questions and columns and try to open yourself to what is being implied. The questionnaire was also designed to overwhelm people and elicit a "Whoa!" That's when the brain clicks in, when you have no other choice but to sit down and really reflect, analyze, and think things out.

Considering the responses I got, I am now more anxious than ever before to see laboratory measurement studies on electrical sensitivity conducted by professionals of different disciplines, such as engineers, medical people, psychologists, and anthropologists. Questionnaires, even using control groups, will not obtain the kind of in-depth observations that we now need to understand what happens to people because of a near-death experience. This is important to know since such scientific findings could well have an impact on our very definition and understanding of what it is to be a human being.

Any individual (or any group) who feels so inclined, please help IANDS initiate this type of study. Send contributions to NDE Research Fund, c/o IANDS, P.O. Box 502, East Windsor Hill, CT 06028. Moneys are tax-deductible.

Before I close this section, I want to impress on you just how much the near-death phenomenon challenges what we think we know about life:

- Since infants, even newborns can accurately remember their experience and the conditions of birth, how much more can they remember and how far back does their memory go? And how does this speak to the penchant in our country to operate on newborns without benefit of anesthesia? If they can remember a near-death experience, can they not remember that surgery?
- Since children and adults alike meet future and past siblings and "babies to be" while on The Other Side, how does this

speak to the so-called randomness of the choices we make, the consequences that follow, and who we affect? And what does this imply about abortion and the theory that the soul enters only at birth?

- Since out-of-body episodes often have components in them that are later verified, some even impossibly so, what does this say about the range of our faculties? Also, what does this say about the relationship between our faculties and our brain? And about our ability to be completely mobile and fully functional *without a body,* and still be in possession of all our faculties?

- Since near-death survivors are physically changed by their experiences, as well as psychologically, what does this say about the real power of subjective experiences? Does this not mean we need to redefine subjectivity itself and its value to the continuance of a healthy life? And what about the structural changes that occur to the brain? What does this mean and how extensive are they?

- Since the part of us that has this experience "separates" from the body to the extent that it does, is that not an indication that not only do we have a soul, but we *are* a soul-resident in a manifested life-form? If that is true, what else is true? About life? About death? About soul? About purpose and mission and Source and Creation?

Some say we have done all the research on the near-death phenomenon that we can, that too many people know about it to avoid bias. But I say we have only begun to research this field. Bias may affect questionnaires and psychological studies, but it will not deter physiological measurements, in-depth consciousness research, or the work being done with children.

Personally, it has been an honor for me to be involved in near-death research and to have met and spoken with so very many people over the years. My role, as I see it, has always been and still is that of a synergist, one who seeks to provide a broader context for meaningful dialogue and greater understanding. I only hope that my contribution to the field can in some way add to the growing body of knowledge that the near-death phenomenon imparts to the world.

Resource Suggestions

What we call the beginning is often the end.
And to make an end is to make a beginning.
The end is where we start from.
—T.S. Eliot

Carl Gustav Jung, the famous psychoanalyst, once said, "There is no birth of consciousness without pain." Transformations, more often than not, are painful, and the near-death experience is no exception. It is painful to be jerked away from your security blanket, whatever it was, flung into a situation you did not ask for, and be returned only to discover that somehow everything changed while you were gone.

You come back, but in a very real sense there is no coming back. What you left isn't the same anymore because you're not the same. You now have a basis of comparison unknown to you previously, and that is both wonderful and not so wonderful. It is confusing at best. Because this is true, I feel *Beyond the Light* would be incomplete without a section devoted to referrals, sources, and resources that *anyone* can use to begin the process of looking around for ideas and inspiration.

This compilation focuses on, in the order of relevance:

Offerings are not meant to comprise a comprehensive index, nor can I make any promises or guarantees about anything so presented. I simply give this to you as a gesture of sharing some of the best of what is currently available. Any choices or results depend on you.

While on The Other Side, I was told, "One book for each death." I was shown what each was to contain, although not how to write them. This book replaces Coming Back to Life as book one of the trilogy. Book two is Future Memory and the Inner-workings of Creation/Consciousness (estimated publication 1995), and book three, A Manual for Developing Humans (by 1996). The trilogy is meant as a celebration of life in all its fullness.

To receive a flier about any of the sessions I offer that you could take advantage of or sponsor in your area, or about informative materials I have available, send a stamped, self-addressed, letter-size envelope to: YOU CAN Change Your Life, P.O. Box 7691, Charlottesville, VA 22906-7691.

THE NEAR-DEATH PHENOMENON

The International Association for Near-Death Studies (IANDS) has several publications: a scholarly magazine called *The Journal of Near-Death Studies*, a general interest newsletter entitled *Vital Signs* (the same name as the magazine they once published), and a handy brochure every hospital and clinic on earth should stock called *Coming Back*. This brochure carries pertinent information experiencers and their families need to deal with the phenomenon.

Audiocassette tapes of IANDS conference speakers are available. There is a large selection, including tapes from the June 1991 Conference on Aftereffects held in Charlottesville, Virginia (Mellen-Thomas Benedict, Margaret Fields Kean, and Vernon Sylvest were among the speakers). When you contact IANDS, request a copy of the *Conference Audio Tape Order List*.

Membership in this nonprofit organization dedicated to educating the public and promoting research on the near-death phenomenon is open to anyone; dues are annual and include various benefits. Donations to cover operating expenses are always needed and always welcome. Individual reports about near-death episodes are solicited for the archives; you will need to fill out a form, so please ask for one. Write or call:

IANDS
P.O. Box 502, East Windsor Hill, CT 06028
(203) 528-5144

Another Research Project

Justine Owens, Ph.D. and Ian Stevenson, M.D. of the Division of Personality Studies, University of Virginia, are conducting a thorough and ongoing study of all types of near-death experiences. Anyone who has had a near-death episode is urged to contact them and volunteer for this project. Participation is via questionnaires and letters. Write to:

Justine Owens, Ph.D., Division of Personality Studies
Box 152, Medical Center, University of Virginia
Charlottesvile, VA 22908

Books on the Near-Death Phenomenon

Researchers (listed by year of first *publication)*

Raymond A. Moody, Jr., M.D.—*Life After Life,* Covington, GA; Mockingbird Books, 1975. *Reflections on Life After Life,* New York, NY; Bantam Books, 1977. *The Light Beyond,* New York, NY; Bantam Books, 1988.

Maurice Rawlings, M.D.—*Beyond Death's Door,* Nashville, TN; Thomas Nelson, Inc., 1978. *Before Death Comes,* Nashville, TN; Thomas Nelson, Inc., 1980. *To Hell and Back,* Nashville, TN; Thomas Nelson, Inc., 1993.

Kenneth Ring, Ph.D.—*Life at Death,* New York, NY; Coward, McCann & Geoghegan, 1980. *Heading Toward Omega: In Search of the Meaning of the Near-Death Experience,* New York, NY; William

Morrow, 1984. *The Omega Project: Near-Death Experiences, UFO Encounters, and Mind at Large*, New York, NY; William Morrow, 1992.

Michael B. Sabom, M.D.—*The Near-Death Experience: A Medical Perspective*, New York, NY; Harper & Row, 1982.

Bruce Greyson, M.D. and Charles Flynn, Ph.D. (eds)—*The Near-Death Experience: Problems, Prospects, Perspectives*, Springfield, IL; C.C. Thomas, 1984.

Margot Grey—*Return From Death*, London, England; Arkana, 1985.

P.M.H. Atwater, Lh.D.—*Coming Back to Life: The After-effects of the Near-Death Experience*, New York, NY; Dodd, Mead & Co., 1988 and Ballantine Books 1989.

Melvin Morse, M.D. with Paul Perry—*Closer to the Light: Learning From the Near-Death Experiences of Children*, New York, NY; Villard Books, 1990.

Commentators/Studies (listed by year of first publication)

George Gallup, Jr.—*Adventures in Immortality*, New York, NY; McGraw-Hill, 1982.

Michael Grosso—*The Final Choice*, Walpole, NH; Stillpoint, 1985.

Charles Flynn, Ph.D.—*After the Beyond*, Englewood Cliffs, NJ; Prentice-Hall, 1986.

Carol Zaleski—*Otherworld Journeys, Accounts of Near-Death Experience in Medieval and Modern Times*, New York, NY; Oxford University Press, Inc., 1987.

D. Scott Rogo—*The Return From Silence: A Study of Near-Death Experiences*, Wellingborough, Northamptonshire, England; Aquarian Press, 1989 (in the United States through Harper & Row).

David Lorimer—*Whole in One: The Near-Death Experience and the Ethic of Interconnectedness*, New York, NY; Penguin, 1992.

Experiencers (year omitted on self-published books)

George Ritchie, M.D.—*Return From Tomorrow*, Waco, TX; Chosen Books, 1978. *My Life After Dying: Becoming Alive to Universal Love*, Norfolk, VA; Hampton Road Publishing Co., Inc., 1991.

Barbara Harris and Lionel C. Bascom—*Full Circle: The Near-Death Experience and Beyond*, New York, NY; Simon and Schuster, 1990.

Betty J. Eadie—*Embraced by the Light,* Placerville, CA; Gold Leaf Press, 1992.

Sidney Saylor Farr—*What Tom Sawyer Learned from Dying,* Norfolk, VA; Hampton Roads Publishing Co., Inc., 1993.

Billy Jo Branson—*Mining the Silver Lining: Taking Triumph From Tragedy.* Available from Sun Coyote Press, 1302 East Street #48, Emporia, KS 66801.

Grace Bubulka—*Beyond Reality: A Personal Account of the Near-Death Experience.* Available from Pacific Business Services, Inc., 2350 W. Shaw, #103, Fresno, CA 93711.

Arthur E. Yensen—*I Saw Heaven.* Still available from his son Eric Yensen at his Dad's address: P.O. Box 369, Parma, ID 83660.

Videos on the Near-Death Phenomenon

Aftereffects of the Near-Death Experience, The. A talk about the positive and negative aftereffects of the near-death experience, given to a live audience by P.M.H. Atwater. From Golden Tree Videos, 1714 Swann St., Fayetteville, NC 28303; (919) 488-3150.

Life After Death. An unusually long and touching account of Reinee Pasarow's near-death experience, interpreted through her Baha'i faith. From New Age Industries, 9 Cupania Circle, Monterey Park, CA 91754; (213) 888-6938.

A Message of Hope. A panel discussion of the near-death phenomenon, featuring the remarkable experience of Howard Storm (his began as hell-like then later turned heaven-like), plus three other experiencers, a psychologist, and a counselor. From The Counseling Institute, 40 Grand Professional Center #304, Ft. Thomas, KY 41075. For more information, call Ed Riess at (606) 781-1344.

Moment of Truth: A Window on Life After Death. The detailed and fascinating account of Jayne Smith's near-death experience. From Starpath Productions, P.O. Box 160, Fayetteville, AR 72702.

Piercing the Illusion of Death. The detailed and fascinating account of Nancy Maier's near-death experience. From Nancy Maier, P.O. Box 5752, Santa Monica, CA 90409; (213) 452-3707.

Round Trip. A comprehensive presentation of the near-death experience, which mixes experiencer accounts with informed commentary to produce a fascinating video geared for any audience. Can be easily segmented for classroom use. From

Tim O'Reilly, 435 West 54th Street, #4RE, New York, NY 10019; (212) 757-3933.

Transcending the Limits: The Near-Death Experience. Filmed at the Pacific Northwest Conference on Near-Death Experiences, this video is a compilation of highlights and features such speakers as Kenneth Ring, Melvin Morse, Kimberly Clark Sharp, and Nancy Evans Bush. From Seattle IANDS, P.O. Box 84333, Seattle, WA 98124; (206) 525-5489.

Audiocassette Tape on Near-Death

Coming Back to Life features P.M.H. Atwater, Lh.D. updating her research on the aftereffects of the near-death phenomenon and how this interfaces with current events. From Mithra Corporation, P.O. Drawer 447, Organ, NM 88052-0447; (505) 382-5449.

Teacher's Text for Classrooms

The Near-Death Experience Teaching Unit was devised by Howard A. Michel, Ph.D. for use in school classrooms. Geared for college-level courses, it can be adapted to various settings. The teaching unit contains a one-hundred-page text of basic introductory material on the near-death phenomenon, a fifty-seven-minute video featuring interviews of five near-death survivors, and a student workbook. A twenty-eight-minute video of Dr. Raymond Moody, Jr., lecturing on the near-death experience while at Wichita State University in 1986, is also available as a separate item. To obtain the teaching unit (a package deal) and/or the Moody video, contact: Theta Project, P.O. Box 618, LaJolla, CA 92038; (619) 456-0523.

Children's Book on Near-Death

The Door to the Secret City, by Kathleen J. Forti, tells in story form what it is like for a child to have a near-death experience and then deal with the aftereffects. The book is available in hardcover and as an audiocassette dramatization. Contact: Kids Want Answers, Too!, 1544 Bay Point Drive, Virginia Beach, VA 23454.

Videos on Life and Death Transformations

Mandalas, Vision of Heaven and Earth and *The Human Journey,* of unusual quality, feature the transformational sculpture and poetry of Mirtala set to music. Especially helpful in hospice and counseling situations, or for anyone seeking a deeper meaning to life. these videos are available from: MACROmedia, P.O. Box 279, Epping, NH 03042. (To obtain a copy of Mirtala's brochure, write: Mirtala, P.O. Box 3237, Sedona, AZ 86336-3237.)

Booklet About An After-Death Experience

One of the most inspiring stories I have come across about an after-death experience concerns the case of Mark Carson, who was killed in a car/bus accident in 1976. In a short booklet entitled *Mark My Words, An After-Death Dialogue,* Mark's stepmother Roberta Carson writes of making contact with him after his death. Because her story typifies what happens so often after a loved one dies, and because most professionals refuse to admit this, her booklet is well worth reading. Obtain directly: Roberta Ayers Carson, 70 Sable Court, Winter Springs, FL 32708; (407) 699-1672.

An Unusual Book on the Interlife

Life Between Life by Joel L. Whitton, M.D., Ph.D. and Joe Fisher, published by Warner Books in 1986, is the best book I have yet discovered about reincarnation as viewed from patterns present in the interlife, the world between death and rebirth. The research in this book closely parallels my own experiences during the sixties and early seventies when I maintained a professional practice as a hypnotherapist specializing in past-life regressions. Try your library if you cannot find the book in stores.

CONCERNING FULL DEATH

A Special Type of Meditation to Use

Letting Go by Richard W. Boerstler, Ph.D., a psychotherapist, explains the ancient technique of "co-meditation," one of the most important yet simple techniques I have found to assist an individual in making his or her transition during the process of death. This ancient Tibetan breathing exercise consists of a single sound toned (expressed) on an out-breath, which is shared in breathing rhythm between the helper and the dying patient. Designed to ease fear and tension, co-meditation has shown remarkable results in assisting patients through the death process, while enabling relatives and caregivers to express themselves in a manner that directly benefits all concerned. For the book and/or any guidance you may desire on the subject contact: Dr. Richard W. Boerstler, 115 Blue Rock Road, South Yarmouth, MA 02664; (617) 394-6520.

An Audiocassette Tape for the Dying

As You Die is an unusual visit with P.M.H. Atwater. Inspired by an AIDS patient in New York City to openly discuss the death process, Atwater takes on the subject with vigor and compassion, focusing on what it feels like to die, and the actual moment when one makes his or her transition. The final section of the tape is designed to be played to the individual after death has occurred to guide the departing soul. Obtain from Mithra Corporation, P.O. Drawer 447, Organ, NM 88052-0447; (505) 382-5449.

Books That Affirm an Afterlife

Death Does Not Part Us, Elsie R. Sechrist. Virginia Beach, VA; A.R.E. Press, 1992.

Final Gifts: Understanding the Special Awareness, Needs and Communications of the Dying, Maggie Callanan and Patricia Kelley. New York, NY; Simon and Schuster, 1992.

Window to Heaven, A: When Children See Life in Death, Diane M. Komp, M.D. Grand Rapids, MI; Zondervan Publishing House, 1992.

Books to Prepare Individuals and Families

Caring for Your Own Dead, Lisa Carlson. Available from Upper Access Publishers, One Upper Access Road, P.O. Box 457, Hinesburg, VT 05461; (802) 482-2988.

Dealing Creatively with Death: A Manual of Death Education and Simple Burial, Ernest Morgan. Bayside, NY; Barclay House

Books, in continuous printing.
Practical Guide to Death and Dying, A, John White. Wheaton, IL;
Theosophical Publishing House, 1988.

Compassion Book Service and Rainbow Collection

For a complete collection of books on death, dying, grief,
compassion, and hope, this service-oriented bookstore is exceptional. While perusing their titles, look for books by Stephen
Levine and Elisabeth Kübler-Ross, outstanding authors on the
topic. For a free catalog, call or write: Compassion Book Service
and Rainbow Collection, 479 Hannah Branch Road, Burnsville,
NC 28714; (704) 675-5909.

The Elisabeth Kübler-Ross Hospice, Grief Counseling
& Death Education Program

The Foundation for Life, Death, and Transition is committed to
working with educators and institutions worldwide to provide an
advocate for research and the development and implementation
of educational and clinical programs in hospice care and administration, home health care, grief and death education, transition
support, counseling, and personal health and healing. For more
information, contact them through Northern New Mexico Community College, El Rito Campus, El Rito, NM 87530; (505)
581-4148.

Hospice Referrals

U.S., Canadian, and International directory of hospice services
and general information, 1-800-331-1620
The National Hospice Organization, 1901 N. Moore Street, Suite
901, Arlington, VA 22209; (703) 243-5900 or 1-800-658-8898
Children's Hospice International, 901 North Washington Street,
Suite 700, Alexandria, VA 22314; (703) 684-0330 or
1-800-242-4453

HEALTH AND HEALING

Because of the brain shift they go through, most near-death
survivors (and others so transformed) return unusually sensitive

or allergic to pharmaceuticals. Such a shift also seems to render the physical body more vulnerable to the effects of subtle stimuli, which probably explains much of the uncontrollable and/or additional psychic phenomena experiencers report. This means that the physical body and its care become extra important. I have seen good nutrition make a demonstrable difference in comprehension levels after a brain shift, and in the ability to control one's own psyche and personal environment. Once the condition of the physical body can be stabilized and health habits revamped, it is much easier to retrain the brain to access new levels of mind. There is no simple rule of thumb to use in accomplishing this, but the following resources represent places where you can begin the process of reeducating yourself.

Acupuncture

American Association of Acupuncture and Oriental Medicine, 1424 16th Street, NW, Suite 501, Washington, DC 20036; (202) 265-2287. Also at 4101 Lake Boone Trail, #210, Raleigh, NC 27607; (919) 787-5181.

Aromatherapy

The Complete Book of Essential Oils & Aromatherapy, Valerie Ann Worwood. San Rafael, CA; New York Library, 1991.

Ayurvedic (Traditional Indian) Medicine

Ayurvedic Educational Programs, P.O. Box 598, South Lancaster, MA 01561; 1-800-858-1808.

Chiropractic

American Chiropractic Association, 1701 Clarendon Blvd., Arlington, VA 22209; (703) 276-8800.
International Chiropractors Association, 1110 N. Glebe Road, Suite 1000, Arlington, VA 22201; (703) 528-5000.

Essence of Flowers

Flower Secrets Revealed: Using Flowers to Heal, Beautify, and Energize Your Life, Carly Wall. Virginia Beach, VA; A.R.E. Press, 1993.

Bach Flower Remedies, 644 Merrick Road, Lynbrook, NY 11563; (516) 593-2206.

Flower Essence Society, P.O. Box 459, Nevada City, CA 95959; (916) 265-9163.

Matrix Flower Essences, RR1, Box 391, Westmoreland, NH 03467; general information phone (603) 399-4916.

Perelandra Rose and Garden Essences, P.O. Box 3603, Warrenton, VA 22186; Twenty-four-hour message phone (703) 937-2153. (Inquire about their book, *Flower Essences: Reordering Our Understanding and Approach to Illness and Health.*)

First-Aid Using Natural Remedies

Handbook of Alternatives to Chemical Medicine, The, Mildred Jackson, N.D. and Terri Teague, N.D. Available from Lawton Teague Publications, P.O. Box 12353, Oakland, CA 94604; and Bookpeople, 7900 Edgewater Drive, Oakland, CA 94621.

Natural Health First-Aid Guide, The: The Definitive Handbook of Natural Remedies for Treating Minor Emergencies, Mark Mayell and the Editors of *Natural Health* magazine. Available from *Natural Health,* 17 Station Street, Box 1200, Brookline, MA 02147; (617) 232-1000.

Healing Hands

Hands of Light: A Guide to Healing Through the Human Energy Field, Barbara Ann Brennan. New York, NY; Bantam Books, 1988.

Therapeutic Touch: How to Use Your Hands to Help or to Heal, Dolores Krieger, Ph.D. Englewood Cliffs, NJ; Prentice-Hall, 1979. And *Living the Therapeutic Touch: Healing as a Lifestyle,* New York, NY; Dodd, Mead & Company, 1987.

Academy of Healing Arts, 2027 Pershing Street, Durham, NC 27705; (919) 286-2055.

Barbara Brennan School of Healing, P.O. Box 2005, East Hampton, NY 11937; (516) 329-0951.

Center for Reiki Training, 29209 Northwestern Hwy., #592, Southfield, MI 48034; (313) 948-8112.

Nurse Healers Professional Associates, Inc., 175 Fifth Avenue, Suite 2755, New York, NY 10010; (212) 886-3776.

Health Centers With a Holistic Approach

A.R.E. Clinic (a division of the Association for Research and Enlightenment), 4018 North 40th Street, Phoenix, AZ 85018; (602) 955-7729 or (602) 955-0551.

Richmond Health & Wellness Center, 5700 West Grace Street, Suite 105, Richmond, VA 23226; (804) 285-6240.

The Shealy Institute, 1328 East Evergreen, Springfield, MO 65803; (417) 865-5940.

Health Practitioners With a Holistic Approach

Directory of Alternative Health-Care Professionals, from Holistic Resources, Inc., P.O. Box 25450, Seattle, WA 98125-2350; (206) 523-2101.

Association of Health Practitioners, P.O. Box 5007, Durango, CO 81301; (303) 259-1091 (for referrals).

Herbs

Health Through God's Pharmacy, Maria Treben. Steyr, Austria; Wilhelm Ennsthaler, 1982 (also available in the United States).

Herbal Medicine: The Natural Way to Get Well and Stay Well, Dian Dincin Buchman. New York, NY; McKay, 1979.

Herb Companion Magazine, published by Interweave Press, Inc., 201 East Fourth Street, Loveland, CO 80537; (303) 669-7672.

New Age Herbalist Magazine, The, Consultant Editor Richard Mabey with Michael McIntyre, Pamela Michael, Gail Duff, and John Stevens. New York, NY; Collier Books, 1988.

Nichols Herb and Rare Seeds Catalog, from Nichols Garden Nursery, 1190 North Pacific Hwy, Albany, OR 97321; (503) 928-9280.

Our Earth, Our Cure: A Handbook of Natural Medicine for Today, Raymond Dextreit. Secaucus, NJ; Citadel Press, 1986.

American Botanical Council, P.O. Box 201660, Austin, TX 78720; 1-800-373-7105.

American Herb Association, P.O. Box 99, Rescue, CA 95672.

School of Herbal Medicine, P.O. Box 168, Suquamish, WA 98392; (206) 697-1287.

Holistic Medical Associations

American Holistic Nurses Association, 4101 Lake Boone Trail, Suite 201, Raleigh, NC 27607; (919) 787-5146.

American Holistic Veterinary Medical Association, 2214 Old Emmorton Road, Bel Air, MD 21014; (410) 569-0795.

Holistic Dental Association, 974 North 21st Street, Neward, OH 43055; (614) 366-3309.

Homeopathy

Everybody's Guide to Homeopathic Medicines, Stephen Cummings and Dana Ullman. Los Angeles, CA; J.P. Tarcher, 1984.

Homeopathic Medicines at Home, Maesimund B. Panos, M.D., and Jane Heimlich. Los Angeles, CA; J.P. Tarcher, 1981.

Homeopathic Educational Services, 2124 Kittredge Street, Berkeley, CA 94704; for general information (415) 653-9270, for ordering 1-800-359-9051.

International Foundation for Homeopathy, 2366 Eastlake Avenue East, Suite 301, Seattle, WA 98102; (206) 324-8230.

National Center for Homeopathy, 801 N. Fairfax Street, Suite 306, Alexandria, VA 22314; (703) 548-7790.

International Holistic Health and Environmental Network

European Headquarters–World Research Foundation, Krieger-strasse 17, D-7000 Stuttgart 1, Germany; phone (0) 711-290813, FAX (O) 711-291180. (Request their holistic health catalog.)

World Headquarters–World Research Foundation, 15300 Ventura Blvd., Suite 405, Sherman Oaks, CA 91403; phone (818) 907-5483, FAX (818) 907-6044. (Request their holistic health catalog.)

Mental Health With a Holistic Approach

Heal Your Body, Louise L. Hay. Available through Hay House, P.O. Box 6204, Carson, CA 90749-6204; 1-800-654-5126. (This small book is an alphabetical listing of probable mental causes for each physical illness, plus metaphysical affirmations to help facilitate recovery. It is truly remarkable. Ask for their catalog of other books and tapes now available.)

I Want to Change But I Don't Know How, Tom Rusk, M.D., and Randy Read, M.D. Los Angeles, CA; Price Stern Sloan, 1986.

Love Is Letting Go of Fear, Gerald G. Jampolsky, M.D. Berkeley, CA; Celestial Arts, 1979.

Make Anger Your Ally: Harnessing Our Most Baffling Emotion, Neil C. Warren. Garden City, NY; Doubleday, 1983.

Who's the Matter With Me, Alice Steadman. Marina Del Rey, CA; DeVorss, 1977.

Your Body Believes Every Word You Say, Barbara Levine. Boulder Creek, CA; Asian Publishing, 1991.

John Bradshaw Center, 7500 E. Hellman Avenue, Rosemead, CA 91770; 1-800-845-4445. Full offering of workshops based on John Bradshaw's philosophy in his book *Healing the Inner Child.*

The Elisabeth Kübler-Ross Center, South Route #616, Head Waters, VA 24442; (703) 396-3441. (Although famous for her work with death and dying, Elisabeth Kübler-Ross, M.D., is now dedicated to the upliftment of life and the practice of unconditional love. Contact her Center for information about membership, a listing of her publications and tapes, and workshop schedules.)

Mental Health With a Holistic Approach for Teenagers

Creative Rebellion: Positive Options for Teens in the 90s, Daniel Shahid Johnson. Available from Mystic Garden Press, Box 51, Crestone, CO 81131-0051; general information (719) 256-4137, ordering 1-800-888-4741. (Inquire too about the teen workshops Johnson holds. Calling himself a "fellow traveler who shares," he combines various cathartic personal awareness techniques to help teens build integrity and a sense of self-worth. Equally outstanding is his *Nine Steps to Better Parent/Teen Relating,* a simple flier every parent should have. Ask for a copy.)

Midway Center for Creative Imagination, 2112 F Street NW, #404, Washington, DC 20037; (202) 296-4466. (*The Journey* is a self-discovery program for teenagers developed by David Oldfield, Director of the Midway Center. This program combines the appeal of fantasy role-playing games with shared group therapy to help today's teenagers find positive solutions to "the necessary crises of adolescence." Ask about program schedules.)

Naturopathy

American Association of Naturopathic Physicians, P.O. Box 20386, Seattle, WA 98102; (206) 323-7610.
Southwest College of Naturopathic Medicine, 6535 East Osborn Road, Scottsdale, AZ 85251; (602) 990-7424.

Nontoxic Environments

Nontoxic, Natural, and Earthwise, Debra Lynn Dadd. Los Angeles, CA; J.P. Tarcher, 1990. And *The Nontoxic Home and Office*, Debra Lynn Dadd. Los Angeles, CA; J.P. Tarcher, 1992.

Publications on Health and Healing

Anatomy of an Illness, Norman Cousins. New York, NY; W.W. Norton & Co., 1979.
Beyond Illness: Discovering the Experience of Health, Larry Dossey, M.D. Boston, MA; Shambhala Publications, 1984.
Confessions of a Medical Heretic, Robert Mendelsohn, M.D. Chicago, IL; Contemporary Books, 1979.
Creation of Health: Merging Traditional Medicine with Intuitive Diagnosis, C. Norman Shealy, M.D., Ph.D., and Caroline Myss, M.A. Walpole, NH; Stillpoint International, 1988.
Encyclopedia of Natural Medcine, Michael Murray, N.D., and Joseph Pizzorno. Allston, MA; Prima Publications, 1991.
Food and Healing, Annemarie Colbin. New York, NY; Ballantine Books, 1986.
Head First: The Biology of Hope and the Healing Power of the Human Spirit, Norman Cousins. New York, NY; Dutton, 1989.
Healing and the Mind, Bill Moyers. New York, NY; Doubleday, 1993.
Health for the Whole Person: The Complete Guide to Holistic Medicine, edited by Arthur C. Hastings, Ph.D., James Fadiman, Ph.D., and James S. Gordon, M.D. Boulder, CO; Westview Press, 1980.

Light, Medicine of the Future, Jacob Liberman, O.D., Ph.D. Santa Fe, NM; Bear & Co., 1991.

Love, Medicine and Miracles: Lessons Learned About Self-Healing From a Surgeon's Experience With Exceptional Patients, Bernie Siegel, M.D. New York, NY; Harper & Row, 1986.

Natural Health, Natural Medicine, Andrew Weil, M.D. Boston, MA; Houghton Mifflin Company, 1991.

Our Bodies Ourselves, The Boston Women's Health Book Collective. New York, NY; Simon and Schuster, 1992.

Quantum Healing, Deepak Chopra, M.D. New York, NY; Bantam Books, 1989.

Vibrational Medicine: New Choices for Healing Ourselves, Richard Gerber, M.D. Santa Fe, NM; Bear & Co., 1988.

Wellness Workbook, John W. Travis, M.D., and Regina Sara Ryan. Berkeley, CA; Ten Speed Press, 1988.

What Your Doctor Won't Tell You, Jane Heimlich. New York, NY; HarperCollins, 1990.

Wise Woman Herbal: Healing Wise, Susan S. Weed. Available from Ash Tree Publishing, P.O. Box 64, Woodstock, NY 12498.

Sources of Health and Nutritional Information

American Holistic Health Sciences Association, 1766 Cumberland Green, Suite 208, St. Charles, IL 60174 (timely newsletter).

Center for Science In The Public Interest, 1875 Connecticut Avenue, NW, Suite 300, Washington, DC 20009-5728; (202) 332-9110 (many services and publications).

Health & Healing Newsletter, Phillips Publishing, Inc., 7811 Montrose Road, Potomac, MD 28854; (301) 424-3700 (by subscription).

International Holistic Health Association,The, Forge House, Mill Road, Liss, Hampshire GU33 7DX, England; phone 0730-894111.

Natural Health Magazine, 17 Station Street, Box 1200, Brookline, MA 02147.

Prevention Magazine, Rodale Press, Emmaus, PA 18098.

Video Workshop on Holistic Health

Energy Anatomy and Self-Diagnosis: The Language of Your Body's Power Centers. This three-hour, two-tape video is of a workshop with Caroline Myss, a medical intuitive and co-author with C. Norman Shealy, M.D., of *Creation of Health*. Produced by MHMH Productions, the tape workshop is available from Myss at 1210 Hirsch Street, Melrose Park, IL 60160 (in either VHS American Format or PAL European Format).

For personalized medical information that relates to a specific condition, you can now contact a service that will do the legwork for you. For a fee these people will either keep you abreast of the latest research and treatment on whatever condition you are concerned with, or prepare specialized reports. Contact: The Health Resources, 209 Katherine Drive, Conway, AR 72032; (501) 329-5272.

There now exists a registry of health-care professionals who are nutritionally oriented. To receive referrals, send a brief letter specifying the geographical area in which you live and/or how far afield you would be willing to travel to receive such care. In your letter, include a legal-size, self-addressed stamped envelope for the reply, along with a six dollar donation. Send to: Price-Pottenger Nutrition Foundation, P.O. Box 2614, La Mesa, CA 91943-2614.

Dean Black's concepts about health and wellness are among the most sensible yet compelling I have heard. His talks and workshops are geared toward helping people realize they must address *the whole*, not just part of the whole, to establish a true context for healing. His ideas challenge the entire medical establishment to reconsider their present models of what constitutes health. To avail yourself of his many books and tapes, inquire through Tapestry Press, P.O. Box 653, Springville, UT 84663; (801) 489-9432 for general information, or 1-800-333-4290 for ordering.

Litany for Handling Fear

I happened across a very powerful and instructive litany during my own struggles to rebuild my life, that made an immense difference in how I was able to understand and handle fear. The more I repeated it to myself the less fearful I became.

The litany came from, of all places, a science fiction series about the planet Dune. There are now six books and a major motion picture, *Dune*, thanks to its author Frank Herbert, and publishers, Berkley Books. Science fiction is not a particular favorite of mine, but the first book in the *Dune* series contained the litany—and I owe a debt of thanks to Frank Herbert for it. With permission from Berkley Books, here is the original version from *Dune*, followed by what I memorized. Why I changed it around I do not know, but I'm glad I found it nonetheless.

Original Version:

I must not fear. Fear is the mind-killer. Fear is the little-death that brings total obliteration. I will face my fear. I will permit it to pass over me and through me. And when it has gone past I will turn the inner eye to see its path. Where the fear has gone there will be nothing. Only I will remain.

What I memorized:

Fear is the mind killer. It is the little death. I will face my fear. It will pass over me, around me and through me, and when it is gone—I WILL remain!

RELIGION

Any religion is a systematized approach to spiritual development based on set standards or dogmas, which may or may not alter as the religion evolves. Don't be distracted, however, by what appears restrictive, for the very purpose of religion is to provide the protection of community support and moral development, plus metaphors to offer guidance and describe what seems mysterious.

At the core of all religions is that moment of enlightenment, that mystical revelation and sacred teaching from which the religion itself grew and prospered.

Before we go too far forward, perhaps it would be wise to first go backward, back to those original "grains of wisdom" that, in ways unique to each, fostered a revolution of consciousness in their time and changed history. There is no easy way to do this, but I urge you to try, nonetheless.

The Christian Bible translation I prefer came directly from ancient Eastern manuscripts thanks to George M. Lamsa. Lamsa was born and raised in a nomadic tribe of the Holy Lands that still spoke the language of Jesus. He was later educated by Christian missionaries and then emigrated to the United States. He dedicated his life to making a direct translation of the Bible from the original scrolls, finding in the process over twelve hundred errors made by other translators. In continuous publication since 1933, the twelfth printing I have is entitled:

> *Holy Bible From the Peshitta: The Authorized Bible of the Church of East,* translated by George M. Lamsa, published by A.J. Holman Co., Philadelphia, PA.

A study of biblical idioms helps one to understand why biblical languages are so difficult to translate.One person well experienced in this subject is Dr. Rocco A. Errico, a student of the late George M. Lamsa. He is a popular speaker and teacher. His three-tape series on biblical idioms is entitled *Enlightenment From the East,* and it can be obtained from the Three Arches Bookstore, P.O. Box 75127, Los Angeles, CA 90075; (213) 388-2181. You might also ask for a copy of Errico's latest book, *The Message of Matthew,* an annotated parallel on the Gospel of St. Matthew (between Aramaic and English versions).

Dr. Lamsa's original book on idioms, first published in 1931, is once again available:

> *Idioms in the Bible Explained and a Key to the Original Gospels,* George M. Lamsa, D.D. New York, NY; Harper & Row, 1985.

For more conventional approaches to The Holy Bible, a particular favorite of mine is the twelve-tape cassette program called *The New Testament, King James Version,* which is narrated by Alexander Scourby. For both Old and New Testament versions, contact: Bible Tapes, P.O. Box 1700, Tampa, FL 33601; (813) 935-0499.

In the Christian religion, The Holy Bible was changed, altered, and subject to several highly political maneuverings, not to mention various translations, before it emerged in its present form. For instance, the concept of The Holy Trinity (Father, Son, Holy Ghost) was not part of the Apostles' original teachings, nor did it enter Christian dogma until the Council of Nicea in the early fourth century. Also, the Bible was divided into chapters only in the thirteenth century, and into verses in the fifteenth century. Thus, the Bible as it exists today is only six hundred years old. To help you understand some of this history, I would recommend the following:

The Dead Sea Scrolls Uncovered, Robert Eisenman and Michael Wise. Rockport, MA; Element Books, 1992.

The Gospel According to Jesus: A New Translation and Guide to His Essential Teachings for Believers and Unbelievers, Stephen Mitchell. New York, NY; HarperCollins, 1991.

The Gospel of Thomas: The Hidden Sayings of Jesus, Marvin Meyer. San Francisco, CA; Harper, 1992.

The Hidden Mystery of the Bible, Jack Ensign Addington. New York, NY; Dodd, Mead & Company, 1969.

The Lost Books of the Bible and the Forgotten Books of Eden, (no editor listed). New York, NY; W.W. Norton & Co., Inc., 1948.

The Other Bible, Willis Barnstone (ed.) New York, NY; Harper & Row, 1984.

The Secret Teachings of Jesus: Four Gnostic Gospels, Marvin W. Meyer. New York, NY; Random House, 1984.

Of the New Thought churches, the three that are the most popular and well established are:

Baha'i

The Baha'i Faith was founded in 1884 on the extensive writings and revelations of Baha u llah, its principal prophet. It is predicated on the concept of unity in diversity. Baha'i people downplay the necessity of a physical "church" and emphasize the importance of family worship and community gatherings. For more information, contact: Baha'i National Center, Wilmette, IL 60091; (708) 869-9039.

Church of Religious Science

Founded in 1927 on the universal principles of spirituality as explained by Ernest Holmes, the one who later wrote the textbook *The Science of Mind,* this church offers a full range of local centers, study groups, publications, prayer services, and educational programs. For more information, contact: The Church of Religious Science Headquarters, P.O. Box 75127, Los Angeles, CA 90075; (213) 388-2181 or 385-0209.

Unity Church of Practical Christianity

Inspired by healing miracles in the lives of Charles and Myrtle Fillmore and founded in 1889, the Unity Church has branched out into a large spiritual network predicated on prayer. The church offers a full range of local centers, extensive publications, prayer services, and educational programs. For more information, contact: Unity, Unity Village, MO 64065; (816) 524-7414 or 524-3550.

For bridging older and newer views about Christianity, and the problems that can occur from religious extremism, refer to the following:

Lost Christianity: A Journey of Rediscovery, Jacob Neddleman. New York, NY; Harper & Row, 1985.

Rescuing The Bible From Fundamentalism, Bishop John Shelby Spong. San Francisco, CA; Harper, 1991.

Toward a New Age in Christian Theology, Richard H. Drummond. Los Angeles, CA; Orbis Books, 1985.

When God Becomes a Drug: Breaking the Chains of Religious Addiction and Abuse, Leo Booth. Los Angeles, CA; J.P. Tarcher, 1991.

SPIRITUALITY

Spirituality is based upon a personal, intimate experience of God. There are no standards or dogmas; only precedents for individual knowing, or gnosis, are honored.

Because spirituality is so personal, methodologies are often elusive or confusing at best. So here is a caution to remember: **There is no system of spiritual enlightenment that can guarantee spiritual attainment.** Just because someone thinks he or she is spiritual doesn't mean that person is. Always look to the results, the consequences, because aftereffects cannot be faked. My own personal credo is: If you can't live what you know to be true, then it isn't worth knowing.

Meditation and prayer are starting points on the spiritual path, and the best, in my opinion. Speaking first of **meditation:** There are many methods and countless styles. One of my favorite teachers on the subject is the practical and humorous Eknath Easwaran. His book, *Meditation: Commonsense Directions for an Uncommon Life,* is excellent. Founder of the Blue Mountain Center for Meditation and a successful college professor, Easwaran has written many books—all of them available through: Nilgiri Press, Box 256, Tomales, CA 94971; (707) 878-2749.

Other Books on Meditation

Adults

Active Meditation, The Western Tradition, Robert R. Leichtman, M.D., and Carl Japikse. Canal Winchester, OH; Ariel Press, 1982.

An Easy Guide to Meditation, Roy Eugene Davis. Available from CSA Press, P.O. Box 7, Lake Rabun Road, Lakemont, GA 30552.

Creative Meditation: Inner Peace is Practically Yours, Richard Peterson. Virginia Beach, VA; A.R.E. Press, 1990.

How to Meditate: A Guide to Self-Discovery, Lawrence LeShan. New York, NY; Bantam Books, 1974.

Meditation in the Silence, E.V. Ingraham. Available from Unity School of Christianity, Unity Village, MO 64065.

Miracle of Mindfulness,The: A Manual on Meditation, Thich Nhat Hanh. Boston, MA; Beacon Press, 1976.

Three Minute Meditator, The, David Harp. San Francisco, CA; Mind's I Press, 1988.

Children

Healthier and Happier Children Through Bedtime Meditations and Stories—Books I and II, Lee and Jim Perkins. In continuous printing from A.R.E. Press, P.O. Box 595, Virginia Beach, VA 23451; 1-800-723-1112. (A cassette tape comes with each book.)

My Magic Garden, Ilse Klipper (a meditation guide for children). Available from Science of Mind Publications, P.O. Box 75127, Los Angeles, CA 90075.

Spinning Inward: Using Guided Imagery With Children, Maureen Murdock. Boston, MA: Shambhala, 1987.

Starbright: Meditations for Children, Maureen Garth. San Francisco, CA; Harper, 1991. And *Moonbeam: A Book of Meditations for Children*, San Francisco, CA; Harper, 1993.

As part of the meditative experience, it is helpful to include reading materials that add "gems" to inspire and uplift. Here are two I especially enjoy:

Quiet Mind, The, a small book containing the sayings of White Eagle. Available in American bookstores or through: General Secretary, The White Eagle Lodge, New Lands, Ranke, Liss, Hampshire, GU33 7HY, England.

Science of Mind, a monthly periodical that contains Daily Guides to Richer Living in the middle of each issue, as well as outstanding articles. To subscribe, contact: *Science of Mind* magazine, P.O. Box 75127, Los Angeles, CA 90075-9985.

A study of the Chakras and the Kundalini system is essential to a healthy understanding of the overall effect of meditation. To practice meditation without some concept of how the technique affects the human body is not wise. An organization dedicated to the study and investigation of what is now called "the Kundalini effect" is the Kundalini Research Network (KRN). Located in Canada, KRN holds regular symposia and reports on research projects worldwide. The work of Gopi Krishna and his seminal book *The Dawn of a New Science* undergirds the organization's basic premise. For more information about this organization, or to inquire about the work of Gopi Krishna, contact: Kundalini Research Network, c/o Dale Pond, R.R. #5, Flesherton, Ontario, NOC 1EO Canada; (519) 924-2681.

Excellent books on the subject:

Eastern viewpoint—*Energy, Ecstasy, and Your Seven Vital Chakras*, Bernard Gunther; N. Hollywood, CA; Newcastle, 1983.

Western viewpoint—*Kundalini Awakening: A Gentle Guide to Chakra Activation and Spiritual Growth*, John Selby; New York, NY; Bantam Books, 1992.

Meditation is a helpful way to facilitate and maintain the inner journey based on commitment and discipline. There is no quick high to be had from meditation and no one has a monopoly on the subject. Meditative life consists of phases and cycles as the process assists with inner cleansing and inner purification. It changes as you change. In no way does meditation offer short-cuts or magic or any form of escapism.

Affirmative prayer accepts as truth the biblical injunction, "It is done unto you in accordance with your belief." Here are some books that may help you to understand this type of dynamic and powerful prayer:

Dynamic Laws of Prayer, The, Catherine Ponder. Available from DeVorss & Company, P.O. Box 550, Marina del Rey, CA 90291.

Receptive Prayer and *A Manual of Receptive Prayer*, both by Grace Adolphsen Brame. Available from Science of Mind Publications, P.O. Box 75127, Los Angeles, CA 90075. When contacting this department of the Church of Religious Science, also inquire about their home-study course for learning how to do Science of Mind Treatments ("treatment" is the word given to the process of affirmative prayer by Ernest Holmes, the author of *Science of Mind*, the textbook).

Words That Heal: Affirmations and Meditations for Daily Living, Douglas Bloch. Available from Pallas Communications, 4226 NE 23rd Avenue, Portland, OR 97211.

Finding good classes and courses in spiritual development has always been difficult. There are none that are better or best, since it depends on the individual—what is helpful to one may not be for another. Many times opportunities are local and can be found through traditional, or conventional, channels. Sometimes the best source of spiritual instruction is from someone you deeply admire. That someone could as easily be a sanitation worker as some "great" guru type. For those of you who would like to expand your spiritual horizons and open yourselves up to other points of view, I have taken the liberty here of listing some places where you might begin. This is by no means a complete list of spiritual learning centers, nor is it meant to be in any way exclusive. Rather, I have merely tried to include a cross section of some organizations that have stood the test of time by consistently offering classes and workshops that are responsible, prag-matic, and psychologically sound. Most offer catalogs or schedules. Feel free to contact them. The listing begins in the western United States, progresses across the country to New York, and then goes abroad:

California
  Institute in Culture and Creation Spirituality
  Holy Names College, 3500 Mountain Blvd., Oakland, CA 94619; (415) 436-1046.

  Institute of Noetic Sciences
  475 Gate Five Road, Suite 300, Sausalito, CA 94965; (415) 331-5650.

  John F. Kennedy University
  Graduate School of Consciousness Studies, 360 Camino Pablo, Orinda, CA 94563; (510) 254-0105.

  Mount Madonna Center
  445 Summit Road, Watsonville, CA 95076; (408) 847-0406.

  Ojai Foundation
  P.O. Box 1620, Ojai, CA 93023; (805) 646-8343.
Montana
  The Feathered Pipe Foundation
  P.O. Box 1682, Helena, MT 59624; (406) 442-8196.
Nevada
  The School of the Natural Order, Inc.
  P.O. Box 150, Baker, NV 89311; (702) 234-7304.
Colorado
  Emissaries of Divine Light Foundation
  4817 North Country Road 29, Loveland, CO 80538; (303) 679-4300.

  Naropa Institute
  2130 Arapahoe Avenue, Boulder, CO 80302; (303) 444-0202.
Arizona
  Teleos Institute (formerly the Love Project)
  P.O. Box 12009-418, Scottsdale, AZ 85267; (602) 948-1800.

Texas
 Guadalupe River Ranch
 P.O. Box 877, Boerne, TX 78006; (512) 537-4837.
Oklahoma
 Sancta Sophia Seminary
 Sparrow Hawk Village, 11 Summit Ridge Drive, Tahlequah, OK
 74464-9215; (918) 456-3421.
Minnesota
 The International Institute of Integral Human Sciences, Inc.
 Midwest Chapter, P.O. Box 1309, Minnetonka, MN 55345; (612)
 934-7355.
Illinois
 The Theosophical Society
 P.O. Box 270, Wheaton, IL 60189; (708) 668-1571.
Georgia
 Center for Spiritual Awareness
 P.O. Box 7, Lake Rabun Road, Lakemont, GA 30552-9990; (404)
 782-4723.
Pennsylvania
 Himalayan Institute
 R.R. 1, Box 400, Honesdale, PA 18431; 1-800-822-4547.

 The Bear Tribe
 P.O. Box 199, Devon, PA 19333; (215) 993-3344.
Virginia
 Atlantic University
 67th Street and Atlantic Avenue, Virginia Beach, VA 23451;
 (804) 428-1512.

 Fellowship of Inner light
 P.O. Box 4100, Virginia Beach, VA 23454; (804) 496-9574

 Sevenoaks Pathwork Center
 Route 1, Box 86, Madison, VA 22727; (703) 948-6544.

 University of Science and Philosophy at Swannanoa
 P.O. Box 520, Waynesboro, VA 22980; (703) 942-5161.
Connecticut
 The Foundation for Shamanic Studies
 Box 670, Belden Station, Norwalk, CT 06852; (203) 454-2825.

Massachusetts
  Kripalu Center for Yoga & Health
  Box 793, Lenox, MA 02140; (413) 637-3280.
New York
  Aegis
  The Abode, Route 1, Box 1030D, New Lebanon, NY 12125; (518) 794-8095.

  New York Open Center
  83 Spring Street, New York, NY 10012; (212) 219-2527.

  Omega Institute
  260 Lake Drive, Rhinebeck, NY 12572-3212; (914) 266-4301.

  The Waldorf Institute
  260 Hungry Hollow Road, Spring Valley, NY 10977; (914) 425-0055.
Abroad
  France—Plum Village (Mindfulness Meditation)
  Sister Annabelle Laity, Meyrac, 47120, Loubes-Bernac, France.

  Scotland—Findhorn
  The Accommodation Secretary, Findhorn Foundation, Cluny Hill College, Forres, IV36 ORD, Scotland; phone Forres (0309) 72288.

  Switzerland—Moral Re-Armament
  The Conference Secretary, Mountain House, Ch-1824, Caux, Switzerland, phone 021-63-48-21.

Helpful Books About Various Aspects of Spirituality

As Above, So Below: Paths to Spiritual Renewal in Daily Life, by the editors of *New Age Journal.* Available from *New Age Journal* Book Order Dept., 342 Western Avenue, Brighton, MA 02135; (617) 787-2005.
Being Peace, Thich Nhat Hanh. Berkeley, CA; Parallax Press, 1987.
Care of the Soul, Thomas Moore. New York, NY; HarperCollins, 1992.
Coming Home: The Experience of Enlightenment in Sacred Traditions, Lex Hixon, Ph.D. Los Angeles, CA; J.P. Tarcher, 1989.
Coming of the Cosmic Christ, The, Matthew Fox. San Francisco, CA;

Harper & Row, 1988.

Course in Miracles, A. An unusual three-volume set about spiritual development available from the Foundation for Inner Peace, P.O. Box 1104, Glen Ellen, CA 95442; (707) 939-0200. Interpretive materials available from Miracle Distribution Center, 1141 East Ash Avenue, Fullerton, CA 92631; (714) 738-8380.

Discovering Your Soul's Purpose, Mark Thurston. Available as a kit from A.R.E. Bookstore, P.O. Box 595, Virginia Beach, VA 23451; 1-800-723-1112. Also available from the same source is *Edgar Cayce's Story of the Soul*, W.H. Church.

Finding Your Life Mission: How to Unleash That Creative Power and Live With Intention, Naomi Stephan, Ph.D. Walpole, NH; Stillpoint Press, 1990.

Gently Lead: How to Teach Your Children About God While Finding Out For Yourself, Polly Berrien Berenda. New York, NY; HarperCollins, 1991.

Homesick for Heaven—You Don't Have to Wait!, Walter Starcke. From Guadalupe Press, P.O. Box 865, Boerne, TX 78006.

Illusions, Richard Bach. New York, NY; Delacorte Press, 1977.

Imprisoned Splendour, The, Raynor Johnson, Norwich, CT; Pelegrin Press (Pilgrim Books), 1989.

Inevitable Grace: Breakthroughs in the Lives of Great Men and Women: Guides to Your Self-Realization, Piero Ferrucci. Los Angeles, CA; J.P. Tarcher, 1990.

Kything: The Art of Spiritual Presence, Louis M. Savary and Patricia H. Berne. Mahwah, NJ; Paulist Press, 1988.

Letters of the Scattered Brotherhood: A Twentieth-Century Spiritual Classic for Those Seeking Serenity and Strength, edited by Mary Strong. San Francisco, CA; Harper, 1991.

Meditations With Hildegarde of Bingen, translated by Gabriele Uhlein. Santa Fe, NM; Bear & Company, 1982.

Meeting of Science and Spirit, The, John White. New York, NY; Paragon House, 1990.

Notebooks of Paul Brunton, The. A library of insightful thoughts written during thirty years of "quiet" by the late Paul Brunton. Available in single volumes or as a set, from: The Paul Brunton Philosophic Foundation, 4936 Route 414, Burdett, NY 14818; (607) 546-9342.

Ordinary People as Monks and Mystics: Lifestyles for Self-Discovery, Marsha Sinetar. Mahwah, NJ; Paulist Press, 1986.

Path With Heart: A Guide Through the Perils and Promises of Spiritual Life, Jack Kornfield. New York, NY; Bantam Books, 1993.

Portable World Bible, The, edited by Robert O. Ballou. New York, NY; Viking Press, 1972 (in print since 1939).

Problem is God,The: The Selection and Care of Your Personal God, C. Alan Anderson, Ph.D. Walpole, NH; Stillpoint Press, 1984. Anderson also wrote *God In a Nutshell* and *Metaphysical Mousetraps*, both available through Three Arches Bookstore, P.O. Box 75127, Los Angeles, CA 90075.

Practical Mysticism, Evelyn Underhill. Available from Ariel Press, 3854 Mason Road, Canal Winchester, OH 43110.

Prophet, The, Kahlil Gibran. New York, NY; Alfred A. Knopf, continuous printings—a timeless classic.

Road Less Traveled,The: A New Psychology of Love, Traditional Values and Spiritual Growth, M. Scott Peck, M.D. New York, NY; Simon and Schuster, 1980.

Seat of the Soul, The, Gary Zukav. New York, NY; Simon and Schuster (A Fireside Book), 1990.

Seeker's Handbook, The: The Complete Guide to Spiritual Pathfinding, John Lash. New York, NY; Harmony Books, 1990.

Silent Pulse,The: The Search for the Perfect Rhythm That Exists in Each of Us, George Leonard. New York, NY; E.P. Dutton, 1986.

Way of the Wolf, The: The Gospel in New Images, Martin Bell. New York, NY; Ballantine Books, 1970.

*Way Without Words, A,*Marsha Sinetar. Mahwah, NJ; Paulist Press, 1992.

Western Spirituality: Historical Roots, Ecumenical Routes, Matthew Fox. Santa Fe, NM; Bear & Company, 1987.

When You Can Walk on Water, Take the Boat, John Harricharan. Marietta, GA; New World Publishing, 1988.

World Scripture: A Comparative Anthology of Sacred Texts, edited by Andrew Wilson. New York, NY; Paragon House, 1991.

Visions of Innocence: Spiritual and Inspirational Experiences of Childhood, Edward Hoffman. Boston, MA; Shambhala, 1992.

An Unusually Excellent Video

Nicholas Roerich, Messenger of Beauty. Contains views of 160 of his breathtaking paintings set to music, with commentary about Roerich himself, a great Russian mystic. From the Nicholas

Roerich Museum, 319 West 107th Street, New York, NY 10025-2799; (212) 864-7752.

A Most Unusual Audiocassette Series

The True Teacher. This is a series of six audiocassette tapes that were recorded live during the last workshop the Reverend Ben Osborne gave. A metaphysician and mystic, Osborne summed up a lifetime of wisdom in this taping, then was murdered several months later. The tapes are rather primitive, but the material is outstanding. Order from Tessa Babcock, 229 Temple, Brighton, MI 48116; (313) 229-7978.

As a reference on millennium fever, there is a bibliography available that examines over nine hundred international millennial movements and lists five thousand more, surveying documents from historical, sociological, literary, and theological sources. Entitled *Millennialism: An International Bibliography* by Theodore T. Daniels, it can be obtained from Garland Publishing, 1000A Sherman Avenue, Hamden, CT 06514; 1-800-627-6273.

Should you wish to contact the **Millennium Watch Institute,** you can reach them at P.O. Box 34021, Philadelphia, PA 19101-4021; (215) 662-5677.

Here is a Zen koan that I feel best addresses the human quest for spirituality in context with the whole of life:

After enlightenment—the laundry.

INTUITION AND THE PSYCHIC

Logic and intuition are equal partners. Without both working together harmoniously, we are neither healthy nor balanced. Logic, a product of conscious and deliberate thought, is considered a left-brain activity. Intuition, a product of subconscious abstractions, is most often associated with the right-brain hemisphere. A healthy brain is a whole brain, where all parts work together effectively. Some books on this subject are:

How Creative Are You? Eugene Raudsepp. New York, NY; Putnam, 1981.

Right-Brain Experience, The: An Intimate Program to Free the Powers of Your Imagination, Marilee Zdenek. New York, NY; McGraw-Hill, 1983.

Whole-Brain Thinking: Working From Both Sides of the Brain to Achieve Peak Job Performance, Jacquelyn Wonder and Priscilla Donovan. New York, NY; William Morrow, 1984.

As we expand our creative and intuitive potential, we develop solid, dependable skills and abilities with which to explore our inner life and dreamscapes. A question to ask is: How can we ever reach and endure transcended states of consciousness until we can first learn to utilize and integrate the inner realities of our own mind? **Visualization and dream interpretation** are positive, safe ways to begin.

Visualization

Creative Visualization, Shakti Gawain. New York, NY; Bantam Books, 1982.

Imagineering for Health, Serge King. Wheaton, IL; Theosophical Publishing House, 1981.

Magic Shop, The: Healing With the Imagination, Helen Graham. York Beach, ME; Samuel Weiser, Inc., 1993.

Visualization: Directing The Movies of Your Mind, Adelaide Bry and Marjorie Bair. New York, NY; Harper & Row, 1979.

Dreams

Dream Dictionary, The, Jo Jean Boushahla and Virginia Reidel-Geubtner.New York, NY; Pilgrim, 1983.

Getting Help From Your Dreams, Henry Reed. Virginia Beach, VA; Inner Vision Publishing Company, 1985.

How to Interpret Your Dreams: An Encyclopedic Dictionary, Tom Chetwynd. New York, NY; P.H. Wyden, 1980.

Inner Eye, The: Your Dreams Can Make You Psychic, Joan Windsor. Englewood Cliffs, NJ; Prentice-Hall, 1985.

Lucid Dreaming: The Power of Being Awake and Aware in Your Dreams, Stephen LaBerge, Ph.D. Los Angeles, CA; J.P. Tarcher, 1985.

Where People Fly and Water Runs Uphill: Using Dreams to Tap the Wisdom of the Unconscious, Jeremy Taylor. New York, NY; Warner Books, 1992.

The dynamics of inner realities are really the same thing as psychic abilities. The only real difference is one of semantics. The psychic and the intuitive are the same! Psychic abilities developed out of context from our practical and spiritual natures represent the negative aspect of inner growth, in my opinion; but psychic abilities developed as part of a balanced, wholesome life are invaluable.

To illustrate what I mean, in 1991 the prestigious Albert Schweitzer Award for Medicine went to Clif Sanderson, who, since meeting his Russian wife Galina in Chernobyl, has produced tangible psychic healings of child victims of the world's most tragic nuclear accident. The couple has since set up the International Foundation for New Science near the Russian lake of Baikal as a model of how psychic and spiritual methods can be successfully used in healing.

Skills of the inner life are just as valid and desirable as skills of the outer life. And anything you can already do, you can always learn to do better.

Credible Organizations That Deal With Psychic Realities

Association for Research and Enlightenment (A.R.E.), P.O. Box 595, Virginia Beach, VA 23451; general phone (804) 428-3588, for information about membership 1-800-333-4499, for publications and books 1-800-723-1112. Extensive services, publications, conferences, and the top-quality magazine *Venture Inward.* (Ask about a kit they produced entitled *Discover the Psychic Within,* as it is well done and quite helpful for beginners.) A.R.E. has active chapters throughout the world.

Fellowship of The Inner Light, P.O. Box 4100, Virginia Beach, VA 23454; (804) 496-9574. Ongoing workshops and classes, plus an excellent ministerial training program. Has affiliated centers in various foreign countries.

Huna Research Associates, 1760 Anna Street, Cape Girardeau, MO 63701; (314) 334-3478. Varied programs, classes, and conference opportunities. Produces an interesting small magazine on Huna.

International Institute of Integral Human Sciences, P.O. Box 1387, Station H, Montreal, Quebec, H3G 2N3 Canada; (514) 937-8359. Chapters in the United States and Europe, as well as an accredited international college degree program. Large international conferences, classes, and workshops. Active in Eastern Europe. (This is where I obtained my doctorate in the humanities.)

Metaphysical Center of New Jersey, P.O. Box 94, Bloomingdale, NJ 07403; (201) 835-7863. Extensive educational programs through adult extension services in the schools. Regular monthly meetings and ongoing class opportunities.

Parapsychological Services, 5575 B Chamblee Dunwoody Road, Suite 323, Atlanta, GA 30338; (404) 391-0991. Founded by William Roll as a nonprofit educational and counseling organization for those wishing to explore psychic phenomena and spiritual states.

The Parapsychology Foundation, 228 East 71st Street, New York, NY 10021; (212) 628-1550. A prestigious research and educational organization dedicated to the exploration of psychism and related phenomena.

Spiritual Advisory Council, 14345 S.E. 103rd Terrace, Summerfield, FL 32691; (904) 288-6607. Numerous conferences and meetings, as well as a ministerial training program. Fascinating bulletins.

Spiritual Frontiers Fellowship, P.O. Box 7868, Philadelphia, PA, 19101-7868; (215) 222-1991. Excellent journal, and one of the best programs for producing nationwide conferences and summer retreats that exists. Various membership services.

Manuals and Books on Psychic/Intuitive Development

Develop Your Psychic Skills and *Expand Your Psychic Skills*, both by Enid Hoffman. Westchester, PA; Para Research, Inc., various years depending on edition.

Harold Sherman's Great ESP Manual. Can still be obtained from his widow, Martha Sherman, HC74, Box 232, Highway 5 South, Mountain View, AR 72560.

Mind Is It, Charles C. Wise, Jr. Available from the Magian Press, P.O. Box 117, Penn Laird, VA 22846.

Natural ESP: A Layman's Guide to Unlocking the Extra Sensory Power of Your Mind, Ingo Swann. New York, NY; Bantam Books, 1987. Swann is currently developing a way to combine various types of psychic information gathering to produce a dependable method of tracking future events and trends.

Practical ESP: A Step by Step Guide for Developing Your Intuitive Potential, Carol Ann Liaros. Available from Blind Awareness Project, 1966 Niagara St., Buffalo, NY 14207; (716) 874-2613.

Psychic Energy Workbook, The, R. Michael Miller and Josephine M. Harper. New York, NY; Sterling Publishers, 1987.

Books for a Better Understanding of the Psychic Field

Adults

Conscious Evolution: Understanding Extrasensory Abilities in Everyday Life, Janet Lee Mitchell, Ph.D. New York, NY; Ballantine Books, 1989.

Personal Mythology: The Psychology of Your Evolving Self, David Feinstein and Stanley Krippner. Los Angeles, CA; J.P. Tarcher, 1988.

Psychic Sourcebook, The: How to Choose and Use a Psychic, Frederick G. Levine. New York, NY; Warner Books, 1988.

Psychic Studies: A Christian's View, Michael Perry. San Bernadino, CA; Borgo Press, 1987.

Synchronicity: The Bridge Between Matter and Mind, F. David Peat. New York, NY; Bantam Books, 1988.

Unobstructed Universe, The, Stewart White. Available from Ariel Press, 3854 Mason Road, Canal Winchester, OH 43110.

Venture Inward, Hugh Lynn Cayce. New York, NY; Harper & Row, 1985.

Children

Secret Life of Kids, The: An Exploration Into Their Psychic Senses, James W. Peterson. Wheaton, IL; Theosophical Publishing House, 1988.

Twelve, Elaine Kittredge (for children of all ages). Chicago, IL; Optex, 1981.

Understanding and Developing Your Child's Natural Psychic Abilities, Alex Tanous and Katherine Fair Donnelly. New York, NY; Fireside Books (Simon and Schuster), 1979.

Reference Texts

Ashby Guidebook for Study of the Paranormal, The, Robert H. Ashby, revised edition edited by Frank C. Tribbe. York Beach, ME; Samuel Weiser, Inc., 1987.

New Age Almanac, J. Gordon Melton. Detroit, MI; Visible Ink Press, 1990.

Paranormal,The: A Scientific Exploration of the Supernatural, Arthur J. Ellison. New York, NY; Dodd, Mead & Company, 1988.

Parapsychology: The Controversial Science, Richard Broughton, Ph.D. New York, NY; Ballantine Books, 1991.

Parapsychology and Psychology: Matches and Mismatches, Gertrude R. Schmeidler. Jefferson, NC; McFarland and Co., 1988.

Special Publications in the Field

Memories and Visions of Paradise: Exploring the Universal Myth of a Lost Golden Age, Richard Heinberg. Los Angeles, CA; J.P. Tarcher, 1989.

Power of Myth, The, Joseph Campbell, with Bill Moyers. New York, NY; Doubleday, 1988.

Secret Teachings of All Ages, The, Manley P. Hall. Los Angeles, CA; Philosophical Research Society, Inc., 1978.

Magazines and Newsletters on the Subject

Body, Mind and Spirit, P.O. Box 701, Providence, RI 02901.
Connecting Link, 9392 Whitneyville Road, Alto, MI 49302-9694.
New Frontiers, Fellowship Farm, Route 1, Oregon, WI 53575.
Woodrew Update, 448 Rabbit Skin Road, Waynesville, NC 28786.

A Unique Board Game

Intuition: The Game You Already Know, developed by Daniel Cappon, Ph.D. Available through the developer, 32 York Valley Cr., North York, Ontario, M2P 1A7 Canada; (416) 736-5252.

A Computerized Database System for Researching Psychism

Exceptional Human Experiences, The PSI Center, 2 Plane Tree Lane, Dix Hills, NY 11746; (516) 271-1243. Anyone is welcome to avail themselves of the service. Pay per use.

Pro and Con Statements About New Age Types of Thinking

Emerging New Age, The, J.L. Simmons, Ph.D. Santa Fe, NM; Bear & Company, 1990.
New Age, The, David Spangler. Issaquah, WA; Moringtown Press, 1988.
New Inquisition, The, Robert Anton Wilson. Phoenix, AZ; Falcon Press, 1987.
Not Necessarily The New Age: Critical Essays, edited by Robert Basil. Buffalo, NY; Prometheus, 1988.
Reimagination of the World: A Critique of The New Age, Science, and Popular Culture, David Spangler and William Irwin Thompson. Santa Fe, NM; Bear & Co., 1991.

Special Groups on The "Leading Edge" of Psychic/Intuitive Development

The Global Intuition Network (G.I.N.) has as its purpose to promote the applied use of intuition in decision making, to share new knowledge on how to use this brain skill as it becomes known, and to promote ongoing research on intuitive processes for practical use in organizations. Initiated by Weston Agor, Ph.D., the Network expands on ideas first introduced by Agor's challenging book: *Intuition in Organizations—Leading and Managing Productively,* (Newbury Park, CA; Sage Publications, 1989). International support and participation have mushroomed since G.I.N. began, making the network an important resource for the practical development and use of intuition as a skills-enhancement tool. For information about membership and their international conferences contact: Global Intuition Network, The University of Texas at El Paso, TX 79968-0614; (915) 747-5227.

The Center for the Investigation and Training of Intuition was started by Helen Palmer after the publication of her book, *The Enneagram,* (New York, NY; HarperCollins, 1988). The *enneagram,* by the way, is an ancient psychological system based on nine personality types and how each interacts with the other. Palmer defines the nine types in her book, then illustrates how each one can lead to higher awareness and greater capacities for behavior such as empathy, compassion, and love. The goal, she believes, is to help individuals become complete human beings. Her non-profit Center focuses on intuition training and, to this end, has become a top-notch networking source for teachers and therapists who practice individualized work with clients in their given areas. To learn more about classroom opportunities or workshops that may be in your area, write or call: Center for the Investigation & Training of Intuition, 1442-A Walnut Street, Suite 377, Berkeley, CA 94709; (510) 843-7621.

The Consciousness Research and Training Project was originated by the famous author and researcher, Lawrence LeShan, Ph.D. Introductory seminars are offered four or five times a year to prescreened applicants, people sincere in their willingness not to charge for effecting a healing experience for others and who understand that the healing is never to be used as a substitute for traditional and licensed forms of treatment. Following the seminars, students are urged to practice what they have learned and to meditate. Advanced sessions are sometimes available. For more information on how to participate in these unique training opportunities, contact: Joyce Goodrich, Ph.D., Project Director, Consciousness Research and Training Project, Inc., 315 East 68th Street, Box 9G, New York, NY 10021. Occasionally, LeShan offers this program outside New York. Be certain to inquire about his schedule.

Dowsing is the most simple yet constructive way I know to explore and expand intuitive/psychic skills. And it's fun! Anyone from a four-year-old to great-grandparents can do it. Contrary to some notions, dowsing is not a "special gift," but is readily teachable as a practical way to access octaves beyond the electromagnetic spectrum. Dowsers are the doers of *Psi*. They emphasize demonstration and results. Two of the best books written on the subject are:

The Divining Hand, Christopher Bird. Black Mountain, NC; New Age Press, 1985.

The Divining Mind, Edward Ross and Richard D. Wright. Rochester, VT; Destiny Books, 1990.

The largest and most established organization devoted to dowsing is the American Society of Dowsers, Danville, VT 05828-0024; (802) 684-3417. They have chapters located throughout the nation and sponsor an excellent national conference each August. Their bookstore is located at 101 Railroad Street, St. Johnsbury, VT 05819; (802) 748-8565. Inquiries are welcome at both places.

MUSIC

To a survivor of death, music often sounds like so much noise! These people usually prefer silence or the sounds nature affords, tuning inward rather than outward. If commercial music can be tolerated, preferences change. For those who alter consciousness naturally or because of a growth event, the idea of music comes to center around that which is melodic and inspirational.

Since music becomes such an issue for near-death survivors and others like them, I have prepared the following as a way to acquaint you with various aspects of music and sound:

Sources for Healthy Holistic Music (request free catalogs)

Backroads Distributing/*The Heartbeats Catalog*
    417 Tamal Plaza, Corte Madera, CA 94925; 1-800-825-4848.
Heartsong Review
    P.O. Box 1084, Cottage Grove, OR 97424.
Steven Halpern's Sound RX
    163 Whittier Avenue, Suite 3, San Rafael, CA 94903; (415) 491-1930.
The Relaxation Company
    20 Lumber Road, Roslyn, NY 11576; (516) 621-2727 and 1-800-788-6670 (formerly Vital Body Marketing).

The different effects from sound and vibration are no small matter once you've experienced near-death or similar states. Here are three books that can help you to reeducate yourself:

The Secret Power of Music: The Transformation of Self and Society Through Musical Energy, David Tame. Rochester, VT; Destiny Books, 1984.

Sound Health: The Music and Sounds That Make Us Whole, Steven Halpern and Louis Savary. New York, NY; Harper & Row, 1985.

The World Is Sound: Music and the Landscape of Consciousness, Joachim-Ernest Berendt. Rochester, VT; Destiny Books, 1983.

To obtain singing **quartz crystal bowls** (incredibly wonderful instruments), contact the main distributor for more information on locating the store nearest you that carries them. Write or call: Crystal Distributing Co., 7320 Ashcroft, Suite 303, Houston, TX 77081; 1-800-833-2328.

The only earthplane music I have yet found that comes close to what is heard on The Other Side is hoomi singing. Originated in Mongolia, **hoomi singing** is a way of using vocal chords plus various other parts of the body to refract sound and create overtones. The goal is to imitate nature without using instruments. While Tibetan lamas developed a type of overtone chanting that is so low it sounds as if it comes from the bowels of the earth, the Mongolians employ the higher harmonics, which have an angelic, bell-like quality. Renamed "harmonic singing," this ancient skill has undergone a revival. The Harmonic Arts Society was the first to commercially produce albums of *hoomi (harmonic) singing.* Performed by David Hykes and the Harmonic Choir, their albums *Hearing Solar Winds* and *Harmonic Meeting* are still available. If you cannot find them at your favorite music store, inquire of Backroads Distributing (listed previously).

Toning: The Creative Power of the Voice, by Laurel Elizabeth Keyes, is a classic in the exploration of the human voice and the effect it can have. Although small in size, this book is dynamic in presenting how all of us can learn to utilize the power of our own voices. Available from DeVorss and Co., P.O. Box 550, Marina del Rey, CA 90291.

Two Leaders in the Creative Exploration of Voice, Sound, and Healing

Jill Purce was headed for a degree in biophysics when she became sidetracked by a profound desire to learn how patterns of sound seem to direct spirit into matter, being into form. A specialist in *hoomi singing*, chanting, and drumming, she regularly conducts workshops like "The Healing Voice" throughout North America and Europe. To avail yourself of her schedules and chant tapes, write to Gillian McGregor, Garden Flat, 9 Yonge Park, London N4 3NU, England.

Rhoda Beryl Semel is a distinguished classical concert artist, educator, certified hypnotherapist, and sound healer. She offers a series of programs entitled Touching Your Healing Frequency, which includes healing of sound and voice through movement, Chakra balancing, color, and experiencing great music in expanded states. Contact her at 25 Trinity Place, Apt. 102, Montclair, NJ 07041; or phone her public relations coordinator at (201) 316-8361.

Institute For Music, Health, and Education is a place of miracles. Through experiential classroom involvement, people engage in accelerated learning and listening techniques that can and often do facilitate healing. "Music holds the rhythmic and tonal patterns of energy that directly organize thought, speech, and movement," says the Institute's originator, Don G. Campbell. The author of seven books, including *Music and Miracles* and *Music: Physician for Times to Come*, Campbell is internationally known for his innovative techniques in helping people reclaim their health by changing their response to sound. To obtain a catalog of publications as well as workshop and class schedules, contact: Institute for Music, Health, & Education, P.O. Box 1244, Boulder, CO 80306; (303) 443-8484.

EXPANDING WORLDVIEWS

Those who have altered their consciousness see the world differently. They tend to prefer cooperation instead of competition, conservation instead of consumerism, caring instead of apathy. Invariably their worldview expands. The following books provide a starting place. Use your own judgment in making selections:

Concerning the New Sciences

Belonging to the Universe: Explorations on the Frontiers of Science and Spirituality, Fritjof Capra and David Steindl-Rast, with Thomas Matus. San Francisco, CA; Harper, 1992.

The Bone Peddlers: The Selling of Evolution, William R. Fix. New York, NY; Macmillan, 1984.

Chaos: Making a New Science, James Gleick. New York, NY; Viking, 1987.

The Dancing Wu-Li Masters: An Overview of the New Physics, Gary Zukav. New York, NY; Bantam Books, 1979.

Gaia: A New Look at Life on Earth, James E. Lovelock. New York, NY; Oxford University Press, 1982.

The Medium, the Mystic, and the Physicist, Lawrence LeShan. New York, NY; Ballantine Books, 1982.

Tesla, Man Out of Time, Margaret Cheney. Englewood Cliffs, NJ; Prentice-Hall, 1981.

Concerning Economics

The Ecology of Commerce: Doing Good Business, Paul Hawken. New York, NY; HarperBusiness, 1993.

The Findhorn Garden: Pioneering a New Vision of Humanity and Nature in Cooperation, The Findhorn Community. Forres, Scotland; The Findhorn Press, 1988 (available in the United States).

The Living Economy: A New Economics in the Making, Paul Elkins. Available from Technology Development Group, P.O. Box 337, Croton-on-Hudson, NY 10520.

Permaculture: A Designer's Handbook, Bill Mollison. Stanley, Australia; Tagaari, 1981.

The Soul of Economies: Spiritual Evolution Goes to the Marketplace, Denise Breton and Christopher Largent. New York, NY; Idea House Publishing Company, 1991.

Concerning Human Behavior

Builders of the Dawn: Community Lifestyles in a Changing World, Corinne McLaughlin and Gordon Davidson. Walpole, NH; Stillpoint Press, 1985.

The Culture of Disbelief, Stephen L. Carter. New York, NY; Basic Books, 1993.

Faces of the Enemy, Sam Keen. New York, NY; Harper & Row, 1987.

Future Lives: A Fearless Guide to Our Transition Times, J.L. Simmons, Ph.D. Santa Fe, NM; Bear & Company, 1990.

The Immense Journey, Loren Eiseley. New York, NY; Random House, 1957.

The Inner Side of World Events, Corinne McLaughlin and Gordon Davidson. New York, NY; Ballantine Books, 1993.

The Re-Enchantment of the World, Morris Berman. Ithaca, NY; Cornell University, 1981.

Vital Lies, Simple Truths: The Psychology of Self-Deception, Daniel Goleman, Ph.D. New York, NY; Simon and Schuster, 1985.

We're All Doing Time, Bo Lozoff. Available from Human Kindness Foundation, Route 1, Box 201-N, Durham, NC 27705.

When Society Becomes an Addict, Anne Wilson Shaef. New York, NY; Harper & Row, 1987.

A World Waiting to Be Born, M. Scott Peck, M.D. New York, NY; Bantam Books, 1993.

Concerning Children

Babies Remember Birth, David Chamberlain, Ph.D. Los Angeles, CA; J.P. Tarcher, 1988.

For Your Own Good: Hidden Cruelty in Child-Rearing and the Roots of Violence, Alice Miller. New York, NY; Farrar, Straus & Giroux, 1983.

Hope for the Flowers, Trina Paulus. New York, NY; Paulist Press, 1972. (A children's book for all ages.)

The Hour Glass: Sixty Fables for This Moment in Time, Carl Japikse. Canal Winchester, OH; Ariel Press, 1984. (For the child in all of us.)

Kinship With All Life, J. Allen Boone. New York, NY; Harper & Row, 1976. (A timeless children' classic for all ages.)

Mister God, This Is Anna, Flynn. New York, NY; Holt, Rinehart & Winston, 1975.

The Secret Life of the Unborn Child, Thomas Verny and John Kelly. New York, NY; Dell, 1986.

Who Speaks for Wolf, Paula Underwood Spencer. Available from A Tribe of Two Press, P.O. Box 216, San Anselmo, CA 94979. (A timeless classic for children of all ages.)

You—A Source of Strength in Our World, Eleanor Rost. Available from the author at 8 Virginia Road, Montville, NJ 07045. (For grade-school-age children—outstanding.)

Specials

Jesus, The Son of Man, Kahlil Gibran. New York, NY; Knopf, 1928.
The Man Who Tapped the Secrets of the Universe, Glenn Clark. Available from the University of Science and Philosophy, Swannanoa, P.O. Box 520, Waynesboro, VA 22980.
The Wandering Taoist, Deng Ming-Dao. New York, NY; Harper & Row, 1983.

> What you are looking for is what is looking.
> —St. Francis of Assisi

Notes

Let us learn, then, that energy of faith which
enables us to live constantly in the vision of the
good; and let us descend, in action, into the
world of fact, with that vision always before us.
—Bertrand Russell

1. I was one of the original psychic counselors hired when the Professional
   Psychic Counselors Network (Psychic Friends) came on-line. They featured
   me in their first two infomercials that were aired nationally for a year and a
   half. (Yes, I was that "light-haired" grandmother-type sitting on the floor
   tossing rocks [rune casting].) I don't know how other psychic counselors
   operate their business on the line, but I endeavor to be of service in helping
   people gain more clarity in their decision-making process and to offer
   inspiration when needed. I have never conducted myself as some fortune-
   teller trying to amaze anyone. For those who want such entertainment, I
   simply request that they hang up, redial, and seek out someone else more
   suited to that type of performance. If a practical psychic with a hearty laugh
   and a gentle voice interests you, call me sometime. Dial 1-900-737-3225, then
   punch in extension 7039. That's me. There will be a recording to tell you
   when I am next on duty, if I'm not there to answer when you call. At this
   writing, there is a charge of $3.89 *per minute* that you will be billed for the
   call, and it will appear on your monthly telephone statement. Also, the line
   has an automatic half-hour shutoff (in other words, I cannot keep a caller on-
   line more than thirty minutes). I implore discretion here, if you are short of
   funds. I want to thank Mike Warren and all the staff at the Professional
   Psychic Counselors Network for their understanding and their caring. They
   have been wonderful to me. No, I haven't always enjoyed providing this
   service (I usually work the late shift after a full day doing research), but I
   have always been more than rewarded by the remarkable and loving people
   who have called me to seek aid or information. It has been a privilege for me
   to have been part of their lives—if only for a moment! Should you wish to
   contact my employer for any reason, write or call: Professional Psychic
   Counselors Network, 23–25 Walker Avenue, Baltimore, MD 21208; (410)
   486-6452.

2. *I Died Three Times in 1977* came out in 1980. Five hundred copies were printed. *Coming Back to Life: The Aftereffects of the Near-Death Experience* was published in 1988; a total of ten thousand copies were printed in hardcover by Dodd, Mead & Company. Six foreign countries now have editions of their own, although many of them omitted the Resource Section, which concerned me greatly since it continued the text. Ballantine Books has continuously printed their paperback version in the United States and Canada, and I have recently updated that Resource Section.

3. Kenneth Ring wrote: *Life at Death*, Coward, McCann & Geoghegan, New York, NY; 1980; *Heading Toward Omega: In Search of the Meaning of the Near-Death Experience*, William Morrow, New York, NY, 1984; and *The Omega Project: Near-Death Experiences, UFO Encounters, and Mind at Large*, William Morrow, New York, NY, 1992.

4. This quote appears in an article by Allen Josephs entitled, "Hemingway's Out of Body Experience," and was given to me by Charles M. "Tod" Oliver, Editor of The *Hemingway Newsletter* and former editor of The *Hemingway Review*. Hemingway's book *A Farewell to Arms* was originally published by Charles Scribner's Sons, New York, NY in 1920, and remains in print.

5. *Return From Death: An Exploration of the Near-Death Experience*, Margot Grey. London, England; Arkana, 1985.

6. *After the Beyond: Human Transformation and the Near-Death Experience*, Charles Flynn. Englewood Cliffs, NJ; Prentice-Hall, 1986.

7. *Beyond Death's Door*, Maurice Rawlings, M.D. Nashville, TN; Thomas Nelson, 1978.

8. *Before Death Comes* and *To Hell and Back*, Maurice Rawlings, M.D. Nashville, TN; Thomas Nelson 1980 and 1993, respectively.

9. *The Divine Comedy*, Dante Alighieri. New York, NY; Random House, 1955. (Original work published in the fourteenth century.)

10. *A Christmas Carol*, Charles Dickens. New York, NY; Bantam Books, 1983. (Original work published in 1843.)

11. *Our Town*, Thornton Wilder. New York, NY; Coward, McCann, 1938.

12. *The Tibetan Book of the Dead*, edited by W. Y. Evans-Wentz. London, England; Oxford University Press, 1957.

13. The spiritualist camp of Lily Dale was founded in 1879 to provide instruction and sanctuary for people who are psychically inclined. Over the years, it has expanded into a major educational center emphasizing holistic health, the healing arts, and spiritual mediumship. Public demonstrations and lectures are given on a regular basis. Anyone may inquire or visit, contact: Lily Dale Assembly, 5 Melrose Park, Lily Dale, NY 14752; (716) 595-8721.

14. *I Saw Heaven*, by Arthur E. Yensen, is still available through his son Eric at P.O. Box 369, Parma, ID 83660.

15. Mellen-Thomas Benedict, founder of Benedict & Associates, is presently working with many corporate and technical research groups as an intuitive consultant. His insight and ability to work in altered states of consciousness has quite a track record, from inventing toys and tools to doing DNA and subtle energy research. He is available for consultations and lectures on a wide variety of subjects, and is currently writing a book about his near-death experience focusing on the four hundred years in the future that he was shown. Contact him at: Benedict & Associates, 1714 Swann Street, Fayetteville, NC 28303; (910) 488-3150. His motto: If it's difficult, we do it immediately. If it's impossible, it takes a little longer. Miracles by appointment only!!! (Obviously, this man has a sense of humor.)

16. Refer to Spiritual Emergence/Emergencies for more information about the extensive services, training, and opportunities available to anyone through the Smith Mountain Lake Retreat Center operated by Margaret Fields Kean and her husband, Leonard Kean. You may reach the Center yourself by contacting: Smith Mountain Lake Retreat and Healing Center, Route 1, Box 77A, Huddleston, VA 24104; (703) 297-1828.
17. George G. Ritchie, Jr., M.D., wrote: *Return From Tomorrow* (with Elizabeth Sherrill), Spire Books, Old Tappan, NJ, 1978; and *My Life After Dying: Becoming Alive to Universal Love*, Hampton Roads Publishing Company, Inc., Norfolk, VA, 1991.
18. *What Tom Sawyer Learned From Dying*, Sidney Saylor Farr. Norfolk, VA; Hampton Roads Publishing Company, Inc., 1993.
19. *Embraced by the Light*, Betty J. Eadie. Placerville, CA; Gold Leaf Press, 1992.
20. Rudolf Steiner's anthroposophy is a comprehensive and innovative revamping of biodynamic agriculture, medicine, architecture, arts, social therapy, and many other areas of human interaction and development. For more information, contact: The Waldorf Institute, 260 Hungry Hollow Road, Spring Valley, NY 10977; (914) 425-0055.
21. Individuals seeking to contact Nancy Clark for participation in her research study on Near-Death-Like Experiences, should write to her at P.O. Box 835, Dublin, OH 43017. Please include a self-addressed, stamped, letter-sized envelope to receive a research questionnaire in the mail. Confidentiality is assured.
22. To contact either the Institute or the health-care facility, write or call: Vernon Sylvest, M.D., Richmond Health & Wellness Center, 5700 W. Grace Street, Suite 105, Richmond, VA 23226; (804) 285-6240.
23. Their article, "Do 'Near-Death Experiences' Occur Only Near Death?—Revisited," was published in the *Journal of Near-Death Studies*, Fall 1991, pages 41–47. (This question was originally tackled by Gabbard, Twemlow, and Jones ten years earlier.) Available through IANDS, P.O. Box 502, East Windsor Hill, CT 06028-0502.
24. *The Golden Chalice: A Collection of Writings of the Famous Soviet Parapsychologist and Healer Barbara Ivanova*, edited by Larissa Vilenskaya and Maria Mir (1986). Available from H.S. Dakin Company, 3220 Sacramento Street, San Francisco, CA 94115.
25. About angels, here are some suggestions to give you a more well-rounded view of what is currently being said about them:
Angels: The Role of Celestial Guardians and Beings of Light, Paola Giovetti. York Beach, ME; Samuel Weiser, Inc., 1993.
Behaving As If the God In All Life Mattered, Machaelle Small Wright. Available from Perelandra Ltd., P.O. Box 3603, Warrenton, VA 22186.
Commune With the Angels: A Heavenly Handbook, Jane M. Howard. Virginia Beach, VA; A.R.E. Press, 1992.
The Angels Around Us, John Randolph Price. New York, NY; Ballantine Books (Fawcett Columbine), 1993.
To Hear the Angels Sing: An Odyssey of Co-Creation With the Devic Kingdom, Dorothy Maclean. Middletown, WI; Lorian Press, 1983.
Where Angels Walk: True Stories of Heavenly Visitors, a compilation by Joan Wester Anderson. New York, NY; Bantam, 1992.
The most articulate exponent of angel realms today is Karyn Martin-Kuri, an artist of world renown and a student of Rudolf Steiner's teachings. She has initiated national and international conferences on angels that have drawn

together thousands of people in an exploration of how people can better prepare themselves to serve with angels. To contact her organization and inquire about their programs, write or call: Tapestry, P.O. Box 3032, Waquoit, MA 02536; 1-800-28ANGEL.

26. *Threshold to Tomorrow,* Ruth Montgomery. New York, NY; Putnam, 1983.
27. *Messengers of Hope,* Reverend Carol W. Parrish-Harra; New Age Press, 1983. Available from Sancta Sophia Seminary, Sparrow Hawk Village, 11 Summit Ridge Drive, Tahlequah, OK 74464-9215; (918) 456-3421. Inquire also about their seminary programs, if you are interested, as the facility exists to further the "mystery teachings of mysticism" within the Christian framework. It offers accreditation in five emerging ministries: pastor, minister-scholar, minister-priest, theologian, and prophet-seer.
28. *The Omega Project: Near-Death Experiences, UFO Encounters, and Mind at Large,* Kenneth Ring, Ph.D. New York, NY; William Morrow, 1992.
29. *Life After Life,* Raymond A Moody, Jr., M.D. Covington, GA; Mockingbird Books, 1975. (In continuous printings worldwide.)
30. The Elisabeth Kübler-Ross Center is now located at South Rt. 616, Head Waters, VA; 24442; (703) 396-3441. The world's preeminent authority on death and dying, Elisabeth Kübler-Ross no longer travels as much as she used to, preferring instead to hold many of her programs at her large facility in Head Waters. Her Life, Death and Transition Workshops are as dynamic and viable today as when I first attended one in 1978. Write or call about schedules and the many other opportunities that are available. For a small yearly fee, you can subscribe to her newsletter and keep abreast of activities.
31. *Cosmic Consciousness,* Richard Maurice Bucke, M.D. First published in book form by Innes & Sons in 1901. Currently published by Citadel Press, New York, NY. (Continuous printings.)
32. Anyone can inquire about or join the Kundalini Research Network, c/o Dale Pond, R.R. 5, Flesherton, Ontario, Canada NOC 1EO; (519) 924-2681. Recognizing the work of Gopi Krishna (the Vedic tradition of India) as their main reference text, they actively support ongoing research globally to determine the extent, aftereffects, and meaning of Kundalini breakthroughs as an evolutionary force present in the human species. *Kundalini: Dawn of a New Science* is a conference they sponsor, along with many other activities, publications, tapes, bibliographies, and contacts in the academic and medical professions. Their materials and outreach programs are highly recommended. Gopi Krishna's main work is as follows (listed by year of publication):
Kundalini, The Evolutionary Energy in Man, Shambhala, Berkeley, CA, 1967.
The Secrets of Yoga, Harper & Row, New York, NY; 1972.
The Awakening of Kundalini, Dutton, New York, NY; 1975.
33. *Catching the Light: The Entwined History of Light and Mind,* Arthur Zajonc. New York, NY; Bantam Books, 1993.
34. *Creating Minds,* Howard Gardner. New York, NY; Basic Books, 1993.
35. *Portrait of Jesus?* Frank C. Tribbe, available from The Holy Shroud Guild, 294 E. 150th Street, Bronx, NY 10451. (Published in hardcover by Stein & Day, 1983.) The descriptions of Jesus and how he physically appeared are on page 245 in the text.
36. *The Earth's Annular Systems,* Issac N. Vail, published in 1902 (may be difficult to locate). Vail, by the way, was considered a "crackpot" in his time and much of his work was either lost or destroyed. I would suggest that you obtain a copy, instead, of a later work of his, *Waters Above the Firmament,*

which has been kept in continuous print by Donald L. Cyr of *Stonehenge Viewpoint* newspaper, and can be purchased from him. Write: Stonehenge Viewpoint, 2261 Las Positas, Santa Barbara, CA 93105.

37. *A New Science of Life: The Hypothesis of Formative Causation,* Rupert Sheldrake. Los Angeles, CA; J.P. Tarcher/Houghton Mifflin, 1981.

38. Bethe Hagens, Ph.D., a professor in the Graduate School at Union Institute, is currently researching the relationship between archaeoastronomy, ancient mythology, and geometry. She is writing a book on the pervasive symbolism of brains in ancient iconography and calendar systems, tentatively titled *Canoa Cabrata: The Luck of the Broken Canoe.* An anthropologist, she and her husband, Bill Becker, sell educational toys, maps, and models of ancient geometry, through their company, Conservative Technology. To inquire about her theory of the Venus figurines, refer to her article, "Venuses, Turtles, and Other Hand-Held Cosmic Models." Write or call: Conservative Technology, 105 Wolpers Road (2155W.), Part Forest, IL 60466; (708) 481-6168.

39. *Closer to the Light: Learning From the Near-Death Experiences of Children,* Melvin Morse, M.D., with Paul Perry. New York, NY; Villard Books, 1990.

40. *The Body Electric: Electromagnetism and the Foundation of Life,* Robert O. Becker, M.D. and Gary Selden. New York, NY; William Morrow, 1985.

41. The International Society For The Study of Subtle Energies & Energy Medicine is a membership organization open to anyone interested in building bridges across disciplines and providing dialogue opportunities between modern science and traditional healing practices. Contact them directly for more information: ISSSEEM, 356 Goldco Circle, Golden, CO 80403; (303) 278-2228.

42. *Evolution's End: Claiming the Potential of Our Intelligence,* Joseph Chilton Pearce. San Francisco, CA; Harper, 1992.

43. Kimberly Clark Sharp, MSW, had a near-death experience in 1970 when she collapsed without warning onto a sidewalk. An improperly activated portable ventilator brought by the volunteer fire department removed oxygen from her body rather than replacing it. She was pronounced dead, but ultimately survived against all odds. Her mission since then has been to mainstream and normalize the near-death experience in our culture, especially in the field of health care. As a clinical assistant professor in social work at the University of Washington, and in her capacity as President of Seattle IANDS, the world's oldest and largest support group for experiencers, she is in great demand as a public speaker and workshop leader. To contact Kimberly Clark Sharp or for information on Seattle IANDS (including their free newsletter), contact: Seattle IANDS, P.O. Box 84333, Seattle, WA 98124; (206) 525-5489. Her book, *A Life After Death,* is due out in 1995 through William Morrow and Company, Inc.

44. There are two systems of rune use: Oracle Runes (masculine/yang) and Casting Runes (feminine/yin). Oracle Runes operate according to instructive definitions and formats and were made popular by Ralph Blum in his *The Book of Runes,* St. Martin's Press, New York, NY, 1982. Casting Runes operate through free-form tossing to illustrate flowing patterns of thought and were made popular in a book I wrote, *The Magical Language of Runes,* Bear & Company, Santa Fe, NM, 1990 (no longer in print). My original work has since been expanded to include past-life as well as present-life castings, and should be available under the title *Goddess Runes* in 1995.

45. *Lithium, Nature in Harmony,* by Haroldine, and published by Borderland Sciences, P.O. Box 429, Garberville, CA 95440-0429. Some of this book may seem nonsensical, parts even apply to a crystal business the author once had but no longer operates. Still, there are gems in this book, gleaned from varied sources and from a long-running research project on lithium that was conducted by Haroldine. I was a participant in that project, working as a fellow researcher with two counselor/psychologists assisting me—they had obtained the cooperation of some of their clients to test our experiments with natural lithium. Although the research we did is not conclusive, test results were positive enough that I feel comfortable recommending natural approaches to lithium, whenever feasible and appropriate.

Life amazes me with the way it brings to the surface just what I ought to recognize.
— Rev. Jesse Jennings